FREEMASONRY
VS.
THE PAPACY

Papal condemnations
of Freemasonry
and its Ideologies

Compiled by

Ann Mary O'Donnell

The Roman Catholic Church has consistently condemned Freemasonry, primarily due to its war against Catholic doctrine and Catholic civilization through promotion of religious indifferentism, naturalism, and secrecy. This book is a collection of the papal encyclicals, bulls, constitutions, and other pronouncements that explain the strict stance of the Church against Freemasonry and its errors and is dedicated to Saint Joseph, Patron of the Universal Church.

NATAL PUBLISHING LLC
ARS LONGA, VITA BREVIS

Copyright© 2025 Natal Publishing

All rights reserved

TABLE OF CONTENTS

Prayer for the Conversion of Freemasons	iii
Canon Law on Freemasonry	iv

Papal Condemnations of Freemasonry

In Eminenti Apostolatus, Papal Bull of Clement XIII (April 28, 1738)	1
Providas Romanorum, Apostolic Constitution of Pope Benedict XIV (May 18, 1751)	5
Ecclesiam a Jesu Christo, Apostolic Constitution of Pope Pius VII (September 13, 1821)	19
Quo Graviora, Apostolic Constitution of Pope Leo XII (March 13, 1826)	25
Qui Pluribus, Encyclical of Pope Pius IX (November 9, 1846)	56
Multiplices Inter, Allocution of Pope Pius IX (September 25, 1865)	97
Etsi Multa, Encyclical of Pope Pius IX (November 21, 1873)	102
Humanum Genus, Encyclical of Pope Leo XIII (April 20, 1884)	130
Dall'Alto Dell'Apostolico Seggio, Encyclical of Pope Leo XIII (October 15, 1890)	152
Au Milieu Des Sollicitudes, Letter of Pope Leo XIII (February 16, 1892)	167

Custodi di Quella Fede, Encyclical of Pope Leo XIII (December 8, 1892)	181
Inimica Vis, Encyclical of Pope Leo XIII (December 8, 1892)	190
Annum Ingressi, Apostolic Letter of Pope Leo XIII (March 18, 1902)	211

Papal Condemnations of Masonic Ideologies

Ut Primum, Constitution of Pope Clement XIII (September 3, 1759)	10
Christianae Reipublicae, Encyclical of Pope Clement XIII (November 25, 1766)	14
Traditi Humilitati, Encyclical of Pope Pius VIII (May 24, 1829)	36
Mirari Vos, Encyclical of Pope Gregory XVI (August 15, 1832)	43
Quanta Cura & the Syllabus of Errors, Encyclical and Syllabus of Bl. Pope Pius IX (December 8, 1864)	72
Etsi Nos, Encyclical of Pope Leo XIII (February 15, 1882)	118
Praeclara Gratulationis Publicae, Apostolic Letter of Pope Leo XIII (June 20, 1894)	195
Pascendi Dominici Gregis, Encyclical of Pope Saint Pius X (September 8, 1907)	235
Other Related Papal Pronouncements	293

✠

PRAYER FOR THE CONVERSION OF FREEMASONS

O LORD JESUS CHRIST, who showest forth thy omnipotence most manifestly when Thou sparest and hast compassion; Thou who didst say, "Pray for those who persecute and calumniate you," we implore the clemency of thy Sacred Heart on behalf of souls, made in the image of GOD, but most miserably deceived by the treacherous snares of Freemasons, and going more and more astray in the way of perdition. Let not the Church, thy spouse, any longer be oppressed by them; but, appeased by the intercession of the blessed Virgin thy Mother and the prayers of the just, be mindful of thy infinite mercy; and, disregarding their perversity, cause these very men to return to Thee, that they may bring consolation to the Church by a most abundant penance, make reparation for their misdeeds, and secure for themselves a glorious eternity; who livest and reignest world without end. Amen.

100 Days, once a day. Leo XIII, Br. August 16, 1898. (#482 from The Raccolta, 1910 edition)

CANON LAW ON FREEMASONRY

The 1917 Code of Canon Law formalized the excommunication of Catholics joining Masonic lodges:

> Canon 2335. Those giving their name to masonic sects or other associations of this sort that machinate against the Church or legitimate civil powers contract by that fact excommunication simply reserved to the Apostolic See.

which was reiterated in the 1983 Code of Canon Law, though the latter did not explicitly name Freemasonry, leading to some ambiguity:

> Can. 1374. A person who joins an association which plots against the Church is to be punished with a just penalty; however, a person who promotes or directs an association of this kind is to be punished with an interdict.

DECLARATION ON MASONIC ASSOCIATIONS
November 26, 1983
Congregation for the Doctrine of the Faith under Pope John Paul II

Though not a papal encyclical or bull, this declaration, issued by the Congregation for the Doctrine of the Faith (CDF) with papal approval, clarified that Catholic membership in Masonic organizations remains prohibited. It states that Masonic principles are irreconcilable with Catholic doctrine, correcting for the ambiguity in the 1983 Code of Canon Law which does not explicitly name Freemasonry in Canon 1374. Addressed confusion following that revision of Canon Law, the Declaration *reaffirms the Church's stance against Freemasonry in the modern era.*

It has been asked whether there has been any change in the Church's decision in regard to Masonic associations since the new Code of Canon Law does not mention them expressly, unlike the previous Code.

This Sacred Congregation is in a position to reply that this circumstance in due to an editorial criterion which was followed also in the case of other associations likewise unmentioned inasmuch as they are contained in wider categories.

Therefore the Church's negative judgment in regard to Masonic association remains unchanged since their principles have always been considered irreconcilable with the doctrine of the Church and therefore membership in them remains forbidden. The faithful who enroll in Masonic associations are in a state of grave sin and may not receive Holy Communion.

It is not within the competence of local ecclesiastical authorities to give a judgment on the nature of Masonic associations which would imply a derogation from what has been decided above, and this in line with the Declaration of this Sacred Congregation issued on 17 February 1981 (cf. *AAS* 73 1981 pp. 240-241; English language edition of *L'Osservatore Romano*, 9 March 1981).

In an audience granted to the undersigned Cardinal Prefect, the Supreme Pontiff John Paul II approved and ordered the publication of this Declaration which had been decided in an ordinary meeting of this Sacred Congregation.

Rome, from the Office of the Sacred Congregation for the Doctrine of the Faith, 26 November 1983.

Joseph Card. RATZINGER
Prefect
+ Fr. Jerome Hamer, O.P.
Titular Archbishop of Lorium
Secretary

✠

IN EMINENTI APOSTOLATUS
Papal Bull of Pope Clement XII
April 28, 1738

The first papal document to explicitly condemn Freemasonry came from the pen of Pope Clement XII in 1738, less than two years before his death. He declared Freemasonry a secret society with principles contrary to Catholic faith, citing its oath-bound secrecy and aims to subvert both Church and state. Clement was concerned about the growing influence of Masonic lodges in Europe. His bull imposed automatic excommunication on Catholics who joined Masonic lodges.

CLEMENT, BISHOP, Servant of the Servants of God to all the faithful, Salutation, and Apostolic Benediction.

Since the divine clemency has placed Us, Whose merits are not equal to the task, in the high watch-tower of the Apostolate with the duty of pastoral care confided to Us, We have turned Our attention, as far as it has been granted Us from on high, with unceasing care to those things through which the integrity of Orthodox Religion is kept from errors and vices by preventing their entry, and by which the dangers of disturbance in the most troubled times are repelled from the whole Catholic World.

Now it has come to Our ears, and common gossip has made clear, that certain Societies, Companies, Assemblies, Meetings, Congregations or Conventicles called in the popular tongue *Liberi Muratori* or *Francs Massons* or by other names according to the various languages, are spreading far and wide and daily growing in strength; and men of any Religion or sect, satisfied with the appearance of natural probity, are joined together, according to their laws and the statutes laid down for them, by a strict and unbreakable bond which obliges them, both by an oath upon the Holy Bible and by a host of grievous punishment, to an inviolable silence about all that they do in secret together. But it is in the nature of crime to betray itself and to show itself by its attendant clamor. Thus these aforesaid Societies or

Conventicles have caused in the minds of the faithful the greatest suspicion, and all prudent and upright men have passed the same judgment on them as being depraved and perverted. For if they were not doing evil they would not have so great a hatred of the light. Indeed, this rumor has grown to such proportions that in several countries these societies have been forbidden by the civil authorities as being against the public security, and for some time past have appeared to be prudently eliminated.

Therefore, bearing in mind the great harm which is often caused by such Societies or Conventicles not only to the peace of the temporal state but also to the well-being of souls, and realizing that they do not hold by either civil or canonical sanctions; and since We are taught by the divine word that it is the part of faithful servant and of the master of the Lord's household to watch day and night lest such men as these break into the household like thieves, and like foxes seek to destroy the vineyard; in fact, to prevent the hearts of the simple being perverted, and the innocent secretly wounded by their arrows, and to block that broad road which could be opened to the uncorrected commission of sin and for the other just and reasonable motives known to Us; We therefore, having taken counsel of some of Our Venerable Brothers among the Cardinals of the Holy Roman Church, and also of Our own accord and with certain knowledge and mature deliberations, with the plenitude of the Apostolic power do hereby determine and have decreed that these same Societies, Companies, Assemblies, Meetings, Congregations, or Conventicles of *Liberi Muratori* or *Francs Massons*, or whatever other name they may go by, are to be condemned and prohibited, and by Our present Constitution, valid for ever, We do condemn and prohibit them.

Wherefore We command most strictly and in virtue of holy obedience, all the faithful of whatever state, grade, condition, order, dignity or pre-eminence, whether clerical or lay, secular or regular, even those who are entitled to specific and individual mention, that none, under any pretext or for any reason, shall dare or presume to enter, propagate or support these aforesaid societies of *Liberi Muratori* or *Francs Massons*, or however else they are called, or to receive them in their houses or dwellings or to hide them, be enrolled among them, joined to them, be present with them, give power or permission for them to meet elsewhere, to help them in any way, to give them in any way advice, encouragement or support either openly or in secret, directly or indirectly, on their own or through others; nor are they to urge others or tell them, incite or persuade them to be enrolled in such societies or to be counted among their number, or to be present or to assist them in any way; but they must stay completely clear of such Societies, Companies, Assemblies, Meetings, Congregations or Conventicles, under pain of excommunication for all the above mentioned people, which is incurred by the very deed without any declaration being required, and from which no one can obtain the benefit of absolution, other than at the hour of death, except through Ourselves or the Roman Pontiff of the time.

Moreover, We Ordain and Mandate, that as well the Bishops and Prelates, Superiors and other Ordinaries of places, as the Inquisitors Deputed for the places of heretical perversity wherever, proceed and search for grounds of accusation against transgressors, of whatever grade, state, condition, order, dignity, or pre-eminence they may be, and punish with fitting penalties and confine those strongly suspected of heresy; for We grant and impart to them, in general, and to each of them unrestricted faculty of going out and searching for grounds against, and of restraining and punishing with suitable punishments, those same transgressors, once the aid of the secular arm also has been called upon for this purpose, if there should be need.

On the other hand, We Ordain, that absolutely the same faith which would be applied to the Original Letter, if they would be produced or shown, be applied to duplicates, likewise to printed copies, of the present letter signed by the hand of some public notary, and secured by the seal of a person constituted in Ecclesiastical Dignity.

It is allowed to no man to falsify this Letter of Our Declaration, Condemnation, Mandate, Prohibition and Interdict, or to oppose it by a rash boldness; but if anyone presumes to attempt this, let him know that he will incur the wrath of Almighty God, and of His Blessed Apostles Peter and Paul.

Given at Rome at Saint Mary Major in the 1738th year of the Incarnation of the Lord on the 28th day of April, in the eighth year of Our Pontificate.

✠

Providas Romanorum
Apostolic Constitution of Pope Benedict XIV
May 18, 1751

Pope Benedict XIV was the immediate successor of Pope Clement XII and wished to confirmed and renew his predecessor's condemnation of Freemasonry. Benedict emphasized the organization's secrecy, oaths and potential to undermine Church authority and Christendom itself. The document clarified that the membership prohibition applied universally to all Catholics, and it bolstered the Church's stance by reinforcing the penalty of excommunication.

We consider it necessary, with a new intervention of Our authority, to support and confirm - as legitimate and serious reasons require - the prudent laws and sanctions of the Roman Pontiffs, Our Predecessors: not only those laws and those sanctions whose strength, either due to the passage of time or the negligence of men, we fear may be weakened or extinguished, but also those that have recently gained strength and full vigor.

1. Indeed, Clement XII, our predecessor of blessed memory, by his apostolic letter of April 28 in the year of the Incarnation of the Lord 1738, the eighth year of his pontificate - a letter addressed to all the faithful and beginning with *In eminenti* - eternally condemned and prohibited certain Societies, Unions, Meetings, Assemblies, Conclaves, or Associations commonly known as Freemasons or *des Francs Macons*, or otherwise named, which were already widely spread in certain countries at that time and which are now increasingly multiplying. He forbade all individual Christians (under penalty of excommunication to be incurred *ipso facto* without any declaration, from which no one could be absolved by anyone else, except in the moment of death, other than by the Roman Pontiff *pro*

tempore) to attempt or dare to enter such Societies, propagate them or give them favor or refuge, to conceal them, to enroll in them, to associate with them or participate in them, and other matters, as is more broadly and extensively contained in the same letter. Here is the text.

2. [The papal bull *In Eminenti Apostolatus* of Pope Clement XII was included here. See page ??]

3. But since, as we have been informed, some have had no difficulty in claiming and publicly spreading that the excommunication imposed by Our Predecessor is no longer in effect because the related Constitution has not been confirmed by Us, as if the explicit confirmation of the successor is necessary for the Apostolic Constitutions to remain valid;

4. And having been suggested to Us, by certain pious and God-fearing people, that it would be very useful to eliminate all the subterfuges of the slanderers and declare the uniformity of Our soul with the intention and will of the same Predecessor, adding to his Constitution the new vow of Our confirmation;

5. We certainly, up to now, when we benignly granted absolution from the incurred excommunication, often before and mainly in the past Jubilee year, to many sincerely repentant and sorrowful faithful for having transgressed the laws of the same Constitution and who assured from the heart that they would completely distance themselves from such Societies and Conventicles, and that in the future they would never return to them; or when we granted the Penitentiaries delegated by Us the authority to impart absolution in Our name and with Our authority to those who approached the Penitentiaries themselves; and when, with diligent vigilance, we did not neglect to ensure that the competent Judges and Courts proceeded in proportion to the crime committed against the violators of the Constitution itself, which was indeed carried out several times; we have certainly provided not only probable but entirely evident and undeniable arguments, through which our intentions and the firm and deliberate will consistent with the censure imposed by the aforementioned Clement Predecessor should have been understood. If opposing opinions were to spread around Us,

We could certainly despise them and submit Our case to the just judgment of Almighty God, pronouncing those words that were once recited during sacred functions: "Grant, O Lord, we beseech You, that We do not care for the calumnies of perverse minds, but having trampled down the very wickedness, we implore You not to allow us to be afflicted by unjust slanders or ensnared by cunning flattery, but rather that we love what You command." Thus reports an ancient Missal attributed to Saint Gelasius, Our Predecessor, and which was included in the Mass titled Against Slanderers by the Venerable Servant of God Cardinal Giuseppe Maria Tommasi.

6. However, in order that it could not be said that we had imprudently omitted anything, in order to easily eliminate the pretexts to the lying calumnies and shut their mouths; having first heard the advice of some Venerable Brothers of ours, Cardinals of the Holy Roman Church, we have decreed to confirm the same Constitution of Our Predecessor, word for word, as above reported in specific form, which shall be considered the broadest and most effective of all: we confirm it, validate it, renew it, and we want and decree that it has perpetual force and efficacy for Our certain knowledge, in the fullness of Our Apostolic authority, according to the tenor of the same Constitution, in everything and for everything, as if it had been promulgated by Our own accord and with Our authority, and had been published for the first time by Us.

7. In truth, among the very serious reasons for the aforementioned prohibitions and condemnation outlined in the above-mentioned Constitution, there is one, by which men of any religion and sect may mutually unite in such Societies and Conventicles; it is clear what harm can be done to the purity of the Catholic Religion. The second reason is the strict and impenetrable promise of secrecy, by which what is done in these meetings is concealed, to which can rightly be applied the statement that Cecilio Natale, at Minucio Felice's place, made in a very different case: 'Honest things always love the public light; wickednesses are secret.' The third reason is the oath with which they commit to inviolably observe said secret, as if it were permissible for anyone, when questioned by legitimate authority, to evade the obligation to

confess everything that is sought, in order to know whether in such groups anything contrary to the stability and laws of Religion and the Republic is taking place. The fourth reason is that these Societies oppose Civil Sanctions no less than Canonical ones, considering that, according to Civil Law, all Colleges and assemblies formed without public authority are prohibited, as stated in the Pandects (book 47, title 22, On Colleges and illegal corporations), and in the famous letter (no. 97 of book 10) by C. Pliny the Younger, who reports that it was prohibited by his Edict, in accordance with the command of the Emperor, for Eteriae to be held, that is to say, for Societies and assemblies to exist and gather without the authorization of the Prince. The fifth reason is that in many countries the aforementioned Societies and Associations have already been proscribed and banned by laws of the Secular Princes. Finally, the last reason is that among prudent and honest men, the aforementioned Societies and Associations were criticized: in their view, anyone who joined them would incur the charge of wickedness and perversion.

8. Finally, the same Predecessor in the above-mentioned Constitution urges the Bishops, the Prelates, and the other Ordinaries of the places not to neglect to invoke the help of the secular arm whenever necessary for the execution of this provision.

9. All these things, even individually, are not only approved and confirmed by Us, but are also recommended and enjoined upon the Ecclesiastical Superiors; but We ourselves, out of duty of Apostolic solicitude, with this Our Letter invoke and seek with heartfelt passion the assistance and help of the Catholic Princes and secular Powers - being the same Supreme Princes and Potentates elected by God as defenders of the faith and protectors of the Church - so that it may be their concern to strive in the most effective way to ensure that the Apostolic Constitutions receive the due respect and the most absolute obedience. This was recalled to their memory by the Fathers of the Council of Trent (sess. 25, cap. 20), and much earlier it had been splendidly stated by Emperor Charlemagne in his Capitularies (tit. I, cap. 2), in which, after commanding all his subjects to observe

Ecclesiastical Sanctions, he added these words: 'In no way can we know how those who show themselves unfaithful to God and disobedient to his priests can be faithful to us.' Consequently, he imposed on all the Presidents and Ministers of his provinces the obligation to ensure that everyone individually heeded the proper obedience to the laws of the Church. Moreover, I impose very serious penalties on those who neglect to do this, adding among other things: "Those who are found negligent and transgressors in these matters (which may not happen), should know that they will not retain honors in our Empire, even if they are our sons; nor will they have a place in the Palace, nor will they have companionship or shared interests with us or our faithful, but rather they will pay the penalty in difficulties and hardships."

10. We then want that copies of this document, even if printed, signed by hand by some public Notary and sealed by a person vested with Ecclesiastical dignity, be given the same credit as would be given to the Letter if it were presented or shown in its original form.

11. Therefore, let no one, absolutely, be allowed to violate, or boldly contradict this page of Our confirmation, innovation, approval, command, invocation, request, decree, and will. If anyone dares to do so, let them know that they will incur the wrath of Almighty God and the Holy Apostles Peter and Paul.

Given in Rome, at Santa Maria Maggiore, on the 18th of March in the year of the Incarnation of the Lord 1751, the eleventh year of Our Pontificate.

✠

UT PRIMUM
Constitution of Pope Clement XIII
Condemnation and Prohibition
September 3, 1759

The work is distributed in several volumes, the title of which is: Encyclopédie, ou Dictionnaire raisonné des Sciences, des Ars, des Métiers par une société de Gens de Lettres mis en ordre, & publié par Mr Diderot de l'Académie Royale des Sciences, & des belles Lettres de Prussia; and quant a la partie Mathématique, par Mr d'Alembert de l'Académie Royale de Sciences de Paris, de celle de Prusse, & de la Société Royale de Londres.

For future reference
For the first time a thick work in several volumes was published, the title of which is – Encyclopedia or Dictionary raisoné des Sciences, des Arts, & des Metiers by a society of Men of Letters, arranged, & published by Mr. Diderot of the Royal Academy of Sciences & of Fine Arts of Prussia; and as for the Mathematical part, by Mr. d'Alembert of the Royal Academy of Sciences of Paris, of that of Prussia, and of the Royal Society of London – not only by public rumor, but also by the judgment of the most serious men of Faith and Religion, ardent in their zeal, we have received that many things are brought out and contained therein, which are not only extremely detrimental to Christian piety and moral discipline, but which attack Religion itself, and either strive to uproot it from the bottom, or certainly undermine its very heads and dogmas: wherefore, having instituted a careful examination of the same work, and by judgment, among the Books condemned and proscribed by the Apostolic See, it was decreed on the 5th of March last. Meanwhile, there were some who, thinking that it would be a public literary and Christian affair, if, after correcting the errors that abound, a

new edition were to be published, rejected, amended, and revised, they set about adorning it, and by adding to certain chapters or articles known to them, they thought that they had brought a suitable remedy for danger and every evil: but since the poison spread and snaked throughout the entire work, and was not such that it could be cured with a mild antidote, they wasted their effort in vain; for it was found that neither was sufficient consultation carried out to the danger and detriment of the readers, nor was the work sufficiently corrected and purged. From time to time, new and serious complaints were brought to our Apostolate against both editions, which, due to the gravity of the matter, seem to demand the help of our authority and vigilance. First, therefore, in the bitterness of our hearts, we greatly grieve that our times have now come to those which the Savior foretold, in which love is cooling off, and moral discipline is deteriorating, and a flood of fallacies and impious doctrines is overflowing through the frenzied license of philosophizing and writing, and faith itself, and on which Divine Revelation rests, is most shamelessly attacked. Unbelief is now not only admitted, but is also openly and openly taught, and so widely propagated that, if it were possible, the Church, which Christ Jesus promised would continue until the end of the world, would be utterly overthrown and destroyed by the doctrines of impious men; for it is that strong City described by Isaiah, in which, as Jerome explains, a wall of good works is placed, and a rampart of right Faith, so that it may be double-walled with a fortress.– perverse and preposterous, both by their actions and by their teaching, they strive to dismember and destroy the wall and the rampart. But we, whom the Lord has set as watchmen and watchmen on the walls of Jerusalem, to stand strong against those who say – empty it, empty it even to the foundation in it.– for the sake of our place and duty, we cannot and should not remain silent any longer; but wishing to guard and protect the deposit of Faith and Religion entrusted to us with all the means we can, lest any harm should befall it, lest the scourge of the destructive work spread further to the Church and the destruction of souls, we have entrusted the work itself, with the notes added, or corrections, to be submitted to a new examination by our

Venerable Brothers, the Cardinals of the same S. R. E., appointed by Apostolic authority as General Inquisitors against heretical wickedness in the entire Christian Republic. They first consulted the Theologians designated to issue the censure, and their judgments were promptly expressed, and then in the General Congregation held before Us on the 5th day of August 2nd, recently passed, they explained to Us in detail by their votes what should be decided about the work itself. Therefore, having disregarded their opinions, and having examined the censures of theologians, we, by our own *Motu proprio*, and from certain knowledge and mature deliberation, and by the fullness of Apostolic power, condemn and reject the aforementioned work, wherever and in whatever language, even with notes or declarations and corrections whatsoever, which have been printed heretofore or which may be printed hereafter, as containing false, pernicious, and scandalous doctrines and propositions, leading to unbelief and contempt of religion, easily opening the way to moral corruption and impiety, and we forbid it to be read, retained, and described in whatever language by all and each of the Christian faithful, even with specific and individual mention and expression, worthy of greater excommunication as regards secular persons, but as regards ecclesiastical persons, even regulars, under penalty of suspension from the Divines ipso facto without any other declaration, the absolution and relative relaxation of which we, and our Roman successors, Pontiff For those who are currently existing, except only as regards the aforementioned excommunication under the article of death, we reserve: Commanding all and each Christian faithful under the same penalties of excommunication and suspension, respectively, who have the same work with them, or into whose hands it has come from time to time, that as soon as our present Letters become known to them, they are bound to hand it over to the local Ordinaries, or Inquisitors of heretical depravity, or to their Vicars, who will see to it that the examples handed over to them are immediately destroyed by fire. To the contrary, without objection to anyone whatsoever. But so that these same present Letters may be brought more easily to the knowledge of all, and that no one may be ignorant of them, we desire and command that they be published at the doors of the Basilica of the Prince of the Apostles, and the Apostolic Chancellery, as well as of the General Curia on Monte Citatorio, and on the Field of the Flower of the City by one of our Cursors, as is the custom, and that copies of them be left affixed there: also copies of the present Letters themselves, or even printed copies signed by the hand of some Notary Public and secured with the seal of a person established in ecclesiastical dignity, the same faith, both in court and outside it, wherever it may be, would be held as would be given to the original Letters themselves, if they were exhibited or shown.

Given at Rome at St. Mary Major under the Fisherman's Ring on the 3rd day of September, 1759, in the Second Year of Our Pontificate.

Cardinal Passionate.

On the day, month and year above, the aforementioned Damnation and Prohibition was affixed and published at the doors of the Basilica of the Prince Apostolic and the Apostolic Chancellery, as well as of the General Curia on Mount Citatori, and on the Field of the Flower, and in other usual and customary places of the City by me Joseph Renzoni, Apostolic Curs.

Philippus Contini Mag. Curs.

✠

CHRISTIANAE REIPUBLICAE
Encyclical of Pope Clement XIII
On the Dangers of Anti-Christian Writings
November 25, 1766

To Our Venerable Brothers, all Patriarchs, Primates, Metropolitans, Archbishops, and Bishops Who Enjoy Grace and Communion with the Apostolic See.

Venerable Brothers, Greetings and Apostolic Blessing.

The well-being of the Christian community which has been entrusted to Us by the Prince of shepherds and the Guardian of souls requires Us to see to it that the unaccustomed and offensive licentiousness of books which has emerged from hiding to cause ruin and desolation does not become more destructive as it triumphantly spreads abroad. The distortion of this hateful error and the boldness of the enemy has so increased, especially at this time, in sowing weeds among the wheat either in word or in writing that unless We lay the scythe to the root and bind up the bad plants in bundles to burn, it will not be long before the growing thorns of evil attempt to choke the seedlings of the Lord Sabaoth. For accursed men who have given themselves over to myths and who do not uphold the stronghold of Sion from all sides vomit the poison of serpents from their hearts for the ruin of the Christian people by the contagious plague of books which almost overwhelms us. They pollute the pure waters of belief and destroy the foundations of religion.

They are abominable in their activity. Secretly sitting in ambush, they draw arrows out of the quiver which they shoot at the righteous in the dark. They have not restrained their impious minds from anything divine, holy, and consecrated by the oldest religion of all time; rather in their attack they have sharpened their tongues like a sword. They have run first of all against God in their pride. Armed with a thick neck, they have strengthened themselves against the Almighty.

They raise again from the ashes the absurdities of the impious which have been destroyed so often. They deny God even though He makes Himself known everywhere and comes before their eyes daily, not because of the dullness of their mind, but only on the urging of their depraved will. Or else they represent God Himself as lazy and indolent. They do not respect His providence nor do they fear His justice. They preach with a detestable and insane freedom of thought that the origin and nature of our soul is mortal although it was created in the image of the supreme creator little lower than the angels. Whether they think matter has been created or foolishly imagine that it is eternal and independent of the causes, they consider that nothing else exists in this universe. Or else if they are forced to admit that spirit exists with matter, they exclude the soul from the spirit's heavenly nature. They are unwilling to understand that in this very weakness of which we are formed something spiritual and incorruptible abides in us. By its power we know, act, will, look to the future, attend to the present, and remember the past.

On the other hand, there are others who, even if they judge correctly that the fog of earthly reasonings should be dispelled and the smoke of worldly wisdom should be driven from the eye of enlightened faith, still dare to examine with human measures the hidden mysteries of faith which surpass all understanding. Having become investigators of greatness, they are not afraid of being overwhelmed by its glory. They ridicule the faith of simple people. They lay open the mysteries of God. They rashly discourse on questions concerning the highest matters. The bold mind of the enquirer takes everything for itself, examines everything, reserves nothing for faith, and deprives faith of merit by seeking proof for it in human reason.

Should we not also be angry with those who use the most wicked indecency of word and example to corrupt pure and strict morals by mortal sin, who recommend to the minds of the unwary an accursed license of living, and who cause an extreme loss of faith? Then consider how they sprinkle their writings with a certain refined splendor, a seductive pleasantness of speech and allurement so as to penetrate more easily into the readers' minds and infect them more deeply with the poison of their error. Thus they will give the snake's poison in the cup of Babylon to the unwary who are seduced and blinded by their smooth speech and so do not recognize the poison that kills them. Finally, who can avoid deep sadness when he sees the bitter enemy exceed the bounds of modesty and due respect and attack with the publication of outrageous books now in open battle, now in dissimulated combat the very See of Peter which the strong redeemer of Jacob has placed as an iron column and as a bronze wall against the leaders of darkness. Perhaps they are led on by the desperate thought that if they shatter the head of the Church, they will be able more freely to tear to pieces its members.

2. Therefore since the Holy Spirit has made you bishops to govern the Church of God and has taught you concerning the unique sacrament of human salvation, We cannot neglect our duty in the face of these evil books. We must arouse the enthusiasm of your devotion so that you, who are called to share in Our pastoral concern join together to oppose this evil with all energy possible. It is necessary to fight bitterly, as the situation requires, and to eradicate with all our strength the deadly destruction caused by such books. The substance of the error will never be removed unless the criminal elements of wickedness burn in the fire and perish. Since you have been constituted stewards of the mysteries of God and armed with His strength to destroy their defenses, exert yourselves to keep the sheep entrusted to you and redeemed by the blood of Christ at a safe distance from these poisoned pastures. For if it is necessary to avoid the company of evildoers because their words encourage impiety and their speech acts like a cancer, what desolation the plague of their books can cause! Well and cunningly written these books are always with us and forever within our reach. They travel with us, stay at home with us, and enter bedrooms which would be shut to their evil and deception.

Since you have been constituted ministers of Christ for the nations, in order to make holy his Gospel, exert yourselves and do everything in your power both by word and example to cut down the shoots of falsehood. Block up the corrupt springs of vice. Sound the trumpet in case as their leader you have to account for the souls who are lost. Act according to the position you hold, according to the rank with which you are vested, and according to the authority which you have received from the Lord. In addition, as nobody could or should avoid sharing in this sadness and insofar as there is one common reason for everyone to grieve and to help in this great crisis of faith and religion, call to your aid when it is necessary the time-honored piety of Catholic leaders. Explain the cause of the Church's sorrow and arouse its beloved sons who have always served it well on many occasions to bring their help. Since they do not carry the sword without cause, urge them with the united authority of state and of priesthood, to vigorously rout those accursed men who fight against the armies of Israel.

It is principally your duty to stand as a wall so that no foundation can be laid other than the one that is already laid. Watch over the most holy deposit of faith to whose protection you committed yourselves on oath at your solemn consecration. Reveal to the faithful the wolves which are demolishing the Lord's vineyard. They should be warned not to allow themselves to be ensnared by the splendid writing of certain authors in order to halt the diffusion of error by cunning and wicked men. In a word, they should detest books which contain elements shocking to the reader; which are contrary to faith, religion, and good morals; and which lack an atmosphere of Christian virtue. We manifest to you Our great happiness in this matter that most of you, following the apostolic customs and energetically defending the laws of the Church, have shown yourselves zealous and watchful in order to avert this pestilence and have not allowed the simple people to sleep soundly with serpents.

Certainly We who are distressed and distracted by Our concern for all the churches and for the salvation of the Christian people, are unsparing of Our efforts, and We promise you assistance too in your own grave danger. Meanwhile, We will not cease to ask God with deep humility to grant you help from His holy place to deflect the cunning of the insidious enemy and to entirely fulfill the duties of your ministry. As a pledge of the desired outcome, we lovingly impart Our apostolic blessing to you and your flock.

Given in Rome in St. Mary Major's on the 25th day of November in the year 1766, the ninth year of Our pontificate.

ECCLESIAM A JESU CHRISTO
Apostolic Constitution of Pope Pius VII
September 13, 1821

Pope Pius VII led the Catholic Church from 1800 until his death in 1823. He served as pope during the Napoleonic Wars and was even exiled and held prisoner by the French Emperor between 1809 and 1813. Once back in Rome he went on to condemn Italian Freemasonry, known as the Carbonari, a militantly anti-clerical and revolutionary group. Pius excommunicated members of both Freemasonry and the Carbonari for conspiring against Church and state. He attempted to expose their secrecy and political plots, especially their lead in the revolutionary movements sweeping across Europe in the early 1800s.

Pope Pius, servant of the servants of God, for the perpetual remembrance of this matter.

The Church founded by Jesus Christ Our Savior upon a firm Rock, and against which Christ Himself has promised that the gates of hell will never prevail, has been so often assaulted, and by such dreadful enemies, that unless that Divine and Unchangeable Promise had intervened, it might seem that it must be feared that the Church itself, besieged be it by their power, their crafts, or their cunning, might entirely perish. But that which has happened in previous times, such also has been done and especially in this certainly sorrowful time of ours, which seems to be that end time foretold by the Apostles so long ago, during which time (Jude v. 18.) mockers will come walking according to their own desires in ungodliness. For It is not concealed from anyone how great the multitude of wicked men will have joined together in these most difficult times against the Lord and against His Anointed One, who are especially solicitous, once the faithful have been ensnared by Philosophy and vain deceit (Col 2:8.) and torn away from the Doctrine of the Church, for weakening and overturning the same Church, although by a useless effort. But in order to succeed more easily, the greater number of them have formed secret groups and clandestine sects, from which they were hoping that they might induce many into the fellowship of their conspiracy and crime.

A long time ago this Holy See, once these sects had been discovered, cried with a great and unbridled Voice against them, and exposed their plans, which had been devised secretly by them against Religion, indeed against civil society. Long ago it called forth the attentiveness of all, that they might beware lest it be allowed to these sects to attempt that which they were heinously contemplating. Indeed it must have grieved these endeavors of the Holy See not to have answered that destruction, which It was observing, and that wicked men had not desisted from their acknowledged plan; whence they at long last attained to those evils which We Ourselves have perceived; indeed, men whose arrogance has always mounted, have dared to begin new secret societies.

Mention must be made in this place of a society, recently born and propagated far and wide in Italy and in other regions, which although it has been divided into several sects, and according to their variety it sometimes assumes names among themselves different and distinct, nevertheless because the entity is a communion of opinions and crimes, and because a certain pact has been entered into, is one, and is generally accustomed to go under the name of the Carbonari. Indeed, they simulate a singular respect and a certain extraordinary zeal toward the Catholic Religion and toward the Person and Doctrine of Jesus Christ Our Savior, Whom at times they also impiously dare to call the Rector and great Teacher of this society. But these ways of speaking, which are seen to be more slippery than oil, are nothing other than darts employed by crafty men, who come in sheep's clothing but are ravenous wolves inside, for more securely wounding the too little cautious.

Surely that most severe oath, by which, imitating for the most part the ancient Priscillianists they promise that they at no time ever, or in no case, either are going to expose to men not enrolled in the society anything which regards the society, or are going to share with those who are in the lower degrees anything which pertains to the higher decrees. In addition, those clandestine and furthermore illegitimate assemblies, which they have, after the manner employed by many heretics, and the selection of men of whatever religion and sect into their society, even if other things were not available, sufficiently convince that it is necessary to have no confidence in their related discourses.

But it is not necessary by conjectures and indications, that it be judged such concerning their sayings, as it was pointed out above. Books published by these very types in which the procedure is described, which is accustomed to be used in the meetings, especially of the higher degrees; their catechisms, statutes, and other authentic and credible documents, and in fact the testimony of those who, when they had abandoned that society to which they had previously adhered, revealed its errors and frauds to Legitimate Judges, have declared openly, that the Carbonari particularly incline in such a way that they give to each one great license for devising by his own genius and from his own ideas for himself a religion which he may practice, once indifference to religion has been introduced, than which hardly anything more destructive can be contrived, such that they profane and defile the passion of Jesus Christ by certain of their impious ceremonies, that they despise the Sacraments of the Church (for which they seem to substitute other new things invented by themselves through their supreme wickedness) and despise the very mysteries of the Catholic Religion and that they overthrow this Apostolic See against which, because on it the Sovereignty of the Apostolic Chair has always flourished, (S. Aug. Epist. 43.) they are roused by a certain unparalleled hate and they devise every dangerous destructive plot.

And the precepts concerning morals, which the society of the Carbonari hand on, are not, as it is certain from their monuments, less wicked, although it boasts confidently that it demands from its own followers, that they cultivate and exercise charity and every kind of virtue, and abstain from every vice. Therefore, it promotes sensual pleasure most shamelessly, it teaches that it is licit to kill those who have not kept the trust offered concerning the secret, which was mentioned above; and although Peter, the Prince of the Apostles, Decrees, that Christians (1 Pet. 2:13.) be subject to every human creature on account of God, whether to the king as pre-eminent, whether to the magistrates as ambassadors to them, etc., and although Paul the Apostle (Tit. 3:1.) commands that every soul be subject to Higher Powers: nevertheless that society teaches that it is allowed, once revolts have been provoked, to deprive of their power kings and other rulers, whom most unjustly it dares indiscriminately to call tyrants.

These and other dogmas and precepts of this society are the ones from which those crimes newly committed by the Carbonari have emerged, which have brought such intense grief to honest and pious men. We, therefore, who have been constituted as the Guardian of the House of Israel, which is Holy Church, and who in accord with Our Pastoral Office ought to beware lest the Lord's flock divinely entrusted to Us suffer any harm, consider in a case so serious that We cannot abstain from repressing the filthy undertakings of men. We are also moved by the example of Clement XII and Benedict XIV, our Predecessors of happy memory, of whom the one on the 28th day of April of the year 1738 by the Constitution *In Eminenti*, the other on the 18th day of March 1751 by the Constitution Providas, have condemned and proscribed the societies de` Liberi Muratori, or Francs-Macons, or called by whatever other name according to the variety of regions and idioms, of which societies the society of the Carbonari, must be considered perhaps the offspring or certainly the imitation. And although We have already gravely prohibited this society with two Edicts published through Our Secretary of State; nevertheless, following Our above mentioned Predecessors, We think that severe penalties must be Decreed with a formality indeed more Solemnly against this society, especially since the Carbonari indiscriminately maintain that they are not included in those two Constitutions of Clement XII and Benedict XIV, and that they are not subject to the judgments and penalties proposed in them.

Therefore, now that the select Congregation of Our Venerable Brothers of the Cardinals of the Holy Roman Church has been heard, indeed from its Counsel, and also by

Our own motion and from Our certain knowledge and mature deliberation, indeed from the fullness of Our Apostolic Power, We have Decreed and Ordained that the society of the Carbonari mentioned above, or called by any other name whatever, its assemblies, meetings, gatherings, fellowships, or associations must be condemned and prohibited, accordingly as We condemn and proscribe by Our present Constitution forever Valid.

Wherefore We Order strictly and in Virtue of Holy Obedience each and every faithful of Christ of whatever state, grade, condition, order, dignity and pre-eminence, be they the laity or Clerics, both Seculars and Regulars and even those worthy of specific and individual mention, that anyone under whatever pretext, or special condition not dare or presume to join or propagate, to foster, the society of the Carbonari mentioned above, or otherwise named, and to admit and hide in their dwellings, or their homes, or any other place, to be enrolled in, to adhere to or to take part in it, indeed whatever degree of it, or to give opportunity or convenience that it may be convened in any place, to furnish it with anything, or otherwise to offer counsel, aid or good will, openly or in secret, directly or indirectly, per se or through others in any way whatever. Likewise no one may dare or presume to exhort, induce, provoke or persuade others to be inscribed in, be reckoned as part of or be among a society of this kind, or any degree of it, nor are they to help and thus support it in any way whatever. On the contrary they must absolutely abstain themselves from the same society and its assemblies, meetings, fellowships, or associations under pain of Excommunication needing to be incurred ipso facto without any declaration by all those offending as above, from which no one is able to obtain the favor of Absolution through anyone except Us, or the Roman Pontiff Reigning at that time, save one determined to be at the point of death.

Furthermore We Order all under the same pain of Excommunication reserved to Us and Our Successors, the Roman Pontiffs, that they are held to declare to the Bishops, or to others whom it pertains all those whom they know to have joined in this society or to have defiled themselves by any one of the crimes mentioned above.

Finally, that every danger of error may efficaciously be prevented, We condemn and We proscribe that all, as they call them, catechisms and books of the Carbonari, and We forbid, under the same pain of Major Excommunication reserved in the same way, every one of the faithful to read or to possess the books mentioned above, and We command that they hand over those materials, either to the Ordinaries, or to others, to whom the right of receiving them pertains.

We Will, however, that absolutely the same Faith which would be applied to the Original Letter, if they would be produced or shown, is to be applied to duplicates, likewise printed copies, of the present Letter signed by the hand of some public notary, and secured by the seal of a person Constituted in Ecclesiastical Dignity.

It is allowed to no man to falsify this Letter of Our Declaration, Condemnation, Mandate, Prohibition and Interdict, or to oppose it by a rash boldness; but if anyone presumes to attempt this, let him know that he will incur the wrath of Almighty God, and of His Blessed Apostles Peter and Paul.

Given in Rome at Santa Maria Maggiore in the year of the Lord's Incarnation one thousand eight hundred twenty-first on the Ides of September in the twenty-second year of our Pontificate.

On the day, month, and year mentioned above, these Apostolic Letters were affixed and published at the doors of the Lateran, Vatican, and Liberian basilicas, as well as at the Apostolic Chancery, the Innocentian Curia, and in other customary places by me, Vincent Benaglia, Apostolic Secretary.

✠

QUO GRAVIORA
Apostolic Constitution of Pope Leo XII
March 13, 1826

Pope Leo XII ruled the Catholic Church from 1823 until his death isn 1829. This apostolic constitution reaffirmed his predecessors' condemnations of Freemasonry, decreeing a perpetual prohibition on Catholic membership in Masonic lodges. It emphasized the incompatibility of Masonic principles with Catholic teachings and the danger of secret societies and solidified the Church's ongoing opposition to Freemasonry, framing the secret society as a persistent threat to faith and social order.

For the perpetual remembrance of the matter.

1. Blessed Peter, Prince of Apostles, and his Successors have been given the Power and Care of Feeding and Ruling the flock of Christ, Our God and Savior. Hence, the more grave the evils threatening the flock, the greater the solicitude the Roman Pontiffs ought to employ in preventing them. For, those who have been placed in the topmost Watch Tower of the Church can discern from afar the artifices which the enemies of the Christian family undertake to destroy the Church of Christ: (which they will never achieve) they can point them out and expose them to the faithful, who may then guard against them; they can drive away and remove them by their Authority. Our Predecessors, the Roman Pontiffs, understanding this most Grievous Duty imposed upon them, have unceasingly kept the watches of a good Shepherd, and by Exhortations, Doctrines, Decrees, and by their very life given for their sheep, have been solicitous about restraining and utterly abolishing the sects threatening the complete ruin of the Church. Neither is the memory of this Pontifical solicitude able to be drawn only from the age of Ecclesiastical Annals. What things have been carried out in our time and in the age of Our Fathers by the Roman Pontiffs, how they

opposed themselves to secret factions of men contriving maliciously against Christ, clearly demonstrate such. For when Clement XII, Our Predecessor, saw that the sect de' Liberi Muratori or des Francs-Macons, or otherwise named, was increasing every day and that they were acquiring new strength, which he knew with certainty from many proofs to be not only suspect but even altogether inimical to the Catholic Church, condemned it with his magnificent Constitution, beginning with *In eminenti*, published on the 28th of April 1738, the text of which is supplied:

2. [For text of the Papal Bull *In Eminenti Apostolatus* of Pope Clement XII, see page ??.)

3. Nevertheless, these things were not enough for Benedict XIV Our Predecessor of celebrated memory. For it had become spread abroad by the discussions of so many that the penalty of Excommunication demanded in the Letter of Clement, having died a short while ago, had already lost its strength, because Benedict had not clearly confirmed that Letter. It was truly absurd to maintain that the Laws of previous Pontiffs become obsolete, if they are not confirmed expressly by one's Successors, and furthermore, it was manifestly evident that the Constitution of Clement had been considered as Valid by Benedict. Nevertheless, Benedict has judged that this sophistry had to be torn away from the hands of sectarians by a new Constitution which was published, the beginning of which was Providas, on the 18th of March in the year 1751, by which Benedict confirmed the Constitution with just as many words, given to in forma specifica, which is held as the strongest and most effective of all. In fact the Constitution of Benedict is as follows:

4. [For text of *Providas Romanorum* by Pope Benedict XIV, see page ??]

5. Would that those who were in charge of matters then had assumed these Decrees to be of such value as the salvation of both the Church and the State was demanding! Would that they had convinced themselves that they ought to

respect in the Roman Pontiffs, Successors of Blessed Peter, not only the Universal Pastors and Teachers of the Church, but also the Vigorous Defenders of their Dignity, and the most diligent heralds of the dangers which threaten! Would that they had used that power of theirs for dismembering the sects whose pernicious devices had been exposed to them by the Apostolic See! Already from that time they had plainly put into effect their cause. And because they judged that this cause was needing to be treated with indifference or at least treated very trivially, whether by the deceit of the sectarians cunningly hiding their affairs, whether by the imprudent counsels of some, from those old Masonic sects which have never languished, very many others have arisen much more dangerous and more audacious than the former. The sect of the Carbonari, which was considered the leader of all the others in Italy and in some other regions, was considered to embrace as if in its bosom all these, and having divided into, as it were, various branches diverse in name only, undertook to fight most vehemently against the Catholic Religion and every topmost legitimate civil power. Which being a disaster, so that he might free Italy and other regions, indeed even the very Pontifical Domain. (into which, because the Pontifical Government had been obstructed for so long a time, the sect had insinuated itself) Pius VII of happy memory, in whose place We have been chosen, condemned with the gravest penalties the sect of the Carbonari, or with the passage of time by whatever other name it might be called according to the diversity of places, of idioms and of men, by a Constitution published on the 13th of September in the year 1821 whose beginning is: *Ecclesiam a Jesu Christo*. We deem that the Original of this must also be inserted in Our Letter.

6. [For text of the Apostolic Constitution *Ecclesiam a Jesu Christo* of Pope Pius VII, see page ??].

7. Not long after the Constitution published by Pius VII, We were elevated to the topmost Chair of Blessed Peter by no merits of Ours; and immediately We turned Our attention to exposing what the state of clandestine sects was, what their number was, what their poser was. Inquiring about these

things We easily understood that their arrogance had grown principally on account of the multitude of them, increased by the new sects. From which sects that one must especially be mentioned which is called Universitaria, because it has a seat and domicile in many universities of learning, in which the young are informed, initiated to, and fashioned for every crime by some teachers, who are zealous not to teach them, but to pervert them by the mysteries of the same sect which ought to be called most truly the mysteries of iniquity.

From this it indeed appears that even after so long a time since the flames of revolution were enkindled and spread abroad, indeed after the remarkable victories reported by the powerful Princes of Europe, by which those flames were expected to be extinguished, their wicked undertakings still have not known an end. For in these very regions in which the early storms seem to have quieted, what fear there is of new disturbances and seditions, which those sects continually devise! Such dread of the impious daggers, which they secretly fix in the bodies of those whom they assign to death! How many and how grave the things, even against their will, are they who rule with power over the same ones not rarely forced to decree for safeguarding public peace?

From this the most painful calamities come forth by which the Church is everywhere fiercely plagued, and which We are not able to relate without pain, without deep sorrow. Its Holy Dogmas and Precepts are fought against most shamelessly; Its Dignity is diminished; and that peace and happiness which It ought to enjoy by a certain right of Its own, was not only being disturbed, but is totally destroyed.

Nor must it be thought that all these evils, and others which have been omitted by Us are attributed to these clandestine sects surely through calumny. Books which they do not hesitate to write about Religion and the State, have been published in their name, with which they scorn dominion, blaspheme majesty; moreover they declare repeatedly that Christ is either a scandal or foolish; indeed, not rarely, that there is no God, and they teach that the soul of man dies together with the body: the codes and statues, by which they explain their goals and ordinances openly declare that all the things which We have already mentioned, and which pertain to the overthrowing of Legitimate Rulers and totally destroying the Church come forth from them. And this has been ascertained and must be considered as certain, that these sects, although in name different, nevertheless have been joined among themselves by an impious bond of filthy goals.

Since matters are in such a state, We judge it to be the Character of our Office to Condemn these clandestine sects again, and in such a manner indeed that no one of them can boast that they are not encompassed by Our Apostolic Pronouncement, and under this pretext lead careless and less sagacious men into error. Therefore, from the Counsel of Our Venerable Brethren, the Cardinals of the Holy Roman Church, and also by Our own motion indeed with Our certain knowledge and mature consideration, We forbid forever under the same penalties which are contained in the Letters of Our Predecessors already reported in this Our Constitution, which Letters We expressly confirm, that all secret societies, those which now are and those which perhaps will afterwards sprout out, and which propose to themselves against the Church and against the highest civil powers those things which We have mentioned above, by whatever name they may finally be called.

Wherefore We Order strictly and in virtue of Holy Obedience each and every faithful of Christ of whatever state, grade, condition, order, dignity and pre-eminence, be they the laity or Clerics, both Seculars and Regulars and even those worthy of specific and individual mention, that anyone, under whatever pretext or special condition, may not dare or presume to join or propagate, or to foster, the societies mentioned above, or by whatever name they may be called, and to admit and hide, in their dwellings, or their homes, or any place, to be enrolled in, to adhere to or to take part in them, indeed to whatever degree of the same, or to give opportunity or convenience that they may be assembled in any place, to furnish the same with anything, or otherwise to offer counsel, aid or good will, openly or in secret, directly or indirectly, per se or through others in any way whatever. Likewise no one may dare or presume to exhort, induce, provoke or persuade others to be inscribed in, be reckoned as part of or be among societies of this kind, or any degree of the same, nor are they to help and thus support them in any way whatever. On the contrary they must absolutely abstain from the same societies and their assemblies, meetings, fellowships, or associations under pain of Excommunication to be incurred ipso facto without any declaration by all those offending as above, from which no one is able to obtain the favor of absolution through anyone except Us, or the Roman Pontiff Reigning at that time, save one determined to be at the point of death.

Furthermore, We order all under the same pain of Excommunication reserved to Us and Our Successors, the Roman Pontiffs, that they are held to declare to the Bishops, or to others whom it concerns, all those whom they know to have joined this society, or to have defiled themselves by any one of the crimes just mentioned above.

In fact, We explicitly condemn and declare invalid particularly that clearly impious and accursed oath, by which they bind those who are received into these sects that they will reveal to none those things which pertain to those sects, and that they will strike with death all those members who expose those things to their superiors, either Ecclesiastics or laity. For what reason? Is not an oath, which must be sworn in justice, in order to establish, as it were, a contract by which someone obliges himself to an unjust murder, and in order to despise the Authority of those, who, when they regulate either the Church or Legitimate civil society, have the right of discerning those things in which the salvation of those societies consists, contrary to Divine Law? Isn't it the most unjust and the greatest indignity to call God as a witness and surety of crimes? Most recently the Fathers of the Lateran Council III have said (Can. 3): "For they must not be called oaths, but rather perjuries, which are taken against Ecclesiastical utility and the Ordinances of the most Holy Fathers." And the shamelessness and madness of the ones among these men who when they say not just in their heart, but also openly and in their public writings: "There is not a God," dare nevertheless demand an oath from all those whom they select for their sects.

These things have been established for suppressing and

condemning all these ravening and criminal sects. But now We not only request but demand your service, Venerable Brothers, the Catholic Patriarchs, Primates, Archbishops, and Bishops. Be attentive for yourselves and for the Universal flock over which the Holy Ghost has placed you as Bishops to Rule the Church of God. Devouring wolves indeed will seize upon you not sparing the flock: but do not fear, not consider your life more precious than yourselves. Maintain that Sacred Truth that the constancy of the men entrusted to you in Religion depends for the most part on you and on things done rightly. For although we may live in those days which are evil, and in that time in which many do not maintain sound Doctrine, nevertheless the Obedience of very many faithful to their Pastors endures, whom they receive with reason as Ministers of Christ and dispensers of His mysteries. Use, therefore, this Authority for the advantage of your sheep, which you maintain over their souls by an imperishable Honor of God. Make known through yourselves the deceits of the sects and with how much diligence they must guard against them and their social intercourse. Let them dread their perverse doctrine which mocks the Most Holy Mysteries of our Religion and the most pure Precepts of Christ, and which attacks every Legitimate Power, while you act as their models and teachers. And finally let Us exhort you with the words of Our Predecessor, Clement XII, in his Encyclical Letter to all the Patriarchs, Primates, Archbishops, Bishops of the Catholic Church of the 14th day of September of the year 1758: "Let Us be filled, I pray, with the Power of the Spirit of the Lord, with discernment and with virtue, lest just as dumb dogs not having the power to bark, We suffer Our flocks to be as pillage and Our sheep forage for the beasts of the field. And let not anything detain Us from giving ourselves up to all battles for the Glory of God and the salvation of souls. Let Us consider Him, who underwent such great contradiction against Himself by sinners. But if We fear the boldness of those wicked ones, it has been from the force of the Episcopate, and from the sublime and Divine Power of Governing the Church; but neither are We able to remain much longer or be any longer Christians, if it has come to this point that We are terrified at the threats or the artifices of the destroyers."

We demand also with great zeal your assistance, dearest sons in Christ, Our Catholic Princes, whom We love with a singular and truly Paternal love. Furthermore We call into memory the words which Leo the Great, whose Successors in Dignity and Heirs We are, although unworthy of the name, used writing to the emperor Leo: "You ought unhesitatingly to recognize that the Royal Power has been conferred to you not only for the Rule of the world, but especially for the defense of the Church, so that by suppressing the heinous undertakings you may defend those Statutes which are good and restore True Peace to those things which have been disordered." Although there is such an interval, the reality remains in this time, so that those sects must be restrained by you not only for defending the Catholic Religion, but also for protecting your safety and that of the people subject to your Rule. In fact, the cause of Religion especially in this time, has been so united with the health of society, that certainly in no way can one be separated from the other. For they who follow those sects, are not less enemies of Religion than of your Power. They assault each one, they devise to overthrow completely each one. But they would not however be allowed, if it were possible, to suppress either Religion or any Royal Power.

And so great is the cunning of the most calculating men that when they are seen especially to be favorable to the increasing of your Power, then they are looking chiefly for the overturning of it. Those men indeed teach very many things such that they advocate that Our Power and that of the Bishops must be diminished and weakened by those who have possession of power, and that many rights must be transferred to them, both from those which are Possessions of this Apostolic See and Principal Church, and from those which pertain to the Bishops, who have been called for a sharing of Our solicitude. But these things those men teach, not only from a most offensive hate by which they are inflamed against Religion, but also according to a plan whereby they hope that people who are subject to your Rule on observing that the limits, which Christ and the Church instituted by Him have established concerning Sacred

Matters, are overturned, may be easily aroused by this example to change and destroy even the form of civil government.

Likewise We look with solicitude, by Our Special Prayer and encouragements, upon you all, O Beloved Sons, who profess the Catholic Religion. Avoid entirely men who consider light darkness, and darkness light. For what utility worthy of the name can arise from agreement with men who think that no consideration for God, no consideration for the more Sublime Powers, is needing to be had, who through intrigues and secret assemblies try to declare war on those things, and who are such that they cry even in public and everywhere that they are the greatest lovers of the public gook, of the Church, and of society; nevertheless they have already declared by all their deeds that they wish to throw all things into disorder and to overturn all things. These are indeed similar to those men to whom John commands in his second Epistle (v. 10) that neither hospitality must be given no "God speed" be said, and whom our Fathers do not hesitate to call the firstborn of the devil. Beware therefore of their flatteries and of their discourses sweetened with honey, by which they will seduce you to enroll in those sects to which they have been admitted. Have it for certain that no one can be a member of those sects, without being guilty of the most serious disgraceful act; and drive away from your ears the words of those who vigorously declare that you may assent to your election to the lower degrees of their sects, that nothing is admitted in those degrees which is opposed to reason, nothing which is opposed to Religion, indeed that there is nothing proclaimed, nothing performed which is not Holy, which is not Right, which is not Undefiled. Truly that abominable oath, which has already been mentioned, and which must be sworn even in that lower echelon, is sufficient for you to understand that it is contrary to Divine Law to be enlisted in those lower degrees, and to remain in them. In the next place, although they are not accustomed to commit those things which are more serious and more criminal to those who have not attained to the higher degrees, nevertheless it is plainly evident that the force and boldness of those most pernicious societies grow on account of the unanimity and the multitude of all who enroll in them. Therefore, even those who have not passed beyond the inferior degrees, must be considered sharers of their crimes. And that passage of the Apostle to the Romans (ch. 1) applies to them: "They who do such things, but also those who consent to those doing them."

Finally, We call very lovingly to Ourselves those who had once been enlightened, and had tasted the Heavenly Gift and had been made partakers, nevertheless, then erred most miserably and follow those sects whether they are engaged in their inferior or abide in their superior degrees. For, the one standing in the place of Him Who has professed that He has not come to call the just but sinners, and Who has likened Himself to a Shepherd, Who, when He has left the remaining flock behind, carefully seeks the sheep He has lost, We exhort and implore them to turn back to Christ. For although they have defiled themselves exceedingly with crime, they ought not despair of Mercy and Clemency from God and Jesus Christ Who has suffered for them also, Who will not despise in any way their repentance, but certainly like a most loving Father, who a long time ago was waiting for his prodigal sons, will very gladly receive it. But We, in order that We may rouse them, inasmuch as it is in Our Power, and pave an easier road for them to penance, suspend for the entire interval of a year, once this Apostolic Letter of Ours has been published in the region in which they live, both the obligation of denouncing their associates in those sects, and also the reservation of censures, into which they, enrolling in those sects, have fallen, and We declare that, even if their associates have not been denounced, they are able to be absolved from those censures by any confessor whatever, provided that he is from the number of those who have been approved by the Ordinaries of the places in which they live.

Which Indulgence also We Authorize to be applied to those who perhaps live at Rome. But if anyone of them whom We address is so unyielding (because God the Father of Mercies turns away) that he acts such that that interval of time, which We have designated, passes without abandoning those sects, and being truly repentant, by that lapse of time immediately both the obligation of denouncing his associates and the reservation of censures revives for him, nor is he able to obtain absolution thereafter, unless once his associates have been denounced before, or at least once an oath has been sworn with respect to denouncing them as soon as possible. Nor is he able to be loosed from those censures by any other than Us, or by Our Successors, or by those who will have obtained the faculty of absolving from the same by the Holy See.

We will, however, that absolutely the same Faith which would be applied to the Original Letter, if they would be produced or shown, is to be applied to duplicates, likewise printed copies, of the present Letter signed by the hand of some public notary, and secured by the Seal of a person constituted in Ecclesiastical Dignity.

It is allowed to no man to falsify this Letter of Our Declaration, condemnations, renewal, ordered prohibition, invocation, examination, decree and will, or to oppose it by a rash boldness. But if anyone presumes to attempt this, let him know that he will incur the wrath of Almighty God, and of His Blessed Apostles Peter and Paul.

Given at Rome in Saint Peter, in the 1826th year of the Incarnation of the Lord, on the 13th day of March, in the second year of Our Pontificate.

TRADITI HUMILITATI
Encyclical of Pope Pius VIII
On His Program for the Pontificate
May 24, 1829

This encyclical, penned by Pope Pius VIII during his brief pontificate, which spanned March 1829 until November 1830, detailed plans for his pontificate. Freemasonry was not the exclusive focus but was of great import, as Pius condemned secret societies and the philosophies promoted by them, especially religious indifferentism. In fact, one of the main concerns of his pontificate was confronting ideologies undermining Catholic doctrine. His encyclical reinforced the Church's condemnation of groups like Freemasonry that warred against Catholicism.

To Our Venerable Brothers, Patriarchs, Primates, Archbishops, and Bishops.

Venerable Brothers, Greetings and Apostolic Benediction.

According to the custom of Our ancestors, We are about to assume Our pontificate in the church of the Lateran. This office has been granted to Us, even though We are humble and unworthy. We open Our heart with joy to you, venerable brothers, whom God has given to Us as helpers in the conduct of so great an administration. We are pleased to let you know the intimate sentiments of Our will. We also think it helpful to communicate those things from which the Christian cause may benefit. For the duty of Our office is not only to feed, rule, and direct the lambs, namely the Christian people, but also the sheep, that is the clergy.

2. We rejoice and praise Christ, who raised up shepherds for the safekeeping of His flock. These shepherds vigilantly lead their flocks so as not to lose even one of those they have received from the Father. For We know well, venerable brothers, your unshakeable faith, your zeal for religion, your

sanctity of life, and your singular prudence. Co-workers such as you make Us happy and confident. This pleasant situation encourages Us when We fear because of the great responsibility of Our office, and it refreshes and strengthens Us when We feel overwhelmed by so many serious concerns. We shall not detain you with a long sermon to remind you what things are required to perform sacred duties well, what the canons prescribe lest anyone depart from vigilance over his flock, and what attention ought to be given in preparing and accepting ministers. Rather We call upon God the Savior that He may protect you with His omnipresent divinity and bless your activities and endeavors with happy success.

3. Although God may console Us with you, We are nonetheless sad. This is due to the numberless errors and the teachings of perverse doctrines which, no longer secretly and clandestinely but openly and vigorously, attack the Catholic faith. You know how evil men have raised the standard of revolt against religion through philosophy (of which they proclaim themselves doctors) and through empty fallacies devised according to natural reason. In the first place, the Roman See is assailed and the bonds of unity are, every day, being severed. The authority of the Church is weakened and the protectors of things sacred are snatched away and held in contempt. The holy precepts are despised, the celebration of divine offices is ridiculed, and the worship of God is cursed by the sinner.

[1] All things which concern religion are relegated to the fables of old women and the superstitions of priests. Truly lions have roared in Israel.[2] With tears We say: "Truly they have conspired against the Lord and against His Christ." Truly the impious have said: "Raze it, raze it down to its foundations."[3]

4. Among these heresies belongs that foul contrivance of the sophists of this age who do not admit any difference among the different professions of faith and who think that the portal of eternal salvation opens for all from any religion.

---

[1] Wis 1.32.
[2] Jer 2.25.
[3] Ps 136.7.

They, therefore, label with the stigma of levity and stupidity those who, having abandoned the religion which they learned, embrace another of any kind, even Catholicism. This is certainly a monstrous impiety which assigns the same praise and the mark of the just and upright man to truth and to error, to virtue and to vice, to goodness and to turpitude. Indeed this deadly idea concerning the lack of difference among religions is refuted even by the light of natural reason. We are assured of this because the various religions do not often agree among themselves. If one is true, the other must be false; there can be no society of darkness with light. Against these experienced sophists the people must be taught that the profession of the Catholic faith is uniquely true, as the apostle proclaims: one Lord, one faith, one baptism.[4] Jerome used to say it this way: he who eats the lamb outside this house will perish as did those during the flood who were not with Noah in the ark.[5] Indeed, no other name than the name of Jesus is given to men, by which they may be saved.[6] He who believes shall be saved; he who does not believe shall be condemned.[7]

5. We must also be wary of those who publish the Bible with new interpretations contrary to the Church's laws. They skillfully distort the meaning by their own interpretation. They print the Bibles in the vernacular and, absorbing an incredible expense, offer them free even to the uneducated. Furthermore, the Bibles are rarely without perverse little inserts to insure that the reader imbibes their lethal poison instead of the saving water of salvation. Long ago the Apostolic See warned about this serious hazard to the faith and drew up a list of the authors of these pernicious notions. The rules of this Index were published by the Council of Trent;[8] the ordinance required that translations of the Bible into the vernacular not be permitted without the approval of the Apostolic See and further required that they be published

---

[4] Eph 4.5.
[5] Epistle to Damasus, the 37th pope.
[6] Acts 4.12.
[7] Mk 16.16.
[8] Rule 4 of the Index, and the addition to same from the decree of the Index of 13 June 1737.

with commentaries from the Fathers. The sacred Synod of Trent had decreed[9] in order to restrain impudent characters, that no one, relying on his own prudence in matters of faith and of conduct which concerns Christian doctrine, might twist the sacred Scriptures to his own opinion, or to an opinion contrary to that of the Church or the popes. Though such machinations against the Catholic faith had been assailed long ago by these canonical proscriptions, Our recent predecessors made a special effort to check these spreading evils.[10] With these arms may you too strive to fight the battles of the Lord which endanger the sacred teachings, lest this deadly virus spread in your flock.

6. When this corruption has been abolished, then eradicate those secret societies of factious men who, completely opposed to God and to princes, are wholly dedicated to bringing about the fall of the Church, the destruction of kingdoms, and disorder in the whole world. Having cast off the restraints of true religion, they prepare the way for shameful crimes. Indeed, because they concealed their societies, they aroused suspicion of their evil intent. Afterwards this evil intention broke forth, about to assail the sacred and the civil orders. Hence the supreme pontiffs, Our predecessors, Clement XII, Benedict XIV, Pius VII, Leo XII,[11] repeatedly condemned with anathema that kind of secret society. Our predecessors condemned them in apostolic letters; We confirm those commands and order that they be observed exactly. In this matter We shall be diligent lest the Church and the state suffer harm from the machinations of such sects. With your help We strenuously take up the mission of destroying the strongholds which the putrid impiety of evil men sets up.

7. We want you to know of another secret society organized not so long ago for the corruption of young people

---

[9] Session 4 on the decree concerning holy books.

[10] Read, among other things, the apostolic letters of Pius VII to the archbishops of Gnesen (1 June 1816) and Mohilev (3 September 1816).

[11] Clement XII, constitution In eminenti; Benedict XIV, constitution Providas; Pius VII, Constitution Ecclesiam a Jesu Christo; Leo XII, constitution Quo graviora.

who are taught in the gymnasia and the lycea. Its cunning purpose is to engage evil teachers to lead the students along the paths of Baal by teaching them un-Christian doctrines. The perpetrators know well that the students' minds and morals are molded by the precepts of the teachers. Its influence is already so persuasive that all fear of religion has been lost, all discipline of morals has been abandoned, the sanctity of pure doctrine has been contested, and the rights of the sacred and of the civil powers have been trampled upon. Nor are they ashamed of any disgraceful crime or error. We can truly say with Leo the Great that for them 'Law is prevarication; religion, the devil; sacrifice, disgrace.'[12] Drive these evils from your dioceses. Strive to assign not only learned, but also good men to train our youth.

8. Also watch the seminaries more diligently. The fathers of Trent made you responsible for their administration.[13] From them must come forth men well instructed both in Christian and ecclesiastical discipline and in the principles of sound doctrine. Such men may then distinguish themselves for their piety and their teaching. Thus, their ministry will be a witness, even to those outside the Church and they will be able to refute those who have strayed from the path of justice. Be very careful in choosing the seminarians since the salvation of the people principally depends on good pastors. Nothing contributes more to the ruin of souls than impious, weak, or uninformed clerics.

9. The heretics have disseminated pestilential books everywhere, by which the teachings of the impious spread, much as a cancer.[14] To counteract this most deadly pest, spare no labor. Be admonished by the words of Pius VII: "May they consider only that kind of food to be healthy to which the voice and authority of Peter has sent them. May they choose such food and nourish themselves with it. May they judge that food from which Peter's voice calls them away to be entirely harmful and pestiferous. May they quickly shrink away from it, and never permit themselves to be caught by its

---

[12] In sermon 5 on fasting of the tenth month, chap. 4.
[13] Session 25, chap. 18, on reform.
[14] 2 Tm 2.17.

appearance and perverted by its allurements."[15]

10. We also want you to imbue your flock with reverence for the sanctity of marriage so that they may never do anything to detract from the dignity of this sacrament. They should do nothing that might be unbecoming to this spotless union nor anything that might cause doubt about the perpetuity of the bond of matrimony. This goal will be accomplished if the Christian people are accurately taught that the sacrament of matrimony ought to be governed not so much by human law as by divine law and that it ought to be counted among sacred, not earthly, concerns. Thus, it is wholly subject to the Church. Formerly marriage had no other purpose than that of bringing children into the world. But now it has been raised to the dignity of a sacrament by Christ the Lord and enriched with heavenly gifts. Now its purpose is not so much to generate offspring as to educate children for God and for religion. This increases the number of worshippers of the true divinity. It is agreed that the union of marriage signifies the perpetual and sublime union of Christ with His Church; as a result, the close union of husband and wife is a sacrament, that is, a sacred sign of the immortal love of Christ for His spouse. Therefore, teach the people what is sanctioned and what is condemned by the rules of the Church and the decrees of the Councils.[16] Also explain those things which pertain to the essence of the sacrament. Then they will be able to accomplish those things and will not dare to attempt what the Church detests. We ask this earnestly of you because of your love of religion.

11. You know now what causes Our present grief. There are also other things, no less serious, which it would take too long to recount here, but which you know well. Shall We hold back Our voice when the Christian cause is in such great need? Shall We be restrained by human arguments? Shall We suffer in silence the rending of the seamless robe of Christ the Savior, which even the soldiers who crucified Him did not dare to rend? Let it never happen that We be found lacking in zealous pastoral care for Our flock, beset as it is by serious

---

[15] In the encyclical letter to all bishops published in Venice.//
[16] Read the Roman catechism for parish priests on matrimony.

dangers. We know you will do even more than We ask, and that you will cherish, augment, and defend the faith by means of teachings, counsel, work, and zeal.

12. With many ardent prayers We ask that, with God restoring the penitence of Israel, holy religion may flourish everywhere. We also ask that the true happiness of the people may continue undisturbed, and that God may always protect the pastor of His earthly flock and nourish him. May the powerful princes of the nations, with their generous spirits, favor Our cares and endeavors. With God's help, may they continue vigorously to promote the prosperity and safety of the Church, which is afflicted by so many evils.

13. Let us ask these things humbly of Mary, the holy Mother of God. We confess that she alone has overcome all heresies and We salute her with gratitude on this day, the anniversary of Our predecessor, Pius VII's, restoration to the city of Rome after he had suffered many adversities. Let us ask these things of Peter, the Prince of the Apostles, and of his coapostle Paul. With Christ's consent, may these two apostles grant that We, firmly established on the rock of the Church's confession, suffer no disturbing circumstances. From Christ Himself We humbly ask the gifts of grace, peace, and joy for you and for the flock entrusted to you. As a pledge of Our affection We lovingly impart the apostolic benediction.

Given in Rome, at St. Peter's, May 24, 1829, the first year of Our pontificate.

✠

MIRARI VOS
Encyclical of Pope Gregory XVI
On Liberalism and Religious Indifferentism
August 15, 1832

Mirari Vos *is one of the most commonly cited papal encyclicals condemining liberalism and religious indifferentism, two of the central philosophies of Freemasonry. Though Pope Gregory XVI (1831-1846) did not specifically name the organization, his criticisms of ideologies that suggest salvation can be attained through any religion are widely interpreted as an implicit condemnation of Freemasonry's religious liberalism.*

To All Patriarchs, Primates, Archbishops, and Bishops of the Catholic World.

Venerable Brothers, Greetings and Apostolic Benediction.

1. We think that you wonder why, from the time of Our assuming the pontificate, We have not yet sent a letter to you as is customary and as Our benevolence for you demanded. We wanted very much to address you by that voice by which We have been commanded, in the person of blessed Peter, to strengthen the brethren.

[1] You know what storms of evil and toil, at the beginning of Our pontificate, drove Us suddenly into the depths of the sea. If the right hand of God had not given Us strength, We would have drowned as the result of the terrible conspiracy of impious men. The mind recoils from renewing this by enumerating so many dangers; instead We bless the Father of consolation Who, having overthrown all enemies, snatched Us from the present danger. When He had calmed this violent storm, He gave Us relief from fear. At once We decided to advise you on healing the wounds of Israel; but the mountain

---

[1] 22.32.

of concerns We needed to address in order to restore public order delayed Us.

2. In the meantime We were again delayed because of the insolent and factious men who endeavored to raise the standard of treason. Eventually, We had to use Our God-given authority to restrain the great obstinacy of these men with the rod.[2] Before We did, their unbridled rage seemed to grow from continued impunity and Our considerable indulgence. For these reasons Our duties have been heavy.

3. But when We had assumed Our pontificate according to the custom and institution of Our predecessors and when all delays had been laid aside, We hastened to you. So We now present the letter and testimony of Our good will toward you on this happy day, the feast of the Assumption of the Virgin. Since she has been Our patron and savior amid so many great calamities, We ask her assistance in writing to you and her counsels for the flock of Christ.

4. We come to you grieving and sorrowful because We know that you are concerned for the faith in these difficult times. Now is truly the time in which the powers of darkness winnow the elect like wheat.[3] "The earth mourns and fades away... And the earth is infected by the inhabitants thereof, because they have transgressed the laws, they have changed the ordinances, they have broken the everlasting covenant."[4]

5. We speak of the things which you see with your own eyes, which We both bemoan. Depravity exults; science is impudent; liberty, dissolute. The holiness of the sacred is despised; the majesty of divine worship is not only disapproved by evil men, but defiled and held up to ridicule. Hence sound doctrine is perverted and errors of all kinds spread boldly. The laws of the sacred, the rights, institutions, and discipline — none are safe from the audacity of those speaking evil. Our Roman See is harassed violently and the bonds of unity are daily loosened and severed. The divine authority of the Church is opposed and her rights shorn off. She is subjected to human reason and with the greatest

---

[2] I Cor 4.21.
[3] Lk 22.53.
[4] Is 24.5.

injustice exposed to the hatred of the people and reduced to vile servitude. The obedience due bishops is denied and their rights are trampled underfoot. Furthermore, academies and schools resound with new, monstrous opinions, which openly attack the Catholic faith; this horrible and nefarious war is openly and even publicly waged. Thus, by institutions and by the example of teachers, the minds of the youth are corrupted and a tremendous blow is dealt to religion and the perversion of morals is spread. So the restraints of religion are thrown off, by which alone kingdoms stand. We see the destruction of public order, the fall of principalities, and the overturning of all legitimate power approaching. Indeed this great mass of calamities had its inception in the heretical societies and sects in which all that is sacrilegious, infamous, and blasphemous has gathered as bilge water in a ship's hold, a congealed mass of all filth.

6. These and many other serious things, which at present would take too long to list, but which you know well, cause Our intense grief. It is not enough for Us to deplore these innumerable evils unless We strive to uproot them. We take refuge in your faith and call upon your concern for the salvation of the Catholic flock. Your singular prudence and diligent spirit give Us courage and console Us, afflicted as We are with so many trials. We must raise Our voice and attempt all things lest a wild boar from the woods should destroy the vineyard or wolves kill the flock. It is Our duty to lead the flock only to the food which is healthful. In these evil and dangerous times, the shepherds must never neglect their duty; they must never be so overcome by fear that they abandon the sheep. Let them never neglect the flock and become sluggish from idleness and apathy. Therefore, united in spirit, let us promote our common cause, or more truly the cause of God; let our vigilance be one and our effort united against the common enemies.

7. Indeed you will accomplish this perfectly if, as the duty of your office demands, you attend to yourselves and to doctrine and meditate on these words: "the universal Church is affected by any and every novelty"[5] and the admonition of

---

[5] St. Celestine, Pope, epistle 21 to Bishop Galliar.

Pope Agatho: "nothing of the things appointed ought to be diminished; nothing changed; nothing added; but they must be preserved both as regards expression and meaning."[6] Therefore may the unity which is built upon the See of Peter as on a sure foundation stand firm. May it be for all a wall and a security, a safe port, and a treasury of countless blessings.[7] To check the audacity of those who attempt to infringe upon the rights of this Holy See or to sever the union of the churches with the See of Peter, instill in your people a zealous confidence in the papacy and sincere veneration for it. As St. Cyprian wrote: "He who abandons the See of Peter on which the Church was founded, falsely believes himself to be a part of the Church."[8]

8. In this you must labor and diligently take care that the faith may be preserved amidst this great conspiracy of impious men who attempt to tear it down and destroy it. May all remember the judgment concerning sound doctrine with which the people are to be instructed. Remember also that the government and administration of the whole Church rests with the Roman Pontiff to whom, in the words of the Fathers of the Council of Florence, "the full power of nourishing, ruling, and governing the universal Church was given by Christ the Lord."[9] It is the duty of individual bishops to cling to the See of Peter faithfully, to guard the faith piously and religiously, and to feed their flock. It behooves priests to be subject to the bishops, whom "they are to look upon as the parents of their souls," as Jerome admonishes.[10] Nor may the priests ever forget that they are forbidden by ancient canons to undertake ministry and to assume the tasks of teaching and preaching "without the permission of their bishop to whom the people have been entrusted; an accounting for the souls of the people will be demanded from the bishop."[11] Finally

---

[6] St. Agatho, Pope, epistle to the emperor, apud Labb., ed. Mansi, vol. 2, p. 235.

[7] St. Innocent, epistle 11 apud Constat.

[8] St. Cyprian, de unitate eccles.

[9] Council of Florence, session 25, in definit. apud Labb., ed. Venet., vol. 18, col. 527.

[10] St. Jerome, epistle 2 to Nepot. a. 1, 24.

[11] From canon ap. 38 apud Labb., ed Mansi, vol. 1, p. 38.

let them understand that all those who struggle against this established order disturb the position of the Church.

9. Furthermore, the discipline sanctioned by the Church must never be rejected or be branded as contrary to certain principles of natural law. It must never be called crippled, or imperfect or subject to civil authority. In this discipline the administration of sacred rites, standards of morality, and the reckoning of the rights of the Church and her ministers are embraced.

10. To use the words of the fathers of Trent, it is certain that the Church "was instructed by Jesus Christ and His Apostles and that all truth was daily taught it by the inspiration of the Holy Spirit."[12] Therefore, it is obviously absurd and injurious to propose a certain "restoration and regeneration" for her as though necessary for her safety and growth, as if she could be considered subject to defect or obscuration or other misfortune. Indeed these authors of novelties consider that a "foundation may be laid of a new human institution," and what Cyprian detested may come to pass, that what was a divine thing "may become a human church."[13] Let those who devise such plans be aware that, according to the testimony of St. Leo, "the right to grant dispensation from the canons is given" only to the Roman Pontiff. He alone, and no private person, can decide anything "about the rules of the Church Fathers." As St. Gelasius writes: "It is the papal responsibility to keep the canonical decrees in their place and to evaluate the precepts of previous popes so that when the times demand relaxation in order to rejuvenate the churches, they may be adjusted after diligent consideration."[14]

11. Now, however, We want you to rally to combat the abominable conspiracy against clerical celibacy. This conspiracy spreads daily and is promoted by profligate philosophers, some even from the clerical order. They have forgotten their person and office, and have been carried away by the enticements of pleasure. They have even dared to

---

[12] Council of Trent, session 13 on the Eucharist, prooemium.

[13] St. Cyprian, epistle 52, ed. Baluz.

[14] St. Gelasius, Pope, in epistle to the bishop of Lucaniae.

make repeated public demands to the princes for the abolition of that *most holy discipline*. But it is disgusting to dwell on these evil attempts at length. Rather, We ask that you strive with all your might to justify and to defend the law of clerical celibacy as prescribed by the sacred canons, against which the arrows of the lascivious are directed from every side.

12. Now the honorable marriage of Christians, which Paul calls "a great sacrament in Christ and the Church,"[15] demands our shared concern lest anything contrary to its *sanctity* and *indissolubility* is proposed. Our predecessor Pius VIII would recommend to you his own letters on the subject. However, troublesome efforts against this sacrament still continue to be made. The people therefore must be zealously taught that a marriage rightly entered upon cannot be dissolved; for those joined in matrimony God has ordained a perpetual companionship for life and a knot of necessity which cannot be loosed except by death. Recalling that matrimony is a sacrament and therefore subject to the Church, let them consider and observe the laws of the Church concerning it. Let them take care lest for any reason they permit that which is an obstruction to the teachings of the canons and the decrees of the councils. They should be aware that those marriages will have an unhappy end which are entered upon contrary to the discipline of the Church or without God's favor or because of concupiscence alone, with no thought of the sacrament and of the mysteries signified by it.

13. Now We consider another abundant source of the evils with which the Church is afflicted at present: indifferentism. This perverse opinion is spread on all sides by the fraud of the wicked who claim that *it is possible to obtain the eternal salvation of the soul by the profession of any kind of religion, as long as morality is maintained*. Surely, in so clear a matter, you will drive this deadly error far from the people committed to your care. With the admonition of the apostle that "there is one God, one faith, one baptism"[16] may those fear who contrive the notion that the safe harbor of

---

[15] Heb 13.4 & Eph 5:32
[16] Eph 4.5.

salvation is open to persons of any religion whatever. They should consider the testimony of Christ Himself that "those who are not with Christ are against Him,"[17] and that they disperse unhappily who do not gather with Him. Therefore "without a doubt, they will perish forever, unless they hold the Catholic faith whole and inviolate."[18] Let them hear Jerome who, while the Church was torn into three parts by schism, tells us that whenever someone tried to persuade him to join his group he always exclaimed: "He who is for the See of Peter is for me."[19] A schismatic flatters himself falsely if he asserts that he, too, has been washed in the waters of regeneration. Indeed Augustine would reply to such a man: "The branch has the same form when it has been cut off from the vine; but of what profit for it is the form, if it does not live from the root?"[20]

14. This shameful font of indifferentism gives rise to that absurd and erroneous proposition which claims that liberty of conscience must be maintained for everyone. It spreads ruin in sacred and civil affairs, though some repeat over and over again with the greatest impudence that some advantage accrues to religion from it. "But the death of the soul is worse than freedom of error," as Augustine was wont to say.[21] When all restraints are removed by which men are kept on the narrow path of truth, their nature, which is already inclined to evil, propels them to ruin. Then truly "the bottomless pit"[22] is open from which John saw smoke ascending which obscured the sun, and out of which locusts flew forth to devastate the earth. Thence comes transformation of minds, corruption of youths, contempt of sacred things and holy laws — in other words, a pestilence more deadly to the state than any other. Experience shows, even from earliest times, that cities renowned for wealth, dominion, and glory perished as a result of this single evil, namely immoderate freedom of opinion, license of free speech, and desire for novelty.

---

[17] Lk 11.23.
[18] Symbols Athanasius.
[19] St. Jerome, epistle 57.
[20] St. Augustine, in psalm. contra part. Donat.
[21] St. Augustine, epistle 166.
[22] Ap 9.3.

15. Here We must include that harmful and never sufficiently denounced freedom to publish any writings whatever and disseminate them to the people, which some dare to demand and promote with so great a clamor. We are horrified to see what monstrous doctrines and prodigious errors are disseminated far and wide in countless books, pamphlets, and other writings which, though small in weight, are very great in malice. We are in tears at the abuse which proceeds from them over the face of the earth. Some are so carried away that they contentiously assert that the flock of errors arising from them is sufficiently compensated by the publication of some book which defends religion and truth. Every law condemns deliberately doing evil simply because there is some hope that good may result. Is there any sane man who would say poison ought to be distributed, sold publicly, stored, and even drunk because some antidote is available and those who use it may be snatched from death again and again?

16. The Church has always taken action to destroy the plague of bad books. This was true even in apostolic times for we read that the apostles themselves burned a large number of books.[23] It may be enough to consult the laws of the fifth Council of the Lateran on this matter and the Constitution which Leo X published afterwards lest "that which has been discovered advantageous for the increase of the faith and the spread of useful arts be converted to the contrary use and work harm for the salvation of the faithful."[24] This also was of great concern to the fathers of Trent, who applied a remedy against this great evil by publishing that wholesome decree concerning the Index of books which contain false doctrine.[25] "We must fight valiantly," Clement XIII says in an encyclical letter about the banning of bad books, "as much as the matter itself demands and must exterminate the deadly poison of so many books;

---

[23] Acts 19.

[24] Acts of the Lateran Council 5, session 10, where the constitution of Leo X is mentioned; the earlier constitution of Alexander VI, Inter multiplices, ought to be read, in which there are many things on this point.

[25] Council of Trent, sessions 18 and 25.

for never will the material for error be withdrawn, unless the criminal sources of depravity perish in flames."[26] Thus it is evident that this Holy See has always striven, throughout the ages, to condemn and to remove suspect and harmful books. The teaching of those who reject the censure of books as too heavy and onerous a burden causes immense harm to the Catholic people and to this See. They are even so depraved as to affirm that it is contrary to the principles of law, and they deny the Church the right to decree and to maintain it.

17. We have learned that certain teachings are being spread among the common people in writings which attack the trust and submission due to princes; the torches of treason are being lit everywhere. Care must be taken lest the people, being deceived, are led away from the straight path. May all recall, according to the admonition of the apostle that "there is no authority except from God; what authority there is has been appointed by God. Therefore he who resists authority resists the ordinances of God; and those who resist bring on themselves condemnation."[27] Therefore both divine and human laws cry out against those who strive by treason and sedition to drive the people from confidence in their princes and force them from their government.

18. And it is for this reason that the early Christians, lest they should be stained by such great infamy deserved well of the emperors and of the safety of the state even while persecution raged. This they proved splendidly by their fidelity in performing perfectly and promptly whatever they were commanded which was not opposed to their religion, and even more by their constancy and the shedding of their blood in battle. "Christian soldiers," says St. Augustine, "served an infidel emperor. When the issue of Christ was raised, they acknowledged no one but the One who is in heaven. They distinguished the eternal Lord from the temporal lord, but were also subject to the temporal lord for the sake of the eternal Lord."[28] St. Mauritius, the unconquered martyr and leader of the Theban legion had this

---

[26] Letter of Clement XIII, Christianae, 25 November 1766.
[27] Rom 13.2.
[28] St. Augustine in psalt. 124, n. 7.

in mind when, as St. Eucharius reports, he answered the emperor in these words: "We are your soldiers, Emperor, but also servants of God, and this we confess freely . . . and now this final necessity of life has not driven us into rebellion: I see, we are armed and we do not resist, because we wish rather to die than to be killed."[29] Indeed the faith of the early Christians shines more brightly, if with Tertullian we consider that since the Christians were not lacking in numbers and in troops, they could have acted as foreign enemies. "We are but of yesterday," he says, "yet we have filled all your cities, islands, fortresses, municipalities, assembly places, the camps themselves, the tribes, the divisions, the palace, the senate, the forum....For what war should we not have been fit and ready even if unequal in forces — we who are so glad to be cut to pieces — were it not, of course, that in our doctrine we would have been permitted more to be killed rather than to kill?...If so great a multitude of people should have deserted to some remote spot on earth, it would surely have covered your domination with shame because of the loss of so many citizens, and it would even have punished you by this very desertion. Without a doubt you would have been terrified at your solitude.... You would have sought whom you might rule; more enemies than citizens would have remained for you. Now however you have fewer enemies because of the multitude of Christians."[30]

19. These beautiful examples of the unchanging subjection to the princes necessarily proceeded from the most holy precepts of the Christian religion. They condemn the detestable insolence and improbity of those who, consumed with the unbridled lust for freedom, are entirely devoted to impairing and destroying all rights of dominion while bringing servitude to the people under the slogan of liberty. Here surely belong the infamous and wild plans of the Waldensians, the Beghards, the Wycliffites, and other such sons of Belial, who were the sores and disgrace of the human race; they often received a richly deserved anathema from the

---

[29] St. Euchenius apud Ruinart. Acts of the Holy Martyrs concerning Saint Maurius and his companions, n. 4.
[30] Tertullian, in apologet., chap. 37.

Holy See. For no other reason do experienced deceivers devote their efforts, except so that they, along with Luther, might joyfully deem themselves "free of all." To attain this end more easily and quickly, they undertake with audacity any infamous plan whatever.

20. Nor can We predict happier times for religion and government from the plans of those who desire vehemently to separate the Church from the state, and to break the mutual concord between temporal authority and the priesthood. It is certain that that concord which always was favorable and beneficial for the sacred and the civil order is feared by the shameless lovers of liberty.

21. But for the other painful causes We are concerned about, you should recall that certain societies and assemblages seem to draw up a battle line together with the followers of every false religion and cult. They feign piety for religion; but they are driven by a passion for promoting novelties and sedition everywhere. They preach liberty of every sort; they stir up disturbances in sacred and civil affairs, and pluck authority to pieces.

22. We write these things to you with grieving mind but trusting in Him who commands the winds and makes them still. Take up the shield of faith and fight the battles of the Lord vigorously. You especially must stand as a wall against every height which raises itself against the knowledge of God. Unsheath the sword of the spirit, which is the word of God, and may those who hunger after justice receive bread from you. Having been called so that you might be diligent cultivators in the vineyard of the Lord, do this one thing, and labor in it together, so that every root of bitterness may be removed from your field, all seeds of vice destroyed, and a happy crop of virtues may take root and grow. The first to be embraced with paternal affection are those who apply themselves to the sacred sciences and to philosophical studies. For them may you be exhorter and supporter, lest trusting only in their own talents and strength, they may imprudently wander away from the path of truth onto the road of the impious. Let them remember that God is the guide to

wisdom and the director of the wise.[31] It is impossible to know God without God who teaches men to know Himself by His word.[32] It is the proud, or rather foolish, men who examine the mysteries of faith which surpass all understanding with the faculties of the human mind, and rely on human reason which by the condition of man's nature, is weak and infirm.

23. May Our dear sons in Christ, the princes, support these Our desires for the welfare of Church and State with their resources and authority. May they understand that they received their authority not only for the government of the world, but especially for the defense of the Church. They should diligently consider that whatever work they do for the welfare of the Church accrues to their rule and peace. Indeed let them persuade themselves that they owe more to the cause of the faith than to their kingdom. Let them consider it something very great for themselves as We say with Pope St. Leo, "if in addition to their royal diadem the crown of faith may be added." Placed as if they were parents and teachers of the people, they will bring them true peace and tranquility, if they take special care that religion and piety remain safe. God, after all, calls Himself "*King of kings and Lord of lords.*"

24. That all of this may come to pass prosperously and happily, let Us raise Our eyes and hands to the most holy Virgin Mary, who alone crushes all heresies, and is Our greatest reliance and the whole reason for Our hope.[33] May she implore by her patronage a successful outcome for Our plans and actions. Let Us humbly ask of the Prince of the Apostles, Peter and his co-apostle Paul that all of you may stand as a wall lest a foundation be laid other than that which has already been laid. Relying on this happy hope, We trust that the Author and Crown of Our faith Jesus Christ will console Us in all these Our tribulations. We lovingly impart the apostolic benediction to you, venerable brothers, and to the sheep committed to your care as a sign of heavenly aid.

---

[31] Wis 7.15.
[32] St. Irenaeus, bk. 14, chap. 10.
[33] St. Bernard, serm de nat. b.M.v., sect. 7.

Given in Rome at St. Mary Major, on August 15, the feast of the Assumption of the Virgin, in the year of Our Lord 1832, the second year of Our Pontificate.

QUI PLURIBUS
Encyclical of Pope Pius IX
November 9, 1846

Qui Pluribus *was the first encyclical of Pope Pius IX published shortly after his election to the papacy in 1846. Though at the time he was though to be a liberal reformer, this document condemns Freemasonry in its overall critique of rationalism, socialism, and communism. It accused secret societies of spreading errors that threatened the Church and society and positioned Freemasonry as one of the leading ideological threats to Christendom during a period of political upheaval.*

ON FAITH AND RELIGION

To All Patriarchs, Primates, Archbishops, and Bishops.

Venerable Brothers, We Greet You and Give You Our Apostolic Blessing.

For many years past We strove with you, venerable brothers, to devote Our best powers to Our episcopal office — an office full of labor and worry. We strove to feed those committed to Our care on the mountains of Israel, at its streams and in its richest pastures. Our illustrious Predecessor, Gregory XVI, whose famous actions are recorded in the annals of the Church in letters of gold, will surely be remembered and admired by future generations. Now though, upon his death, by the mysterious plan of divine providence, We have been raised to the supreme Pontificate. We did not purpose this nor expect it; indeed Our reaction is great disquietude and anxiety. For if the burden of the Apostolic ministry is rightly considered to be at all times exceedingly heavy and beset with dangers, it is to be dreaded most particularly in these times which are so critical for the Christian commonwealth.

2. We are well aware of Our weakness. So when We

reflect on the most serious duties of the supreme apostolate especially in a period of great instability, We would simply have fallen into great sadness, did We not place all Our hope in God who is Our Saviour. For He never abandons those who hope in Him. Time and again, so as to demonstrate what His power can accomplish, He employs weak instruments to rule His Church; in this way, all men may increasingly realize that it is God Himself who governs and protects the Church with his wonderful providence. We are also greatly supported by the comforting consideration that We have you, venerable brothers, as Our helpers and companions in the work of saving souls. For since you have been called to share a portion of Our care, you strive to fulfill your ministry with attentiveness and zeal, and to fight the good fight.

3. For this reason, as soon as We were placed, despite Our unworthiness, on this high See of the prince of the apostles as the representative of the blessed Peter, and received from the eternal Prince of Pastors Himself the most serious divinely given office of feeding and ruling not only the lambs, that is, the whole Christian people, but also the sheep, that is, the bishops, We surely had no greater wish than to address you all with a deep feeling of love. Therefore, since We have now assumed the supreme pontificate in Our Lateran Basilica, We are sending this letter to you without delay, in accordance with the established practice of Our predecessors. Its purpose is to urge that you keep the night-watches over the flock entrusted to your care with the greatest possible eagerness, wakefulness and effort, and that you raise a protecting wall before the House of Israel; do these as you battle with episcopal strength and steadfastness like good soldiers of Christ Jesus against the hateful enemy of the human race.

4. Each of you has noticed, venerable brothers, that a very bitter and fearsome war against the whole Catholic commonwealth is being stirred up by men bound together in a lawless alliance. These men do not preserve sound doctrine, but turn their hearing from the truth. They eagerly attempt to produce from their darkness all sorts of prodigious beliefs, and then to magnify them with all their strength, and to publish them and spread them among ordinary people. We

shudder indeed and suffer bitter pain when We reflect on all their outlandish errors and their many harmful methods, plots and contrivances. These men use these means to spread their hatred for truth and light. They are experienced and skillful in deceit, which they use to set in motion their plans to quench peoples' zeal for piety, justice and virtue, to corrupt morals, to cast all divine and human laws into confusion, and to weaken and even possibly overthrow the Catholic religion and civil society. For you know, venerable brothers, that these bitter enemies of the Christian name, are carried wretchedly along by some blind momentum of their mad impiety; they go so far in their rash imagining as to teach without blushing, openly and publicly, daring and unheard-of doctrines, thereby uttering blasphemies against God.

[1] They teach that the most holy mysteries of our religion are fictions of human invention, and that the teaching of the Catholic Church is opposed to the good and the prerogatives of human society. They are not even afraid to deny Christ Himself and God.

5. In order to easily mislead the people into making errors, deceiving particularly the imprudent and the inexperienced, they pretend that they alone know the ways to prosperity. They claim for themselves without hesitation the name of "philosophers." They feel as if philosophy, which is wholly concerned with the search for truth in nature, ought to reject those truths which God Himself, the supreme and merciful creator of nature, has deigned to make plain to men as a special gift. With these truths, mankind can gain true happiness and salvation. So, by means of an obviously ridiculous and extremely specious kind of argumentation, these enemies never stop invoking the power and excellence of human reason; they raise it up against the most holy faith of Christ, and they blather with great foolhardiness that this faith is opposed to human reason.

6. Without doubt, nothing more insane than such a doctrine, nothing more impious or more opposed to reason itself could be devised. For although faith is above reason, no real disagreement or opposition can ever be found between

---

[1] Ap 13.6.

them; this is because both of them come from the same greatest source of unchanging and eternal truth, God. They give such reciprocal help to each other that true reason shows, maintains and protects the truth of the faith, while faith frees reason from all errors and wondrously enlightens, strengthens and perfects reason with the knowledge of divine matters.

7. It is with no less deceit, venerable brothers, that other enemies of divine revelation, with reckless and sacrilegious effrontery, want to import the doctrine of human progress into the Catholic religion. They extol it with the highest praise, as if religion itself were not of God but the work of men, or a philosophical discovery which can be perfected by human means. The charge which Tertullian justly made against the philosophers of his own time "who brought forward a Stoic and a Platonic and a Dialectical Christianity"[2] can very aptly apply to those men who rave so pitiably. Our holy religion was not invented by human reason, but was most mercifully revealed by God; therefore, one can quite easily understand that religion itself acquires all its power from the authority of God who made the revelation, and that it can never be arrived at or perfected by human reason. In order not to be deceived and go astray in a matter of such great importance, human reason should indeed carefully investigate the fact of divine revelation. Having done this, one would be definitely convinced that God has spoken and therefore would show Him rational obedience, as the Apostle very wisely teaches.[3] For who can possibly not know that all faith should be given to the words of God and that it is in the fullest agreement with reason itself to accept and strongly support doctrines which it has determined to have been revealed by God, who can neither deceive nor be deceived?

8. But how many wonderful and shining proofs are ready at hand to convince the human reason in the clearest way that the religion of Christ is divine and that "the whole principle of our doctrines has taken root from the Lord of the heavens

---

[2] Tertullian, de Praescript., chap. 8.
[3] Rom 13.1.

above";[4] therefore nothing exists more definite, more settled or more holy than our faith, which rests on the strongest foundations. This faith, which teaches for life and points towards salvation, which casts out all vices and is the fruitful mother and nurse of the virtues, has been established by the birth, life, death, resurrection, wisdom, wonders and prophecies of Christ Jesus, its divine author and perfector! Shining forth in all directions with the light of teaching from on high and enriched with the treasures of heavenly wealth, this faith grew famed and notable by the foretellings of so many prophets, the lustre of so many miracles, the steadfastness of so many martyrs, and the glory of so many saints! It made known the saving laws of Christ and, gaining in strength daily even when it was most cruelly persecuted, it made its way over the whole world by land and sea, from the sun's rising to its setting, under the single standard of the Cross! The deceit of idols was cast down and the mist of errors was scattered. By the defeat of all kinds of enemies, this faith enlightened with divine knowledge all peoples, races and nations, no matter how barbarous and savage, or how different in character, morals, laws and ways of life. It brought them under the sweet yoke of Christ Himself by proclaiming peace and good tidings to all men!

9. Now, surely all these events shine with such divine wisdom and power that anyone who considers them will easily understand that the Christian faith is the work of God. Human reason knows clearly from these striking and certain proofs that God is the author of this faith; therefore it is unable to advance further but should offer all obedience to this faith, casting aside completely every problem and hesitation. Human reason is convinced that it is God who has given everything the faith proposes to men for belief and behavior.

10. This consideration too clarifies the great error of those others as well who boldly venture to explain and interpret the words of God by their own judgment, misusing their reason and holding the opinion that these words are like a human work. God Himself has set up a living authority to

---

[4] St. John Chrysostom, hom. 1 in Isaiah.

establish and teach the true and legitimate meaning of His heavenly revelation. This authority judges infallibly all disputes which concern matters of faith and morals, lest the faithful be swirled around by every wind of doctrine which springs from the evilness of men in encompassing error. And this living infallible authority is active only in that Church which was built by Christ the Lord upon Peter, the head of the entire Church, leader and shepherd, whose faith He promised would never fail. This Church has had an unbroken line of succession from Peter himself; these legitimate pontiffs are the heirs and defenders of the same teaching, rank, office and power. And the Church is where Peter is,[5] and Peter speaks in the Roman Pontiff,[6] living at all times in his successors and making judgment,[7] providing the truth of the faith to those who seek it.[8] The divine words therefore mean what this Roman See of the most blessed Peter holds and has held.

11. For this mother and teacher[9] of all the churches has always preserved entire and unharmed the faith entrusted to it by Christ the Lord. Furthermore, it has taught it to the faithful, showing all men truth and the path of salvation. Since all priesthood originates in this church,[10] the entire substance of the Christian religion resides there also.[11] The leadership of the Apostolic See has always been active,[12] and therefore because of its preeminent authority, the whole Church must agree with it. The faithful who live in every place constitute the whole Church.[13] Whoever does not gather with this Church scatters.[14]

12. We, therefore, placed inscrutably by God upon this

---

[5] St. Ambrose on Ps 40.
[6] Council of Chalcedon, Act. 2.
[7] Synod of Ephes., Act. 3.
[8] St. Peter Chrysologus, epistle to Eutyches.
[9] Council of Trent, session 7 on baptism.
[10] St. Cyprian, epistle 55 to Pope Cornelius.
[11] Synod. Letter of John of Constantinople to Pope Hormisdas and Sozomen, Hist., III. 8.
[12] St. Augustine, epistle 162.
[13] St. Irenaeus, Adv. Haer. III, 3.
[14] St. Jerome, epistle to Pope Damasus.

Qui Pluribus

Chair of truth, eagerly call forth in the Lord your outstanding piety, venerable brothers. We urge you to strive carefully and zealously to continually warn and exhort the faithful entrusted to your care to hold to these first principles. Urge them never to allow themselves to be deceived and led into error by men who have become abominable in their pursuits. These men attempt to destroy faith on the pretext of human progress, subjecting it in an impious manner to reason and changing the meaning of the words of God. Such men do not shrink from the greatest insults to God Himself, who cares for the good and the salvation of men by means of His heavenly religion.

13. You already know well, venerable brothers, the other portentous errors and deceits by which the sons of this world try most bitterly to attack the Catholic religion and the divine authority of the Church and its laws. They would even trample underfoot the rights both of the sacred and of the civil power. For this is the goal of the lawless activities against this Roman See in which Christ placed the impregnable foundation of His Church. This is the goal of those secret sects who have come forth from the darkness to destroy and desolate both the sacred and the civil commonwealth. These have been condemned with repeated anathema in the Apostolic letters of the Roman Pontiffs who preceded Us[15] We now confirm these with the fullness of Our Apostolic power and command that they be most carefully observed.

14. This is the goal too of the crafty Bible Societies which renew the old skill of the heretics and ceaselessly force on people of all kinds, even the uneducated, gifts of the Bible. They issue these in large numbers and at great cost, in vernacular translations, which infringe the holy rules of the Church. The commentaries which are included often contain perverse explanations; so, having rejected divine tradition, the doctrine of the Fathers and the authority of the Catholic Church, they all interpret the words of the Lord by their own private judgment, thereby perverting their meaning. As a result, they fall into the greatest errors. Gregory XVI of happy

---

[15] Clement XII, constitution Providas; Pius VII, constitution Ecclesiam a Jesu Christo; Leo XII, constitution Ubi graviora.

memory, Our superior predecessor, followed the lead of his own predecessors in rejecting these societies in his apostolic letters.[16] It is Our will to condemn them likewise.

15. Also perverse is the shocking theory that it makes no difference to which religion one belongs, a theory which is greatly at variance even with reason. By means of this theory, those crafty men remove all distinction between virtue and vice, truth and error, honorable and vile action. They pretend that men can gain eternal salvation by the practice of any religion, as if there could ever be any sharing between justice and iniquity, any collaboration between light and darkness, or any agreement between Christ and Belial.

16. The sacred celibacy of clerics has also been the victim of conspiracy. Indeed, some churchmen have wretchedly forgotten their own rank and let themselves be converted by the charms and snares of pleasure. This is the aim too of the prevalent but wrong method of teaching, especially in the philosophical disciplines, a method which deceives and corrupts incautious youth in a wretched manner and gives it as drink the poison of the serpent in the goblet of Babylon. To this goal also tends the unspeakable doctrine of Communism, as it is called, a doctrine most opposed to the very natural law. For if this doctrine were accepted, the complete destruction of everyone's laws, government, property, and even of human society itself would follow.

17. To this end also tend the most dark designs of men in the clothing of sheep, while inwardly ravening wolves. They humbly recommend themselves by means of a feigned and deceitful appearance of a purer piety, a stricter virtue and discipline; after taking their captives gently, they mildly bind them, and then kill them in secret. They make men fly in terror from all practice of religion, and they cut down and dismember the sheep of the Lord. To this end, finally — to omit other dangers which are too well known to you — tends the widespread disgusting infection from books and pamphlets which teach the lessons of sinning. These works, well-written and filled with deceit and cunning, are scattered at immense cost through every region for the destruction of

---

[16] Gregory XVI, encyclical letter Inter praecipuas machinationes.

the Christian people. They spread pestilential doctrines everywhere and deprave the minds especially of the imprudent, occasioning great losses for religion.

18. As a result of this filthy medley of errors which creeps in from every side, and as the result of the unbridled license to think, speak and write, We see the following: morals deteriorated, Christ's most holy religion despised, the majesty of divine worship rejected, the power of this Apostolic See plundered, the authority of the Church attacked and reduced to base slavery, the rights of bishops trampled on, the sanctity of marriage infringed, the rule of every government violently shaken and many other losses for both the Christian and the civil commonwealth. Venerable brothers, We are compelled to weep and share in your lament that this is the case.

19. Therefore, in this great crisis for religion, because We are greatly concerned for the salvation of all the Lord's flock and in fulfillment of the duty of Our Apostolic ministry, We shall certainly leave no measure untried in Our vigorous effort to secure the good of the whole Christian family. Indeed, We especially call forth in the Lord your own illustrious piety, virtue and prudence, venerable brothers. With these and relying on heavenly aid, you may fearlessly defend the cause of God and His holy Church as befits your station and the office for which you are marked. You must fight energetically, since you know very well what great wounds the undefiled Spouse of Christ Jesus has suffered, and how vigorous is the destructive attack of Her enemies. You must also care for and defend the Catholic faith with episcopal strength and see that the flock entrusted to you stands to the end firm and unmoved in the faith. For unless one preserves the faith entire and uninjured, he will without doubt perish forever.[17]

20. So, in accordance with your pastoral care, work assiduously to protect and preserve this faith. Never cease to instruct all men in it, to encourage the wavering, to convince dissenters, to strengthen the weak in faith by never tolerating and letting pass anything which could in the slightest degree

---

[17] Ex Symbolo Quicumque.

defile the purity of this faith. With the same great strength of mind, foster in all men their unity with the Catholic Church, outside of which there is no salvation; also foster their obedience towards this See of Peter on which rests the entire structure of our most holy religion. See to it with similar firmness that the most holy laws of the Church are observed, for it is by these laws that virtue, religion and piety particularly thrive and flourish.

21. "It is an act of great piety to expose the concealments of the impious and to defeat there the devil himself, whose slaves they are.[18] Therefore We entreat you to use every means of revealing to your faithful people the many kinds of plot, pretense, error, deceit and contrivance which our enemies use. This will turn them carefully away from infectious books. Also exhort them unceasingly to flee from the sects and societies of the impious as from the presence of a serpent, earnestly avoiding everything which is at variance with the wholeness of faith, religion and morality. Therefore, never stop preaching the Gospel, so that the Christian people may grow in the knowledge of God by being daily better versed in the most holy precepts of the Christian law; as a result, they may turn from evil, do good, and walk in the ways of the Lord. You know that you are acting as deputies for Christ, who is meek ant humble, and who came not to call the just but sinners. This is the example that we should follow. When you find someone disregarding the commandments and wandering from the path of truth and justice, rebuke them in the spirit of mildness and meekness with paternal warnings; accuse, entreat and reprove them with all kindness, patience and doctrine. "Often benevolence towards those who are to be corrected achieves more than severity, exhortation more than threats, and love more than power."[19]

22. Strive to instruct the faithful to follow after love and search for peace, diligently pursuing the works of love and peace so that they may love one another with reciprocal charity. They should abolish all disagreements, enmities, rivalries and animosities, thus achieving compatibility. Take

---

[18] St. Leo. sermon 8.4.
[19] Council of Trent, session 13, chap. on reform.

pains to impress on the Christian people a due obedience and subjection to rulers and governments. Do this by teaching, in accordance with the warning of the Apostle,[20] that all authority comes from God. Whoever resists authority resists the ordering made by God Himself, consequently achieving his own condemnation; disobeying authority is always sinful except when an order is given which is opposed to the laws of God and the Church.

23. However, priests are the best examples of piety and God's worship,"[21] and people tend generally to be of the same quality as their priests. Therefore devote the greatest care and zeal to making the clergy resplendent for the earnestness of their morals, the integrity, holiness and wisdom of their lives. Let the ecclesiastical training be zealously preserved in compliance with the sacred canons, and whenever it has been neglected, let it be restored to its former splendor. Therefore, as you are well aware, you must take the utmost care, as the Apostle commands, not to impose hands on anyone in haste. Consecrate with holy orders and promote to the performance of the sacred mysteries only those who have been carefully examined and who are virtuous and wise. They can consequently benefit and ornament your dioceses.

24. These are men who avoid everything which is forbidden to clerics, devoting their time instead to reading, exhorting and teaching, "an example to the faithful in word, manner of life, in charity, in faith, in chastity."[22] They win the highest respect from all men, and fashion, summon forth and inspire the people with the Christian way of life. "For it would certainly be better," as Benedict XIV, Our Predecessor of undying memory very wisely advises, "to have fewer ministers if they be upright, suitable and useful, than many who are likely to accomplish nothing at all for the building up of the body of Christ, which is the Church."[23] You must examine with greater diligence the morals and the knowledge of men who are entrusted with the care and guidance of souls,

---

[20] Rom 12.1-2.
[21] Council of Trent, session 22. chap. 1 on reform.
[22] Tm 4.12.
[23] Benedict XIV, encyclical letter Ubi primum.

that they may be eager to continuously feed and assist the people entrusted to them by the administration of the sacraments, the preaching of God's word and the example of good works. They should be zealous in molding them to the whole plan and pattern of a religious way of life, and in leading them on to the path of salvation.

25. When ministers are ignorant or neglectful of their duty, then the morals of the people also immediately decline, Christian discipline grows slack, the practice of religion is dislodged and cast aside, and every vice and corruption is easily introduced into the Church. The word of God, which was uttered for the salvation of souls, is living, efficacious and more piercing than a two-edged sword.[24] So that it may not prove to be unfruitful through the fault of its ministers, never cease, venerable brothers, from encouraging the preachers of this divine word to carry out most religiously the ministry of the Gospel. This should not be carried out by the persuasive words of human wisdom, nor by the profane seductive guise of empty and ambitious eloquence, but rather as a demonstration of the spirit and power.

26. Consequently, by presenting the word of truth properly and by preaching not themselves but Christ crucified, they should clearly proclaim in their preaching the tenets and precepts of our most holy religion in accordance with the teaching of the Catholic Church and the Fathers. They should explain precisely the particular duties of individuals, frighten them from vice, and inspire them with a love of piety. In this way the faithful will avoid all vices and pursue virtues, and so, will be able to escape eternal punishment and gain heavenly glory.

27. In your pastoral care, continuously urge all ecclesiastics to think seriously of their holy ministry. Urge them to carefully fulfill their duties, to greatly love the beauty of God's house, to urgently pray and entreat with deep piety, and to say the canonical hours of the breviary as the Church commands. By these means they will be able both to pray efficaciously for God's help in fulfilling the heavy demands of their duty, and to graciously reconcile God and the

---

[24] Heb 4.12.

Christian people.

28. You know that suitable ministers can only come from clergy who are very well trained, and that the proper training greatly influences the whole future life of clerics. Therefore, continually strive to ensure that young clerics are properly molded even from their earliest years. They should be molded not only in piety and real virtue, but also in literature and the stricter disciplines, especially the sacred ones. So your greatest desire should be, in obedience to the prescript of the fathers at Trent,[25] to set up skillfully and energetically, seminaries if they do not yet exist. If necessary expand those already established, supplying them with the best directors and teachers. Watch continuously and zealously that the young clerics in them are educated in a holy and religious manner, in the fear of the Lord and in ecclesiastical discipline. See that they are carefully and thoroughly improved, especially by the sacred sciences, according to Catholic doctrine, far from all danger of any error. They should also be improved by the traditions of the Church and the writings of the holy Fathers, as well as by sacred ceremonies and rites. Thus you will have energetic, industrious workers endowed with an ecclesiastical spirit, properly prepared by their studies, who in time will be able to tend the Lord's field carefully and fight strenuously in the Lord's battles.

29. Furthermore, you realize that spiritual exercises contribute greatly to the preservation of the dignity and holiness of ecclesiastical orders. Therefore do not neglect to promote this work of salvation and to advise and exhort all clergy to often retreat to a suitable place for making these exercises. Laying aside external cares and being free to meditate zealously on eternal divine matters, they will be able to wipe away stains caused by the dust of the world and renew their ecclesiastical spirit. And stripping off the old man and his deeds, they will put on the new man who was created in justice and holiness.

30. Do not regret that We have spoken at length on the education and training of the clergy. For you are very well

---

[25] Council of Trent, session 23, chap. 18, on reform.

aware many men are weary of the difference, instability and changing nature of their errors, and therefore want to profess our most holy religion. These men, with God's good help, will more easily embrace and practice the teaching, precepts and way of life of this religion if they see that the clergy surpass all others in their piety, integrity and wisdom, and in the noble example they give of all the virtues.

31. We recognize your many worthy attributes: your burning charity towards God and men, your exalted love of the Church, your almost angelic virtues, your episcopal bravery, and your prudence. Being inspired to do His holy will, you are all followers in the footsteps of the Apostles. As bishops, you are the deputies, and thus the imitators of Christ. In your harmonious pursuits you have become a sincere model for your flock, and you enlighten your clergy and faithful people with the splendor of your sanctity. In your compassionate mercy you seek out and overtake with your love the straying and perishing sheep, as the shepherd in the Gospel did. You place them paternally on your shoulders ant lead them back to the fold. At no time do you spare either cares or plans or toils in religiously fulfilling your pastoral duties and defending all Our beloved sheep who, redeemed by Christ, have been entrusted to your care from the rage, assault and snares of ravening wolves. You keep them away from poisonous pasture land and drive them on to safe ground, and in all possible ways you lead them by deed, word and example to the harbor of eternal salvation.

32. Therefore, to assure the greater glory of God and the Church, venerable brothers, join together with all eagerness, care and wakefulness to repulse error and to root out vice. When this is accomplished, faith, religion, piety and virtue will increase daily. Then all the faithful, as sons of light, casting aside the works of darkness, may walk worthily, pleasing God in all things and being fruitful in every good work. And in the very great straits, difficulties and dangers which must beset your serious ministry as bishops, especially in these times, do not ever be terrified; rather, be comforted by the strength of the Lord "who looks down on us who carry out his work, approves those who are willing, aids those who

do battle, and crowns those who conquer."[26]

33. Nothing is more pleasing to Us than to assist you, whom We love, with affection, advice, and exertion. We devote Ourselves wholeheartedly together with you to protect and spread the glory of God and the Catholic faith; We also endeavor to save souls for whom We are ready to sacrifice life itself, should it be necessary. Come to Us as often as you feel the need of the aid, help and protection of Our authority and that of this See.

34. We hope that Our political leaders will keep in mind, in accordance with their piety and religion, that "the kingly power has been conferred on them not only for ruling the world but especially for the protection of the Church."[27] Sometimes We "act both for the sake of their rule and safety that they may possess their provinces by peaceful right."[28] We hope that with their aid and authority they will support the objects, plans and pursuits which we have in common, and that they will also defend the liberty and safety of the Church, so that "the right hand of Christ may also defend their rule."[29]

35. We hope that all these matters may turn out well and happily. Let us together entreat God in urgent and unceasing prayers, to make up for Our weakness by an abundance of every heavenly grace, to overwhelm with His all-powerful strength those who attack us, and to increase everywhere faith, piety, devotion and peace. Then when all enemies and errors have been overcome, His holy Church may enjoy the tranquillity it so greatly desires. Then too there may be one fold and one shepherd.

36. That the Lord may more readily respond to Us, let us call as intercessor Her who is always with Him, the most holy Virgin Mary, Immaculate Mother of God. She is the most sweet mother of us all; she is our mediatrix, advocate, firmest hope, and greatest source of confidence. Furthermore, her patronage with God is strongest and most efficacious. Let us

---

[26] St. Cyprian, epistle 77 to Nemesianus and other martyrs.
[27] St. Leo, epistle 156 (123) to Emperor Leo.
[28] St. Leo, epistle 43 (34) to Emperor Theodosius.
[29] Ibid.

invoke too the prince of the Apostles to whom Christ Himself gave the keys of the kingdom of heaven, and whom He made the rock of His Church, against which the gates of hell will never prevail; let us also invoke his fellow-apostle Paul, and all the heavenly saints who are already crowned and hold the palm of victory. We ask that they implore for all Christians the abundance of divine favor which they desire.

37. Finally, as an augury of all the heavenly gifts and as witness of Our great charity towards you, receive the Apostolic Blessing which from deep in Our heart We most lovingly impart to yourselves, venerable brothers, and to all clerics and the faithful laity who are entrusted to your care.

Given in Rome at St. Mary Major's on the 9th of November 1846 in the first year of Our Pontificate.

QUANTA CURA
Encyclical of Blessed Pope Pius IX
Condemning Current Errors
December 8, 1864

Quanta Cura *condemns various modern political and philosophical ideologies that the Church views as threats to herself and Christendom. It specifically denounces religious indifferentism, secularization, socialism and the idea that civil authority should have supremacy over religious matters, ideas all espoused by Freemasonry. The encyclical defends the Church's right to teach moral truth, maintain its independence from state control and uphold traditional social order.* Quanta Cura *is accompanied by the* Syllabus of Errors, *which lists specific condemned propositions, reinforcing the Church's rejection of Freemasonry's liberalism and modernism.*

To Our Venerable Brethren, all Patriarchs, Primates, Archbishops, and Bishops having favor and Communion of the Holy See.

Venerable Brethren, Health and Apostolic Benediction.

With how great care and pastoral vigilance the Roman Pontiffs, our predecessors, fulfilling the duty and office committed to them by the Lord Christ Himself in the person of most Blessed Peter, Prince of the Apostles, of feeding the lambs and the sheep, have never ceased sedulously to nourish the Lord's whole flock with words of faith and with salutary doctrine, and to guard it from poisoned pastures, is thoroughly known to all, and especially to you, Venerable Brethren. And truly the same, Our Predecessors, asserters of justice, being especially anxious for the salvation of souls, had nothing ever more at heart than by their most wise Letters and Constitutions to unveil and condemn all those heresies and errors which, being adverse to our Divine Faith, to the doctrine of the Catholic Church, to purity of morals, and to the eternal salvation of men, have frequently excited violent tempests, and have miserably afflicted both Church and State. For which cause the same Our Predecessors, have, with Apostolic fortitude, constantly resisted the nefarious enterprises of wicked men, who, like raging waves of the sea foaming out their own confusion, and promising liberty whereas they are the slaves of corruption, have striven by their deceptive opinions and most pernicious writings to raze the foundations of the Catholic religion and of civil society, to remove from among men all virtue and justice, to deprave persons, and especially inexperienced youth, to lead it into the snares of error, and at length to tear it from the bosom of the Catholic Church.

2. But now, as is well known to you, Venerable Brethren, already, scarcely had we been elevated to this Chair of Peter (by the hidden counsel of Divine Providence, certainly by no merit of our own), when, seeing with the greatest grief of Our soul a truly awful storm excited by so many evil opinions, and (seeing also) the most grievous calamities never sufficiently to be deplored which overspread the Christian people from so many errors, according to the duty of Our Apostolic Ministry, and following the illustrious example of Our Predecessors, We raised Our voice, and in many published Encyclical Letters and Allocutions delivered in Consistory, and other Apostolic Letters, we condemned the chief errors of this most unhappy age, and we excited your admirable episcopal vigilance, and we again and again admonished and exhorted all sons of the Catholic Church, to us most dear, that they should altogether abhor and flee from the contagion of so dire a pestilence. And especially in our first Encyclical Letter written to you on Nov. 9, 1846, and in two Allocutions delivered by us in Consistory, the one on Dec. 9, 1854, and the other on June 9, 1862, we condemned the monstrous portents of opinion which prevail especially in this age, bringing with them the greatest loss of souls and detriment of civil society itself; which are grievously opposed also, not only to the Catholic Church and her salutary doctrine and venerable rights, but also to the eternal natural law engraven by God in all men's hearts, and to right reason; and from which almost all other errors have their origin.

3. But, although we have not omitted often to proscribe and reprobate the chief errors of this kind, yet the cause of the Catholic Church, and the salvation of souls entrusted to us by God, and the welfare of human society itself, altogether demand that we again stir up your pastoral solicitude to exterminate other evil opinions, which spring forth from the said errors as from a fountain. Which false and perverse opinions are on that ground the more to be detested, because they chiefly tend to this, that that salutary influence be impeded and (even) removed, which the Catholic Church, according to the institution and command of her Divine Author, should freely exercise even to the end of the world, not only over private individuals, but over nations, peoples, and their sovereign princes; and (tend also) to take away that mutual fellowship and concord of counsels between Church and State which has ever proved itself propitious and salutary, both for religious and civil interests.[1]

For you well know, venerable brethren, that at this time men are found not a few who, applying to civil society the impious and absurd principle of "naturalism," as they call it, dare to teach that "the best constitution of public society and (also) civil progress altogether require that human society be conducted and governed without regard being had to religion any more than if it did not exist; or, at least, without any distinction being made between the true religion and false ones." And, against the doctrine of Scripture, of the Church, and of the Holy Fathers, they do not hesitate to assert that "that is the best condition of civil society, in which no duty is recognized, as attached to the civil power, of restraining by enacted penalties, offenders against the Catholic religion, except so far as public peace may require." From which totally false idea of social government they do not fear to foster that erroneous opinion, most fatal in its effects on the Catholic Church and the salvation of souls, called by Our Predecessor, Gregory XVI, an "insanity,"[2] viz., that "liberty of conscience and worship is each man's personal right, which ought to be legally proclaimed and asserted in every

---

[1] Gregory XVI, encyclical epistle "Mirari vos," 15 August 1832.
[2] Ibid.

rightly constituted society; and that a right resides in the citizens to an absolute liberty, which should be restrained by no authority whether ecclesiastical or civil, whereby they may be able openly and publicly to manifest and declare any of their ideas whatever, either by word of mouth, by the press, or in any other way." But, while they rashly affirm this, they do not think and consider that they are preaching "liberty of perdition;"[3] and that "if human arguments are always allowed free room for discussion, there will never be wanting men who will dare to resist truth, and to trust in the flowing speech of human wisdom; whereas we know, from the very teaching of our Lord Jesus Christ, how carefully Christian faith and wisdom should avoid this most injurious babbling."[4]

4. And, since where religion has been removed from civil society, and the doctrine and authority of divine revelation repudiated, the genuine notion itself of justice and human right is darkened and lost, and the place of true justice and legitimate right is supplied by material force, thence it appears why it is that some, utterly neglecting and disregarding the surest principles of sound reason, dare to proclaim that "the people's will, manifested by what is called public opinion or in some other way, constitutes a supreme law, free from all divine and human control; and that in the political order accomplished facts, from the very circumstance that they are accomplished, have the force of right." But who, does not see and clearly perceive that human society, when set loose from the bonds of religion and true justice, can have, in truth, no other end than the purpose of obtaining and amassing wealth, and that (society under such circumstances) follows no other law in its actions, except the unchastened desire of ministering to its own pleasure and interests? For this reason, men of the kind pursue with bitter hatred the Religious Orders, although these have deserved extremely well of Christendom, civilization and literature, and cry out that the same have no legitimate reason for being permitted to exist; and thus (these evil men) applaud the calumnies of heretics. For, as Pius VI, Our Predecessor,

---

[3] St. Augustine, epistle 105 (166).
[4] St. Leo, epistle 14 (133), sect. 2, edit. Ball.

taught most wisely, "the abolition of regulars is injurious to that state in which the Evangelical counsels are openly professed; it is injurious to a method of life praised in the Church as agreeable to Apostolic doctrine; it is injurious to the illustrious founders, themselves, whom we venerate on our altars, who did not establish these societies but by God's inspiration."[5] And (these wretches) also impiously declare that permission should be refused to citizens and to the Church, "whereby they may openly give alms for the sake of Christian charity"; and that the law should be abrogated "whereby on certain fixed days servile works are prohibited because of God's worship;" and on the most deceptive pretext that the said permission and law are opposed to the principles of the best public economy. Moreover, not content with removing religion from public society, they wish to banish it also from private families. For, teaching and professing the most fatal error of "Communism and Socialism," they assert that "domestic society or the family derives the whole principle of its existence from the civil law alone; and, consequently, that on civil law alone depend all rights of parents over their children, and especially that of providing for education." By which impious opinions and machinations these most deceitful men chiefly aim at this result, viz., that the salutary teaching and influence of the Catholic Church may be entirely banished from the instruction and education of youth, and that the tender and flexible minds of young men may be infected and depraved by every most pernicious error and vice. For all who have endeavored to throw into confusion things both sacred and secular, and to subvert the right order of society, and to abolish all rights, human and divine, have always (as we above hinted) devoted all their nefarious schemes, devices and efforts, to deceiving and

depraving incautious youth and have placed all their hope in its corruption. For which reason they never cease by every wicked method to assail the clergy, both secular and regular, from whom (as the surest monuments of history conspicuously attest), so many great advantages have abundantly flowed to Christianity, civilization and literature,

---

[5] Epistle to Cardinal De la Rochefoucault, 10 March 1791.

and to proclaim that "the clergy, as being hostile to the true and beneficial advance of science and civilization, should be removed from the whole charge and duty of instructing and educating youth."

5. Others meanwhile, reviving the wicked and so often condemned inventions of innovators, dare with signal impudence to subject to the will of the civil authority the supreme authority of the Church and of this Apostolic See given to her by Christ Himself, and to deny all those rights of the same Church and See which concern matters of the external order. For they are not ashamed of affirming "that the Church's laws do not bind in conscience unless when they are promulgated by the civil power; that acts and decrees of the Roman Pontiffs, referring to religion and the Church, need the civil power's sanction and approbation, or at least its consent; that the Apostolic Constitutions,[6] whereby secret societies are condemned (whether an oath of secrecy be or be not required in such societies), and whereby their frequenters and favourers are smitten with anathema — have no force in those regions of the world wherein associations of the kind are tolerated by the civil government; that the excommunication pronounced by the Council of Trent and by Roman Pontiffs against those who assail and usurp the Church's rights and possessions, rests on a confusion between the spiritual and temporal orders, and (is directed) to the pursuit of a purely secular good; that the Church can decree nothing which binds the conscience of the faithful in regard to their use of temporal things; that the Church has no right of restraining by temporal punishments those who violate her laws; that it is conformable to the principles of sacred theology and public law to assert and claim for the civil government a right of property in those goods which are possessed by the Church, by the Religious Orders, and by other pious establishments." Nor do they blush openly and publicly to profess the maxim and principle of heretics from which arise so many perverse opinions and errors. For they repeat that the "ecclesiastical power is not by divine right

---

[6] Clement XII, "In eminenti;" Benedict XIV, "Providas Romanorum;" Pius VII, "Ecclesiam;" Leo XII, "Quo graviora."

distinct from, and independent of, the civil power, and that such distinction and independence cannot be preserved without the civil power's essential rights being assailed and usurped by the Church." Nor can we pass over in silence the audacity of those who, not enduring sound doctrine, contend that "without sin and without any sacrifice of the Catholic profession assent and obedience may be refused to those judgments and decrees of the Apostolic See, whose object is declared to concern the Church's general good and her rights and discipline, so only it does not touch the dogmata of faith and morals." But no one can be found not clearly and distinctly to see and understand how grievously this is opposed to the Catholic dogma of the full power given from God by Christ our Lord Himself to the Roman Pontiff of feeding, ruling and guiding the Universal Church.

6. Amidst, therefore, such great perversity of depraved opinions, we, well remembering our Apostolic Office, and very greatly solicitous for our most holy Religion, for sound doctrine and the salvation of souls which is intrusted to us by God, and (solicitous also) for the welfare of human society itself, have thought it right again to raise up our Apostolic voice. Therefore, by our Apostolic authority, we reprobate, proscribe, and condemn all the singular and evil opinions and doctrines severally mentioned in this letter, and will and command that they be thoroughly held by all children of the Catholic Church as reprobated, proscribed and condemned.

7. And besides these things, you know very well, Venerable Brethren, that in these times the haters of truth and justice and most bitter enemies of our religion, deceiving the people and maliciously lying, disseminate sundry and other impious doctrines by means of pestilential books, pamphlets and newspapers dispersed over the whole world. Nor are you ignorant also, that in this our age some men are found who, moved and excited by the spirit of Satan, have reached to that degree of impiety as not to shrink from denying our Ruler and Lord Jesus Christ, and from impugning His Divinity with wicked pertinacity. Here, however, we cannot but extol you, venerable brethren, with great and deserved praise, for not having failed to raise with all zeal your episcopal voice against impiety so great.

8. Therefore, in this our letter, we again most lovingly address you, who, having been called unto a part of our solicitude, are to us, among our grievous distresses, the greatest solace, joy and consolation, because of the admirable religion and piety wherein you excel, and because of that marvellous love, fidelity, and dutifulness, whereby bound as you are to us. and to this Apostolic See in most harmonious affection, you strive strenuously and sedulously to fulfill your most weighty episcopal ministry. For from your signal pastoral zeal we expect that, taking up the sword of the spirit which is the word of God, and strengthened by the grace of our Lord Jesus Christ, you will, with redoubled care, each day more anxiously provide that the faithful entrusted to your charge "abstain from noxious verbiage, which Jesus Christ does not cultivate because it is not His Father's plantation."[7] Never cease also to inculcate on the said faithful that all true felicity flows abundantly upon man from our august religion and its doctrine and practice; and that happy is the people whose God is their Lord.[8] Teach that "kingdoms rest on the foundation of the Catholic Faith;[9] and that nothing is so deadly, so hastening to a fall, so exposed to all danger, (as that which exists) if, believing this alone to be sufficient for us that we receive free will at our birth, we seek nothing further from the Lord; that is, if forgetting our Creator we abjure his power that we may display our freedom."[10] And again do not fail to teach "that the royal power was given not only for the governance of the world, but most of all for the protection of the Church;"[11] and that there is nothing which can be of greater advantage and glory to Princes and Kings than if, as another most wise and courageous Predecessor of ours, St. Felix, instructed the Emperor Zeno, they "permit the Catholic Church to practise her laws, and allow no one to oppose her liberty. For it is certain that this mode of conduct is beneficial to their interests, viz., that where there is

---

[7] St. Ignatius M. to the Philadelphians, 3.
[8] Ps 143.
[9] St. Celestine, epistle 22 to Synod. Ephes. apud Const., p. 1200.
[10] St. Innocent. 1, epistle 29 ad Episc. conc. Carthag. apud Coust., p. 891.
[11] St. Leo, epistle 156 (125).

question concerning the causes of God, they study, according to His appointment, to subject the royal will to Christ's Priests, not to raise it above theirs."[12]

9. But if always, venerable brethren, now most of all amidst such great calamities both of the Church and of civil society, amidst so great a conspiracy against Catholic interests and this Apostolic See, and so great a mass of errors, it is altogether necessary to approach with confidence the throne of grace, that we may obtain mercy and find grace in timely aid. Wherefore, we have thought it well to excite the piety of all the faithful in order that, together with us and you, they may unceasingly pray and beseech the most merciful Father of light and pity with most fervent and humble prayers, and in the fullness of faith flee always to Our Lord Jesus Christ, who redeemed us to God in his blood, and earnestly and constantly supplicate His most sweet Heart, the victim of most burning love toward us, that He would draw all things to Himself by the bonds of His love, and that all men inflamed by His most holy love may walk worthily according to His heart, pleasing God in all things, bearing fruit in every good work. But since without doubt men's prayers are more pleasing to God if they reach Him from minds free from all stain, therefore we have determined to open to Christ's faithful, with Apostolic liberality, the Church's heavenly treasures committed to our charge, in order that the said faithful, being more earnestly enkindled to true piety, and cleansed through the sacrament of Penance from the defilement of their sins, may with greater confidence pour forth their prayers to God, and obtain His mercy and grace.

10. By these Letters, therefore, in virtue of our Apostolic authority, we concede to all and singular the faithful of the Catholic world, a Plenary Indulgence in the form of Jubilee, during the space of one month only for the whole coming year 1865, and not beyond; to be fixed by you, venerable brethren, and other legitimate Ordinaries of places, in the very same manner and form in which we granted it at the beginning of our supreme Pontificate by our Apostolic

---

[12] Pius VII, encyclical epistle "Diu satis," 15 May 1800.

Letters in the form of a Brief, dated November 20, 1846, and addressed to all your episcopal Order, beginning, "Arcano Divinae Providentiae consilio," and with all the same faculties which were given by us in those Letters. We will, however, that all things be observed which were prescribed in the aforesaid Letters, and those things be excepted which we there so declared. And we grant this, notwithstanding anything whatever to the contrary, even things which are worthy of individual mention and derogation. In order, however, that all doubt and difficulty be removed, we have commanded a copy of said Letters be sent you.

11. "Let us implore," Venerable Brethren, "God's mercy from our inmost heart and with our whole mind; because He has Himself added, 'I will not remove my mercy from them.' Let us ask and we shall receive; and if there be delay and slowness in our receiving because we have gravely offended, let us knock, because to him that knocketh it shall be opened, if only the door be knocked by our prayers, groans and tears, in which we must persist and persevere, and if the prayer be unanimous . . . let each man pray to God, not for himself alone, but for all his brethren, as the Lord hath taught us to pray."[13] But in order that God may the more readily assent to the prayers and desires of ourselves, of you and of all the faithful, let us with all confidence employ as or advocate with Him the Immaculate and most holy Virgin Mary, Mother of God, who has slain all heresies throughout the world, and who, the most loving Mother of us all, "is all sweet . . . and full of mercy . . . shows herself to all as easily entreated; shows herself to all as most merciful; pities the necessities of all with a most large affection;"[14] and standing as a Queen at the right hand of her only begotten Son, our Lord Jesus Christ, in gilded clothing, surrounded with variety, can obtain from Him whatever she will. Let us also seek the suffrages of the Most Blessed Peter, Prince of the Apostles, and of Paul, his Fellow-Apostle, and of all the Saints in Heaven, who having now become God's friends, have arrived at the

---

[13] St. Cyprian, epist. 11.
[14] St. Bernard, Serm. "de duodecim praerogativis B. M. V. ex verbis Apocalyp."

heavenly kingdom, and being crowned bear their palms, and being secure of their own immortality are anxious for our salvation.

12. Lastly, imploring from our great heart for You from God the abundance of all heavenly gifts, we most lovingly impart the Apostolic Benediction from our inmost heart, a pledge of our signal love towards you, to yourselves, venerable brethren, and to all the clerics and lay faithful committed to your care.

Given at Rome, from St. Peter's, the 8th day of December, in the year 1864, the tenth from the Dogmatic Definition of the Immaculate Conception of the Virgin Mary, Mother of God, in the nineteenth year of Our Pontificate.

✠

THE SYLLABUS OF ERRORS
Blessed Pope Pius IX
December 8, 1864

The Syllabus of Errors, *issued by Pope Pius IX in 1864, is a list of 80 condemned propositions summarizing modern ideological trends opposed by the Catholic Church – many of which are supported by Freemasonry. Attached to the encyclical* Quanta Cura, *it rejects secularism, socialism, liberalism, rationalism and separation of Church and state. It affirms papal authority and defend's the Church's role in public life, education and morality. The* Syllabus *delineates the errors of modernism and is a defining document of 19th-century Catholic resistance to modernity. It laid the groundwork for the First Vatican Council.*

I. PANTHEISM, NATURALISM AND ABSOLUTE RATIONALISM

1. There exists no Supreme, all-wise, all-provident Divine Being, distinct from the universe, and God is identical with the nature of things, and is, therefore, subject to changes. In effect, God is produced in man and in the world, and all things are God and have the very substance of God, and God is one and the same thing with the world, and, therefore, spirit with matter, necessity with liberty, good with evil, justice with injustice. — Allocution "Maxima quidem," June 9, 1862.

2. All action of God upon man and the world is to be denied. — Ibid.

3. Human reason, without any reference whatsoever to God, is the sole arbiter of truth and falsehood, and of good and evil; it is law to itself, and suffices, by its natural force, to secure the welfare of men and of nations. — Ibid.

4. All the truths of religion proceed from the innate

strength of human reason; hence reason is the ultimate standard by which man can and ought to arrive at the knowledge of all truths of every kind. — Ibid. and Encyclical "Qui pluribus," Nov. 9, 1846, etc.

5. Divine revelation is imperfect, and therefore subject to a continual and indefinite progress, corresponding with the advancement of human reason. — Ibid.

6. The faith of Christ is in opposition to human reason and divine revelation not only is not useful, but is even hurtful to the perfection of man. — Ibid.

7. The prophecies and miracles set forth and recorded in the Sacred Scriptures are the fiction of poets, and the mysteries of the Christian faith the result of philosophical investigations. In the books of the Old and the New Testament there are contained mythical inventions, and Jesus Christ is Himself a myth.

II. MODERATE RATIONALISM

8. As human reason is placed on a level with religion itself, so theological must be treated in the same manner as philosophical sciences. — Allocution "Singulari quadam," Dec. 9, 1854.

9. All the dogmas of the Christian religion are indiscriminately the object of natural science or philosophy, and human reason, enlightened solely in an historical way, is able, by its own natural strength and principles, to attain to the true science of even the most abstruse dogmas; provided only that such dogmas be proposed to reason itself as its object. — Letters to the Archbishop of Munich, "Gravissimas inter," Dec. 11, 1862, and "Tuas libenter," Dec. 21, 1863.

10. As the philosopher is one thing, and philosophy another, so it is the right and duty of the philosopher to subject himself to the authority which he shall have proved to be true; but philosophy neither can nor ought to submit to any such authority. — Ibid., Dec. 11, 1862.

11. The Church not only ought never to pass judgment on philosophy, but ought to tolerate the errors of philosophy, leaving it to correct itself. — Ibid., Dec. 21, 1863.

12. The decrees of the Apostolic See and of the Roman

congregations impede the true progress of science. — Ibid.

13. The method and principles by which the old scholastic doctors cultivated theology are no longer suitable to the demands of our times and to the progress of the sciences. — Ibid.

14. Philosophy is to be treated without taking any account of supernatural revelation. — Ibid.

III. INDIFFERENTISM, LATITUDINARIANISM

15. Every man is free to embrace and profess that religion which, guided by the light of reason, he shall consider true. — Allocution "Maxima quidem," June 9, 1862; Damnatio "Multiplices inter," June 10, 1851.

16. Man may, in the observance of any religion whatever, find the way of eternal salvation, and arrive at eternal salvation. — Encyclical "Qui pluribus," Nov. 9, 1846.

17. Good hope at least is to be entertained of the eternal salvation of all those who are not at all in the true Church of Christ. — Encyclical "Quanto conficiamur," Aug. 10, 1863, etc.

18. Protestantism is nothing more than another form of the same true Christian religion, in which form it is given to please God equally as in the Catholic Church. — Encyclical "Noscitis," Dec. 8, 1849.

IV. SOCIALISM, COMMUNISM, SECRET SOCIETIES, BIBLICAL SOCIETIES, CLERICO-LIBERAL SOCIETIES

Pests of this kind are frequently reprobated in the severest terms in the Encyclical "Qui pluribus," Nov. 9, 1846, Allocution "Quibus quantisque," April 20, 1849, Encyclical "Noscitis et nobiscum," Dec. 8, 1849, Allocution "Singulari quadam," Dec. 9, 1854, Encyclical "Quanto conficiamur," Aug. 10, 1863.

V. ERRORS CONCERNING THE CHURCH AND HER RIGHTS

19. The Church is not a true and perfect society, entirely free- nor is she endowed with proper and perpetual rights of her own, conferred upon her by her Divine Founder; but it appertains to the civil power to define what are the rights of the Church, and the limits within which she may exercise those rights. — Allocution "Singulari quadam,&quuot; Dec. 9, 1854, etc.

20. The ecclesiastical power ought not to exercise its authority without the permission and assent of the civil government. — Allocution "Meminit unusquisque," Sept. 30, 1861.

21. The Church has not the power of defining dogmatically that the religion of the Catholic Church is the only true religion. — Damnatio "Multiplices inter," June 10, 1851.

22. The obligation by which Catholic teachers and authors are strictly bound is confined to those things only which are proposed to universal belief as dogmas of faith by the infallible judgment of the Church. — Letter to the Archbishop of Munich, "Tuas libenter," Dec. 21, 1863.

23. Roman pontiffs and ecumenical councils have wandered outside the limits of their powers, have usurped the rights of princes, and have even erred in defining matters of faith and morals. — Damnatio "Multiplices inter," June 10, 1851.

24. The Church has not the power of using force, nor has she any temporal power, direct or indirect. — Apostolic Letter "Ad Apostolicae," Aug. 22, 1851.

25. Besides the power inherent in the episcopate, other temporal power has been attributed to it by the civil authority granted either explicitly or tacitly, which on that account is revocable by the civil authority whenever it thinks fit. — Ibid.

26. The Church has no innate and legitimate right of acquiring and possessing property. — Allocution "Nunquam fore," Dec. 15, 1856; Encyclical "Incredibili," Sept. 7, 1863.

27. The sacred ministers of the Church and the Roman pontiff are to be absolutely excluded from every charge and

dominion over temporal affairs. — Allocution "Maxima quidem," June 9, 1862.

28. It is not lawful for bishops to publish even letters Apostolic without the permission of Government. — Allocution "Nunquam fore," Dec. 15, 1856.

29. Favours granted by the Roman pontiff ought to be considered null, unless they have been sought for through the civil government. — Ibid.

30. The immunity of the Church and of ecclesiastical persons derived its origin from civil law. — Damnatio "Multiplices inter," June 10, 1851.

31. The ecclesiastical forum or tribunal for the temporal causes, whether civil or criminal, of clerics, ought by all means to be abolished, even without consulting and against the protest of the Holy See. — Allocution "Nunquam fore," Dec. 15, 1856; Allocution "Acerbissimum," Sept. 27, 1852.

32. The personal immunity by which clerics are exonerated from military conscription and service in the army may be abolished without violation either of natural right or equity. Its abolition is called for by civil progress, especially in a society framed on the model of a liberal government. — Letter to the Bishop of Monreale "Singularis nobisque," Sept. 29, 1864.

33. It does not appertain exclusively to the power of ecclesiastical jurisdiction by right, proper and innate, to direct the teaching of theological questions. — Letter to the Archbishop of Munich, "Tuas libenter," Dec. 21, 1863.

34. The teaching of those who compare the Sovereign Pontiff to a prince, free and acting in the universal Church, is a doctrine which prevailed in the Middle Ages. — Apostolic Letter "Ad Apostolicae," Aug. 22, 1851.

35. There is nothing to prevent the decree of a general council, or the act of all peoples, from transferring the supreme pontificate from the bishop and city of Rome to another bishop and another city. — Ibid.

36. The definition of a national council does not admit of any subsequent discussion, and the civil authority car assume this principle as the basis of its acts. — Ibid.

37. National churches, withdrawn from the authority of the Roman pontiff and altogether separated, can be

established. — Allocution "Multis gravibusque," Dec. 17, 1860.

38. The Roman pontiffs have, by their too arbitrary conduct, contributed to the division of the Church into Eastern and Western. — Apostolic Letter "Ad Apostolicae," Aug. 22, 1851.

VI. ERRORS ABOUT CIVIL SOCIETY, CONSIDERED BOTH IN ITSELF AND IN ITS RELATION TO THE CHURCH

39. The State, as being the origin and source of all rights, is endowed with a certain right not circumscribed by any limits. — Allocution "Maxima quidem," June 9, 1862.

40. The teaching of the Catholic Church is hostile to the well- being and interests of society. — Encyclical "Qui pluribus," Nov. 9, 1846; Allocution "Quibus quantisque," April 20, 1849.

41. The civil government, even when in the hands of an infidel sovereign, has a right to an indirect negative power over religious affairs. It therefore possesses not only the right called that of "exsequatur," but also that of appeal, called "appellatio ab abusu." — Apostolic Letter "Ad Apostolicae," Aug. 22, 1851

42. In the case of conflicting laws enacted by the two powers, the civil law prevails. — Ibid.

43. The secular Dower has authority to rescind, declare and render null, solemn conventions, commonly called concordats, entered into with the Apostolic See, regarding the use of rights appertaining to ecclesiastical immunity, without the consent of the Apostolic See, and even in spite of its protest. — Allocution "Multis gravibusque," Dec. 17, 1860; Allocution "In consistoriali," Nov. 1, 1850.

44. The civil authority may interfere in matters relating to religion, morality and spiritual government: hence, it can pass judgment on the instructions issued for the guidance of consciences, conformably with their mission, by the pastors of the Church. Further, it has the right to make enactments regarding the administration of the divine sacraments, and the dispositions necessary for receiving them. — Allocutions "In

consistoriali," Nov. 1, 1850, and "Maxima quidem," June 9, 1862.

45. The entire government of public schools in which the youth- of a Christian state is educated, except (to a certain extent) in the case of episcopal seminaries, may and ought to appertain to the civil power, and belong to it so far that no other authority whatsoever shall be recognized as having any right to interfere in the discipline of the schools, the arrangement of the studies, the conferring of degrees, in the choice or approval of the teachers. — Allocutions "Quibus luctuosissimmis," Sept. 5, 1851, and "In consistoriali," Nov. 1, 1850.

46. Moreover, even in ecclesiastical seminaries, the method of studies to be adopted is subject to the civil authority. — Allocution "Nunquam fore," Dec. 15, 1856.

47. The best theory of civil society requires that popular schools open to children of every class of the people, and, generally, all public institutes intended for instruction in letters and philosophical sciences and for carrying on the education of youth, should be freed from all ecclesiastical authority, control and interference, and should be fully subjected to the civil and political power at the pleasure of the rulers, and according to the standard of the prevalent opinions of the age. — Epistle to the Archbishop of Freiburg, "Cum non sine," July 14, 1864.

48. Catholics may approve of the system of educating youth unconnected with Catholic faith and the power of the Church, and which regards the knowledge of merely natural things, and only, or at least primarily, the ends of earthly social life. — Ibid.

49. The civil power may prevent the prelates of the Church and the faithful from communicating freely and mutually with the Roman pontiff. — Allocution "Maxima quidem," June 9, 1862.

50. Lay authority possesses of itself the right of presenting bishops, and may require of them to undertake the administration of the diocese before they receive canonical institution, and the Letters Apostolic from the Holy See. — Allocution "Nunquam fore," Dec. 15, 1856.

51. And, further, the lay government has the right of

deposing bishops from their pastoral functions, and is not bound to obey the Roman pontiff in those things which relate to the institution of bishoprics and the appointment of bishops. — Allocution "Acerbissimum," Sept. 27, 1852, Damnatio "Multiplices inter," June 10, 1851.

52. Government can, by its own right, alter the age prescribed by the Church for the religious profession of women and men; and may require of all religious orders to admit no person to take solemn vows without its permission. — Allocution "Nunquam fore," Dec. 15, 1856.

53. The laws enacted for the protection of religious orders and regarding their rights and duties ought to be abolished; nay, more, civil Government may lend its assistance to all who desire to renounce the obligation which they have undertaken of a religious life, and to break their vows. Government may also suppress the said religious orders, as likewise collegiate churches and simple benefices, even those of advowson and subject their property and revenues to the administration and pleasure of the civil power. — Allocutions "Acerbissimum," Sept. 27, 1852; "Probe memineritis," Jan. 22, 1855; "Cum saepe," July 26, 1855.

54. Kings and princes are not only exempt from the jurisdiction of the Church, but are superior to the Church in deciding questions of jurisdiction. — Damnatio "Multiplices inter," June 10, 1851.

55. The Church ought to be separated from the State, and the State from the Church. — Allocution "Acerbissimum," Sept. 27, 1852.

VII. ERRORS CONCERNING NATURAL AND CHRISTIAN ETHICS

56. Moral laws do not stand in need of the divine sanction, and it is not at all necessary that human laws should be made conformable to the laws of nature and receive their power of binding from God. — Allocution "Maxima quidem," June 9, 1862.

57. The science of philosophical things and morals and also civil laws may and ought to keep aloof from divine and

ecclesiastical authority. — Ibid.

58. No other forces are to be recognized except those which reside in matter, and all the rectitude and excellence of morality ought to be placed in the accumulation and increase of riches by every possible means, and the gratification of pleasure. — Ibid.; Encyclical "Quanto conficiamur," Aug. 10, 1863.

59. Right consists in the material fact. All human duties are an empty word, and all human facts have the force of right. — Allocution "Maxima quidem," June 9, 1862.

60. Authority is nothing else but numbers and the sum total of material forces. — Ibid.

61. The injustice of an act when successful inflicts no injury on the sanctity of right. — Allocution "Jamdudum cernimus," March 18, 1861.

62. The principle of non-intervention, as it is called, ought to be proclaimed and observed. — Allocution "Novos et ante," Sept. 28, 1860.

63. It is lawful to refuse obedience to legitimate princes, and even to rebel against them. — Encyclical "Qui pluribus," Nov. 9, 1864; Allocution "Quibusque vestrum," Oct. 4, 1847; "Noscitis et Nobiscum," Dec. 8, 1849; Apostolic Letter "Cum Catholica."

64. The violation of any solemn oath, as well as any wicked and flagitious action repugnant to the eternal law, is not only not blamable but is altogether lawful and worthy of the highest praise when done through love of country. — Allocution "Quibus quantisque," April 20, 1849.

VIII. ERRORS CONCERNING CHRISTIAN MARRIAGE

65. The doctrine that Christ has raised marriage to the dignity of a sacrament cannot be at all tolerated. — Apostolic Letter "Ad Apostolicae," Aug. 22, 1851.

66. The Sacrament of Marriage is only a something accessory to the contract and separate from it, and the sacrament itself consists in the nuptial benediction alone. — Ibid.

67. By the law of nature, the marriage tie is not indissoluble, and in many cases divorce properly so called

may be decreed by the civil authority. — Ibid.; Allocution "Acerbissimum," Sept. 27, 1852.

68. The Church has not the power of establishing diriment impediments of marriage, but such a power belongs to the civil authority by which existing impediments are to be removed. — Damnatio "Multiplices inter," June 10, 1851.

69. In the dark ages the Church began to establish diriment impediments, not by her own right, but by using a power borrowed from the State. — Apostolic Letter "Ad Apostolicae," Aug. 22, 1851.

70. The canons of the Council of Trent, which anathematize those who dare to deny to the Church the right of establishing diriment impediments, either are not dogmatic or must be understood as referring to such borrowed power. — Ibid.

71. The form of solemnizing marriage prescribed by the Council of Trent, under pain of nullity, does not bind in cases where the civil law lays down another form, and declares that when this new form is used the marriage shall be valid.

72. Boniface VIII was the first who declared that the vow of chastity taken at ordination renders marriage void. — Ibid.

73. In force of a merely civil contract there may exist between Christians a real marriage, and it is false to say either that the marriage contract between Christians is always a sacrament, or that there is no contract if the sacrament be excluded. — Ibid.; Letter to the King of Sardinia, Sept. 9, 1852; Allocutions "Acerbissimum," Sept. 27, 1852, "Multis gravibusque," Dec. 17, 1860.

74. Matrimonial causes and espousals belong by their nature to civil tribunals. — Encyclical "Qui pluribus," Nov. 9 1846; Damnatio "Multiplices inter," June 10, 1851, "Ad Apostolicae," Aug. 22, 1851; Allocution "Acerbissimum," Sept. 27, 1852.

IX. ERRORS REGARDING THE CIVIL POWER OF THE SOVEREIGN PONTIFF

75. The children of the Christian and Catholic Church are divided amongst themselves about the compatibility of the temporal with the spiritual power. — "Ad Apostolicae,"

Aug. 22, 1851.

76. The abolition of the temporal power of which the Apostolic See is possessed would contribute in the greatest degree to the liberty and prosperity of the Church. — Allocutions "Quibus quantisque," April 20, 1849, "Si semper antea," May 20, 1850.

X. ERRORS HAVING REFERENCE TO MODERN LIBERALISM

77. In the present day it is no longer expedient that the Catholic religion should be held as the only religion of the State, to the exclusion of all other forms of worship. — Allocution "Nemo vestrum," July 26, 1855.

78. Hence it has been wisely decided by law, in some Catholic countries, that persons coming to reside therein shall enjoy the public exercise of their own peculiar worship. — Allocution "Acerbissimum," Sept. 27, 1852.

79. Moreover, it is false that the civil liberty of every form of worship, and the full power, given to all, of overtly and publicly manifesting any opinions whatsoever and thoughts, conduce more easily to corrupt the morals and minds of the people, and to propagate the pest of indifferentism. — Allocution "Nunquam fore," Dec. 15, 1856.

80. The Roman Pontiff can, and ought to, reconcile himself, and come to terms with progress, liberalism and modern civilization.- -Allocution "Jamdudum cernimus," March 18, 1861.

The faith teaches us and human reason demonstrates that a double order of things exists, and that we must therefore distinguish between the two earthly powers, the one of natural origin which provides for secular affairs and the tranquillity of human society, the other of supernatural origin, which presides over the City of God, that is to say the Church of Christ, which has been divinely instituted for the sake of souls and of eternal salvation.... The duties of this twofold power are most wisely ordered in such a way that to God is given what is God's (Matt. 22:21), and because of God to

Caesar what is Caesar's, who is great because he is smaller than heaven. Certainly the Church has never disobeyed this divine command, the Church which always and everywhere instructs the faithful to show the respect which they should inviolably have for the supreme authority and its secular rights....

... Venerable Brethren, you see clearly enough how sad and full of perils is the condition of Catholics in the regions of Europe which We have mentioned. Nor are things any better or circumstances calmer in America, where some regions are so hostile to Catholics that their governments seem to deny by their actions the Catholic faith they claim to profess. In fact, there, for the last few years, a ferocious war on the Church, its institutions and the rights of the Apostolic See has been raging.... Venerable Brothers, it is surprising that in our time such a great war is being waged against the Catholic Church. But anyone who knows the nature, desires and intentions of the sects, whether they be called masonic or bear another name, and compares them with the nature the systems and the vastness of the obstacles by which the Church has been assailed almost everywhere, cannot doubt that the present misfortune must mainly be imputed to the frauds and machinations of these sects. It is from them that the synagogue of Satan, which gathers its troops against the Church of Christ, takes its strength. In the past Our predecessors, vigilant even from the beginning in Israel, had already denounced them to the kings and the nations, and had condemned them time and time again, and even We have not failed in this duty. If those who would have been able to avert such a deadly scourge had only had more faith in the supreme Pastors of the Church! But this scourge, winding through sinuous caverns, . . . deceiving many with astute frauds, finally has arrived at the point where it comes forth impetuously from its hiding places and triumphs as a powerful master. Since the throng of its propagandists has grown enormously, these wicked groups think that they have already become masters of the world and that they have almost reached their pre-established goal. Having sometimes obtained what they desired, and that is power, in several countries, they boldly turn the help of powers and authorities which they have secured to trying to submit the Church of God to the most cruel servitude, to undermine the foundations on which it rests, to contaminate its splendid qualities; and, moreover, to strike it with frequent blows, to shake it, to overthrow it, and, if possible, to make it disappear completely from the earth. Things being thus, Venerable Brothers, make every effort to defend the faithful which are entrusted to you against the insidious contagion of these sects and to save from perdition those who unfortunately have inscribed themselves in such sects. Make known and attack those who, whether suffering from, or planning, deception, are not afraid to affirm that these shady congregations aim only at the profit of society, at progress and mutual benefit. Explain to them often and impress deeply on their souls the Papal constitutions on this subject and teach, them that the masonic associations are anathematized by them not only in Europe but also in America and wherever they may be in the whole world.

To the Archbishops and Bishops of Prussia concerning the situation of the Catholic Church faced with persecution by that Government....

But although they (the bishops resisting persecution) should be praised rather than pitied, the scorn of episcopal dignity, the violation of the liberty and the rights of the Church, the ill treatment which does not only oppress those dioceses, but also the others of the Kingdom of Prussia, demand that We, owing to the Apostolic office with which God has entrusted us in spite of Our insufficient merit, protest against laws which have produced such great evils and make one fear even greater ones; and as far as we are able to do so with the sacred authority of divine law, We vindicate for the Church the freedom which has been trodden underfoot with sacrilegious violence. That is why by this letter we intend to do Our duty by announcing openly to all those whom this matter concerns and to the whole Catholic world, that these laws are null and void because they are absolutely contrary to the divine constitution of the Church. In fact, with respect to matters which concern the holy ministry, Our Lord did not put the mighty of this century in charge, but Saint Peter, whom he entrusted not only with feeding his sheep, but also the goats; therefore no power in the world, however great it may be, can deprive of the pastoral office those whom the Holy Ghost has made Bishops in order to feed the Church of God.

✠

MULTIPLICES INTER
Allocution of Pope Pius IX
Condemning Freemasonry
September 25, 1865

This Apostolic letter, given to Cardinals gathered in Consistory, explicitly condemned Freemasonry, reiterating its incompatibility with Catholic doctrine due to its promotion of naturalism and religious indifferentism. It called for vigilance against secret societies undermining the Church and strengthened Pope Pius IX's campaign against Freemasonry during a time of increasing tension between the Church and secular movements.

Venerable Brethren: Amongst the numerous machinations and means by which the enemies of the Christian name have dared to attack the Church of God and have tried, though in vain, to beat it down and to destroy it, it is certainly necessary to include that perverse society of men, commonly called "Masonic," which, first contained in darkness and obscurity, has since come to light for the common ruin of religion and human society.

Since Our predecessors the Roman Pontiffs, faithful to their pastoral office, discovered its snares and deceptions, they deemed there was not a moment to spare in reprimanding by their authority, striking with condemnation and exterminating as with a sword this sect breathing forth iniquity and attacking holy as well as public things. That is why Our predecessor Clement XII, by his apostolic letters, proscribed and condemned this sect, and turned away all the faithful not only from associating with it, but also from propagating and encouraging it in any manner whatsoever, under the pain of incurring excommunication ipso facto. Benedict XIV confirmed by his constitution this just and legitimate sentence of condemnation, and he did not fail to exhort Catholic sovereigns to devote all their strength and solicitude to suppressing this profoundly perverse sect and to defending society against common peril.

Would to Heaven that the monarchs had heeded the words of Our predecessor! Would to Heaven that in such a grave matter they had acted with less softness! Certainly We (and our fathers also) would never then have had to lament so many seditious movements, so many incendiary wars which have put all of Europe on fire, or so many bitter evils which have afflicted and still do afflict the Church. But the fury of the wicked having been far from appeased, Pius VII, Our predecessor, anathematized a sect of recent origins, the Carbonari, which especially propagated itself in Italy, where it gained a great number of followers; and, inflamed with the same zeal for souls, Leo XII condemned through his apostolic letters not only the secret societies We have just mentioned, but also all the others, by whatever name they be called, conspiring against the Church and civil authority, and he strictly forbade them to all the faithful under pain of excommunication.

However, these efforts of the Apostolic See did not have the success for which one had hoped. The Masonic sect of which We speak was neither defeated nor struck down: on the contrary, it grew so much that in these difficult days it shows itself everywhere with impunity, and lifts its head more boldly than ever before. We have therefore judged it necessary to return to this subject, considering that due to the ignorance one might have of the nefarious schemings which take place in these clandestine meetings, one might believe falsely that the nature of this society is inoffensive, that this institution has no other aim than to help men and to come to their aid in adversity, and that there is after all nothing to fear for the Church of God.

But who does not see how much such an idea is far removed from the truth? What is it then that this association of men of every religion and every belief claims? Why these clandestine meetings and why such a strict oath mandated for its initiates, who promise to disclose nothing of what might be relayed there? And why the alarming severity of punishments to which the initiates bind themselves, in case they should happen to break the oath? Certainly, it must be impious and criminal, a society that flees the day and the light in this way; for the one who does evil, says the Apostle, hates the light. How different from such an association the pious societies of the faithful which flourish in the Catholic Church! Among them, nothing is hidden, there are no secrets. The rules which govern them are before the eyes of all, and all can also see the works of charity practiced according to the teaching of the Gospel.

Also, it is not without sorrow that We have seen Catholic societies of this kind, so salutary, so well made for exciting piety and coming to the aid of the poor, attacked and even destroyed in certain places, while on the other hand the dark Masonic society is encouraged or at least tolerated, so inimical to God and to the Church, so dangerous even for the security of kingdoms.

We experience, Venerable Brethren, bitterness and pain in seeing that when it is a matter of condemning this sect according to the constitutions of Our predecessors, many of those whose duty and office's responsibility ought to render them full of vigilance and ardor for so serious a matter, show themselves indifferent and, so to speak, asleep. If some think that the apostolic constitutions issued against the secret sects and their followers and abettors under pain of anathema have no force in the countries where these sects are tolerated by the civil authority, they are most certainly in very great error. As you know, Venerable Brethren, We have already reproved this false and evil doctrine, and today we again reprove and condemn it. This supreme authority to feed all of the Lord's flock, which the Roman Pontiffs have received from Christ in the person of the blessed apostle Peter, and consequently the supreme magisterium they must exercise in the Church, are they dependent upon the civil authority and can they be stopped without reason and restrained by the latter?

In this situation, fearing that imprudent men, and especially the youth, allow themselves to be misled, and that Our silence occasion anyone to protect error, We have resolved, Venerable Brethren, to raise Our apostolic voice; and, confirming here, before you, the constitutions of Our predecessors, by Our apostolic authority, We reprove and condemn this Masonic society and the others of the same

Multiplices Inter

kind, which, while differing in appearance, gather every day for the same goal, and conspire either openly or clandestinely against the Church and the legitimate authorities; and We order under the same penalties as those specified in the preceding constitutions of Our predecessors all Christians of every condition, every rank, every dignity, and every country, to regard these same societies as proscribed and condemned by Us. Now there only remains for Us, in order to satisfy the desires and solicitude of Our paternal heart, to warn and exhort the faithful who would associate themselves with sects of this kind of the necessity to obey wiser inspirations and to abandon these baneful secret meetings, so that they not be led into the abyss of eternal ruin. As for all of the other faithful, full of solicitude for souls, We strongly exhort you to guard yourselves against the perfidious discourse of the sectarians who, beneath an apparent decency, are inflamed with an ardent hatred for the religion of Christ and for legitimate authority, and who have but one single thought as one single goal, namely to annihilate all divine and human laws. May they be well aware that the affiliates of these sects are as the wolves Christ Our Lord foretold must come, covered with sheepskin in order to devour the flock! May they know it is necessary to count them among those whom the Apostle so much forbade us their company and access, that he expressly prohibited even saying to them *ave* (greetings)! [cf. 2 Jn 10-11]

May God, Who is rich in mercy, graciously hearing the prayers of us all, have, with the help of His grace, the senseless come back to reason and men who are astray return to the path of justice! May God rebuke the fury of depraved men who, with the help of the aforementioned societies, prepare impious and criminal acts, and may the Church and human society be able to rest a little from such numerous and inveterate evils! And so that our desires may be graciously heard, let us also pray to our advocate before the most clement God, the Most Holy Virgin, His Mother, immaculate from the beginning, to whom it was given to strike down the enemies of the Church and the monsters of error! Let us also implore the protection of the blessed apostles Peter and Paul, by whose glorious blood this noble city was consecrated! We have confidence that with their help and assistance We shall more easily obtain what We ask the Divine Goodness.

ETSI MULTA
Encyclical of Pope Pius IX
On the Church in Italy, Germany and Switzerland
November 21, 1873

Etsi Multa addresses the challenges facing the Church, including Freemasonry's influence in secularizing society, particularly in Italy after the unification and loss of the Papal States. It condemned Masonic efforts to promote secular education and reduce Church influence.

To all Patriarchs, Primates, Archbishops, Bishops, and other Ordinaries in Favor and Communion with the Apostolic See.

Venerable Brothers Greetings and the Apostolic Blessing.

It has been Our lot from the very beginning of Our Pontificate to suit many grievous and painful occurrences from various causes, which We have often explained to you in encyclical letters; in these last years the burden of distress has grown so that, if the divine goodness did not sustain Us, we would be all but overwhelmed. Indeed things have reached such a point that death itself would seem preferable to life tossed about by so many waves; with eyes lifted to heaven, we are compelled to cry out from time to time: "it is better for us to die, than to witness the ruin of our sanctuary."[1] Forsooth, from the time when this Our beloved city was forcibly captured and subjected to the rule of men who are disdainers of right and enemies of religion, men to whom all things human and divine are one and the same, scarcely no day has gone by without some new wound beings invited on Our already wounded heart.

---

[1] I Mc 3.59.

Evils Which Have Befallen Catholicism

2. We still hear lamentations of men and women of religious congregations, who driven from their houses and in need, are dispersed in a hostile manner; this usually happens when the dominating faction has as its aim the perversion of the social order. As the great St. Anthony, on the testimony of Athanasius, says, "The devil hates all Christians indeed, but cannot tolerate in any way upright monks and virgins of Christ." We have also seen recently something We never expected would happen, namely Our Gregorian University has been suppressed and abolished. It was instituted for this purpose: that to it would come (in the words of an ancient author writing for Anglo-Saxons about the Roman School) young clerics, even from distant regions, to be educated in Catholic doctrine and faith, so nothing contrary to Catholic unity would be taught in their Churches. Thus strengthened in firm faith, they might return to their own people. Little by little all defenses and instruments by which We are able to rule and direct the universal Church are nefariously taken away from Us. It was aimed that once the city was taken from Us, the Roman Pontiff would still have complete freedom in the exercise of spiritual ministry and in carrying out religious matters. This is far from true. As we predicted, the purpose of the sacrilegious usurpation of Our rule is the destruction of the force and efficacy of the papal primacy and eventually the Catholic religion itself.

3. However, it was not Our intention to write to you concerning these evils by which this Our city and all of Italy as well is infested; indeed, We would perhaps have suppressed these Our troubles in mournful silence, if it were permitted by divine clemency that We could lessen the bitter sorrows by which so many venerable brothers, bishops, and laity are tortured in other regions.

Problems in Switzerland

4. For you are well aware, that certain cantons of the Swiss Federation have perverted all order and have undermined the very foundation of the constitution of the Church of Christ. This was brought about not so much by heterodox men, some of whom even find fault with the crime,

as by followers of sects who today have gained power far and wide. They not only subvert all of justice and reason, but they even go against their publicly declared trust as well. For it was solemnly pledged, with the approval and authority of the laws of the Federation as well, that religious liberty for Catholics would remain safe and sound. We deplored, indeed, in Our allocution of last 23 December the force applied to the religious situation by the government of those cantons "whether in decisions about dogmas of the Catholic faith or by the favoring of apostates or by interfering with the exercise of episcopal power." We made these just complaints known when We sent Gestore to the Federal Council as Our negotiator, but they were wholly neglected. Nor were protests from Catholics of all ranks nor those repeatedly sent from the Swiss episcopacy treated any better; indeed the earlier injuries inflicted were greatly increased by worse ones.

New Laws Promulgated

5. The violent banishment of Our venerable brother Gaspar, bishop of Hebron and Vicar Apostolic of Geneva took place as decorously and gloriously for him who endured it as it was foul and indecorous for those who ordered and carried it out. After this banishment the government of Geneva on 12 March and 27 August of this year promulgated two laws fully in keeping with the edict proposed the previous October, the one with which We found fault in Our allocution mentioned previously. In effect the same government arrogated the right to itself of refashioning in that canton the constitution of the Catholic Church and of conforming it to the democratic form. This subjects the bishop, both in the exercise of his proper jurisdiction and administration and in the delegation of his power, to the civil authority. It forbids him to live in the canton and defines the number and limit of parishes. It also proposes the conditions for the election of pastors and vicars and the method of their recall or suspension from office. Furthermore it grants to laics the right of nominating them, entrusting to the same laity the temporal administration of cult and in general setting them in charge, as if inspectors, of ecclesiastical affairs.

Why the Laws Are Invalid

6. These same laws provide that without the government's favor, which is revocable, the pastors and vicars could not exercise any functions and could not accept any office more extensive than those which they received through popular election. Furthermore, they are compelled by the civil power to take an oath, the words of which denote apostasy. Everyone sees that laws of this nature are void and useless because lay legislators, who are for the most part heterodox men, do not have the power to make such laws. They are also invalid because in what they teach, they are opposed to dogmas of the Catholic faith and ecclesiastical discipline sanctioned by the Ecumenical Council of Trent and by pontifical constitutions. We must therefore condemn and disapprove them.

Condemnation of the New Laws

7. Therefore as is required by the duty of Our offices, with Our Apostolic authority We solemnly condemn them, declaring at the same time that the oath they impose is illicit and clearly sacrilegious; therefore all those who in Geneva or elsewhere are elected according to the decrees of these laws or in a similar way, by the vote of the people and with the confirmation of the civil power, and who subsequently dare to undertake the tasks of ecclesiastical ministry incur a major excommunication reserved specially to this Holy See and also incur other canonical penalties. Furthermore, they must all be avoided by the faithful according to the divine admonition, as aliens and thieves who come only to rob, kill, and destroy.[2]

Other Adversities

8. Sad and calamitous as these events are which We have just recounted, more dreadful things have happened in five of the seven cantons which constitute the diocese of Basel, namely Solothurn, Bern, Basel-Landschaft, Aargau, and Zurich. Laws have also been passed there concerning parishes, the election of pastors, and vicars and their recall.

---

[2] Jn 10.5 10.

These laws overturn the rule of the Church and its divine institution, subjugating ecclesiastical ministry to secular power. One of them, that passed by the Governor of Solothurn on 23 December 1872, is completely schismatical. We condemn it and decree that it be forever considered condemned. Indeed Our venerable brother, Eugene, Bishop of Basel, with just indignation and apostolic constancy, rejected certain articles drawn up and presented to him in his meeting. They call said meeting a diocesan conference, to which delegates of the five aforesaid cantons came. In rejecting the articles, he said that they were harmful to episcopal authority, subversive of hierarchical rule, and openly favorable to heresy. For this reason he was deprived of his bishopric, taken from his residence, and violently driven into exile. After this they omitted no type of fraud or vexation to lead the clergy and faithful in the previously mentioned cantons into schism. They forbade the clergy to have any communication with the exiled bishop. Additionally, they ordered the cathedral chapter of Basel to convene for the election of a vicar or administrator of the diocese, just as if the episcopal see were really vacant. The chapter strenuously rejected this proposal.

Difficulties in the Territory of Jura

9. Meanwhile by a decree and vote of the civil magistrates of Bern, sixtynine pastors of the territory of Jura were first forbidden to carry out the functions of their ministry and then deprived of office. This was because they had openly attested that they recognized only Eugene as legitimate bishop and pastor, or were unwilling to separate themselves dishonorably from Catholic unity. This whole territory, has constantly held onto the Catholic faith and was earlier joined to the canton of Bern under the legal stipulation and agreement that it preserve the exercise of its religion free and inviolate. But now it is deprived of parish sermons, solemn baptisms, weddings, and funerals. The multitude of the faithful is protesting in vain that on account of consummate injury done to them, they are compelled either to accept schismatic and heretical pastors forced on them by the political authority or else be deprived of any priestly

ministry and aid.

10. We, for Our part, give thanks to God who, with the same grace with which He formerly strengthened and confirmed martyrs, sustains and strengthens that select part of the Catholic flock which courageously supports their bishop as he builds a wall in defense of the house of Israel that it may stand in battle the day of the Lord.[3] Without fear they follow in the footsteps of the head of the martyrs of Jesus Christ; while offering the gentleness of the lamb to the ferocity of wolves, they constantly and readily fight for their faith.

11. This noble constancy of the faithful Swiss is emulated with no less commendation by the clergy and faithful in Germany, who themselves follow the illustrious example of their ecclesiastical leaders. The Germans, assuming the shield of Catholic truth and the helms of salvation, fight the battles of the Lord and are a wonder to the world, to the angels, and to men who look on them from every side. All the more is their fortitude of spirit and unbroken constancy admired and extolled with outstanding praise as the bitter persecution set in motion against them in the German Empire and especially in Prussia increases with each day.

Unwarranted Power Given to Laity

12. In addition to many grave injuries inflicted on the Catholic Church last year, the government of Prussia with harsh, iniquitous laws totally different from previous ones have subjected the whole institution and education of clerics to lay power. One can now legitimately ask how clerics are to be educated and formed for the priestly and pastoral life. Going further still, the government grants to the same lay power the right to bestow any office or ecclesiastical benefice and even the right to deprive sacred pastors of office and benefice.

13. Moreover so that the ecclesiastical government and the hierarchical order of subordination constituted by Christ Himself may be more quickly and fully subverted, these same

---

[3] 3 Ez 13.5.

laws impose many obstacles on bishops so that they cannot provide, through canonical censures and punishments, for the salvation of souls, the soundness of doctrine in Catholic schools, and the obedience due them from clerics. These same laws forbid bishops to do these things unless they are in accord with the wishes of the civil authority and the norms proposed by it. And so that nothing be lacking in the total oppression of the Catholic Church, a royal tribunal for ecclesiastical affairs has been instituted. Bishops and holy pastors can be summoned before it, both by private individuals and by public magistrates, so as to stand trial like criminals and be coerced in the exercise of their spiritual functions

Existence of Church Threatened

14. Thus the holy Church of Christ, whose necessary and full freedom of which religion had repeatedly been guaranteed by public pacts and the highest princes, has in these same places been deprived of all its rights and exposed to hostile men. Its final extinction now threatens. For the new laws, to be sure, have as their intent its destruction.

15. No wonder, then, that the former religious tranquility has been gravely disturbed in that Empire by this kind of law and other plans and actions of the Prussian government most hostile to the Church. But who would wish to falsely cast the blame of this disturbance on the Catholics of the German Empire! For if they are faulted for not acquiesing in such laws in which they could not acquiesce with good conscience, for the same reason the apostles of Jesus Christ ant the martyrs, who preferred to undergo most dreadful tortures and death itself than to betray their duty and violate the rights of their most holy religion by obeying the commands of the princes who persecuted them, must also be faulted.

16. If no other laws than these of the civil authority existed and if they were of the highest order, it would be wrong to transgress them. If, moreover, these same civil laws constituted the norm of conscience, as some maintain both impiously and absurdly, the early martyrs and their followers would have been worthy of reprehension rather than honor and praise. Indeed it would have been against the laws and

the wish of princes to hand down the Christian faith, propagate it, and found the Church. Nevertheless the faith teaches and human reason demonstrates that there is a twofold order of things. Two kinds of powers must be distinguished on earth-one natural that looks to the tranquility and secular business of human society; the other, whose origin is above nature, which is in charge of the Church of Christ, divinely instituted for the salvation and peace of souls. The offices of these two powers are wisely coordinated so that things which belong to God are returned to God and, because of God, those of Caesar to Caesar, who "for this reason is great because he is less than heaven for he belongs to Him whom heaven and all creatures belong."[4]

17. From this divine command, to be sure, the Church has never turned aside. It always and everywhere attempts to inculcate in the faithful an inviolable obedience towards their supreme rulers and their rights, insofar as they are secular, and it has taught, with the Apostle, that they are rulers not for fear of good works but of evil, teaching the faithful to be subject not only because of fear, because the prince bears the sword to carry out his ire against him who has done evil, but also because of conscience because in his office he is a minister of God.[5] However, this fear of princes the Church limits to evil acts, excluding the same totally from the observance of the divine law, being mindful of what blessed Peter taught the faithful; "May none of you suffer for being a murderer, a thief, a criminal or an informer, but if any of you should suffer for being a Christian, then he is not to be ashamed of it; let him glorify God in that name."[6]

18. Since these things are so, you understand how sad We must have been when We read in the recent letter from the German Emperor the unexpected accusation against certain of his Catholic subjects, especially against the Catholic clergy, and bishops. The reason for this accusation is that they, fearing neither bonds nor tribulations and not

---

[4] Tertullian, apolog., chap. 30.
[5] Rom 13.3f.
[6] I Pt 4.14, 15.

placing any great value on their lives,[7] refuse to obey the aforementioned laws. They protest with that same firmness shown before the passing of these laws. They pointed out their faults by serious, clear and most solid explanations which, with the approval of the whole Catholic world and even of some heterodox men, they delivered to the Prince, his administrators and the supreme council of the kingdom.

19. For the same reason now they are accused of treason, as if they were conspiring with those who strive to upset all orders of human society. No attention is paid to the excellent arguments in which they clearly attest their unbroken loyalty and obedience to the Prince and their lively devotion to their fatherland. Indeed We Ourselves are asked to exhort Catholics and holy pastors there to observe these laws; this would be equivalent to Our contributing to the oppression and dispersion of the flock of the Christ. However, supported by God, We are confident that the most serene Emperor, having more carefully weighed things, will reject the empty suspicion conceived against his most loyal subjects and will no longer allow their honor to be reviled with foul detraction. In addition, he will end the unmerited persecution against them. Moreover, We would have willingly passed over the imperial letter if it had not been published, against Our knowledge and in a most unusual fashion, by an official newspaper in Berlin. It was published together with other material written by Us, in which We appealed for justice from the Emperor for the Catholic Church in Prussia.

Harassing of the Church

20. What We have recounted so far is common knowledge. Monks and virgins devoted to God are deprived of the common liberty of ordinary citizens and ejected with enormous cruelty, Catholic schools are daily being taken away from the care of the Church, and sodalities for pious works and even seminaries are dissolved. Additionally, the liberty of evangelical preaching is interfered with, hindered, teaching religion in the native language is forbidden in certain parts of the kingdom. Curates are withdrawn from

---

[7] Acts 20.24.

their parishes, and prelates themselves are deprived of revenues coerced in many ways, and frightened with threat of imprisonment. While Catholics are vexed with all kinds of harassment such as these, how can We possibly acquiesce to what is suggested and not invoke the religion of Jesus Christ and the truth?

Government Support for Heretics

21. Nor is this the limit of the injuries which are committed against the Catholic Church. In addition the Prussian and other governments of the German Empire openly support those recent heretics who call themselves Old Catholics. Their abuse of such a name would be plainly ridiculous if it were not for the fact that so many monstrous errors of this sect against the principal teachings of the Catholic faith, so many sacrileges in divine service and the administration of the sacraments, so many grave scandals, and so much ruin of souls redeemed by the blood of Christ did not force tears from Our eyes.

Further Heresies

22. And surely what these sons of perdition intend is quite clear from their other writings, especially that impious and most imprudent one which has only recently been published by the person whom they recently constituted as a pseudo-bishop. For these writings attack and pervert the true power of jurisdiction of the Roman Pontiff and the bishops, who are the successors of blessed Peter and the apostles; they transfer it instead to the people, or, as they say, to the community. They obstinately reject and oppose the infallible magisterium both of the Roman Pontiff and of the whole Church in teaching matters. Incredibly, they boldly affirm that the Roman Pontiff and all the bishops, the priests and the people conjoined with him in the unity of faith and communion fell into heresy when they approved and professed the definitions of the Ecumenical Vatican Council. Therefore they deny also the indefectibility of the Church and blasphemously declare that it has perished throughout the world and that its visible Head and the bishops have erred. They assert the necessity of restoring a legitimate episcopacy

in the person of their pseudo-bishop, who has entered not by the gate but from elsewhere like a thief or robber and calls the damnation of Christ upon his head.

23. These unhappy men undermine the foundations of religion, overturn all its marks and properties, and invent so many foul errors, or rather, draw forth from the ancient store of heretics and gather them together and publish them. Yet they do not blush to call themselves Catholics and Old Catholics, while in their doctrine, novelty, and number they show themselves in no way to be either old or Catholic. Certainly the Church rises up with greater right against them than it once did through Augustine against the Donatists. Diffused among all people, the Church was built by Christ the Son of the living God upon the rock, against which the gates of Hell will not prevail, and with which He Himself, to Whom all power in heaven and on earth is given, said He would be with until the consummation of the world. "The Church cries to her Spouse: Why do certain men withdrawing from me murmur against me? Why do these lost men claim that I have perished? Announce to me the length of my days, how long I will be in this world? Tell me on account of those who say: it was and is no longer; on account of those who say: the scriptures have been fulfilled, all nations have believed, but the Church has apostatized and perished from all nations. And He announced and the voice was not vain. What did He announce? 'Behold I am with you all days even to the consummation of the world.' Moved by your voices and your false opinions, it asked of God that He announce to it the length of its days and it found that God said 'Behold I am with you all days even to the consummation of the world.' Here you will say: He spoke about us; we are as we will be until the end of the world. Christ Himself is asked; He says 'and this gospel will be preached in the whole world, in testimony to all nations, and then will come the end.' Therefore the Church will be among all nations until the end of the world. Let heretics perish as they are, and let them find that they become what they are not."[8]

---

[8] Augustine on Ps 101, enarratio 2, nos. 8, 9.

Pseudo-bishop

24. But these men having progressed more boldly in the ways of wickedness and destruction, as happens to heretical sects from God's just judgment, have wished to create a hierarchy also for themselves, as we have intimated. They have chosen and set up a pseudo-bishop, a certain notorious apostate from the Catholic faith, Joseph Hubert Reinkens. So that nothing be lacking in their impudence, for his consecration they have had refuge to those very Jansenists of Utrecht, whom they themselves, before they separated from the Church, considered as heretics and schismatics, as do all other Catholics. However, this Joseph Hubert dares to say that he is a bishop, and, what passes belief, he is recognized and named in an explicit decree by the most serene Emperor of Germany and is proposed to all his subjects as a lawful bishop. But as even the rudiments of Catholic faith declare, no one can be considered a bishop who is not linked in communion of faith and love with Peter, upon whom is built the Church of Christ; who does not adhere to the supreme Pastor to whom the sheep of Christ are committed to be pastured; and who is not bound to the confirmer of fraternity which is in the world. And indeed "the Lord spoke to Peter; to one person therefore, so that He might found unity from one";[9] to Peter, "the divine dignity granted a great and wonderful consortium of his power, and if He wished anything to be common with him and the rest of the princes, He never gave, except through him, what He did not deny to the others."[10] Hence it is from this Apostolic See, where blessed Peter "lives and presides and grants the truth of faith to those seeking it,"[11] that the "rights of venerable communion flow to all";[12] and this same See "for the

---

[9] Pacian, epistle 3 to Sympronius, no. 11; Cyprian, de unit. Eccl; Optatus, contra Parmen., bk. 7, no. 3; Siricius, epistle 5 to the Bishops of Africa; Innocent 1, epistles to Victricius and the Councils of Carthage and Milevis.

[10] St. Leo the Great, sermon 3 on his elevation; Optatus, bk. 2, no. 2.

[11] Peter Chrysologus, epistle to Eutyches.

[12] Council of Aquileia; Ambrose, epistle 11, no. 4; Jerome, epistles 14 and 16 to Damasus.

Churches spread throughout the whole world is certainly the head, as it were, of their members, from which if one cuts himself off, he becomes an exile from the Christian religion, as soon as he begins not to belong to its structure."[13]

25. Therefore the holy martyr Cyprian, writing about schism, denied to the pseudobishop Novatian even the title of Christian, on the grounds that he was cut off and separated from the Church of Christ. "Whoever he is," he says, "and whatever sort he is, he is not a Christian who is not in the Church of Christ. Let him boast and preach his philosophy and eloquence with a proud voice; he who does not have fraternal charity and does not retain ecclesiastical unity, loses also what he previously had. Since by Christ one Church was founded divided into many members throughout the world, so likewise one episcopate, diffused in the harmonious multiplicity of many bishops. Subsequent to the teaching of God and the conjoined unity of the Catholic Church, he attempts to build a human church. Therefore, he who does not retain unity of spirit nor communion of peace and thus separates himself from the bond of the Church and the college of the priesthood cannot have the power nor the honor of a bishop because he kept not the unity or the peace of the episcopacy.[14]

Excommunication

26. We have been undeservingly placed on this supreme seat of Peter to preserve the Catholic faith and the unity of the universal Church. Therefore following the custom and example of Our Predecessors and of holy legislation, by the power granted to Us from heaven, We declare the election of the said Joseph Hubert Reinkens, performed against the sanctions of the holy canons to be illicit, null, and void. We furthermore declare his consecration sacrilegious. Therefore, by the authority of Almighty God, We excommunicate and hold as anathema Joseph Hubert himself and all those who attempted to choose him, and who aided in his sacrilegious consecration. We additionally excommunicate whoever has

---

[13] Boniface 1, epistle 14 to the Bishops of Thessalonica.
[14] Cyprian, contra Novatian, epistle 52 to Antonianus.

adhered to them and belonging to their party has furnished help, favor, aid, or consent. We declare, proclaim, and command that they are separated from the communion of the Church. They are to be considered among those with whom all faithful Christians are forbidden by the Apostle to associate and have social exchange to such an extent that, as he plainly states, they may not even be greeted.[15]

27. From these matters We have touched upon more by way of deploring than narrating them, venerable brothers, you understand how sad and full of danger is the condition of Catholics in those regions of Europe which We indicated. Nor, truly, are things much better or more peaceful in America, several of whose regions are so hostile to Catholics that their governments seem to deny in deeds their Catholic faith. For there, some years past, a most severe war was begun against the Church, its institutions, and the rights of this Apostolic See. If We were to pursue these matters, We would find much to say; since, however, because of the gravity of the situation, they cannot be touched on in passing, We will treat them more thoroughly at another time and place.

28. Some of you may perchance wonder that the war against the Catholic Church extends so widely. Indeed each of you knows well the nature, zeal, and intention of sects, whether called Masonic or some other name. When he compares them with the nature, purpose, and amplitude of the conflict waged nearly everywhere against the Church, he cannot doubt but that the present calamity must be attributed to their deceits and machinations for the most part. For from these the synagogue of Satan is formed which draws up its forces, advances its standards, and joins battle against the Church of Christ.

29. Our Predecessors, as watchers in Israel, denounced these forces from the very beginnings to rulers and nations. Against them they have struck out again and again with their condemnations. We Ourselves have not been deficient in Our duty. Would that the Pastors of the Church had more loyalty from those who could have averted such a pernicious plague! But, creeping through sinuous openings, never stinting in toil,

---

[15] 2 Jn 1.10.

deceiving many by clever fraud, it has reached such an outcome that it has burst forth from its hiding places and boasts itself lord and master. Grown immense by a multitude of followers, these nefarious bands think that they have been made masters of their desire and have all but achieved their goal. The have at last achieved what they have so long desired, that is, that in many places they obtained supreme power and won for themselves bulwarks of men and authority. Now they boldly turn to this, to hand over the Church of God to a most harsh servitude, to tear up the supports on which it rests, and to attempt to distort the marks by which it stands out gloriously. What more? They would, if possible, completely wipe it out from the world after they had shaken it with frequent blows, ruined it, and overturned it.

Efforts to Defeat Heresies

30. Since these things are so, venerable brothers, apply all your effort to protect the faithful committed to your care against the snares and contagion of these sects. Bring back those who have unhappily joined these sects. Expose especially the error of those who have been deceived or those who assert now that only social utility, progress, and the exercise of mutual benefits are the intention of these dark associations. Explain to them often and fix deeper in their minds the pontifical decrees on this matter. Teach them that these decrees refer not only to Masonic groups in Europe, but also those in America and in other regions of the world.

31. As for the rest since we have fallen on these evil times let us take care first and foremost, as good soldiers of Christ, not to lose heart. Indeed, in the very storms in which we are tossed, there is a certain hope of achieving future tranquility and greater serenity in the Church. So let us arouse ourselves and the toiling clergy and laity, propped up by divine help and inspired by that most noble statement of Chrysostom: "Many waves and dire storms, press on but we do not fear lest we be submerged, for we stand on a rock. Let the sea rage, it cannot dissolve the rock. Let the waves rise, they cannot sink the bark of Christ. Nothing is stronger than the Church. The Church is stronger than the heavens. Heaven and earth shall pass away, but my words will not pass away.

What words? Thou art Peter and upon this rock I will build my Church and the gates of Hell will not prevail against it. If you do not trust the words, trust the deeds. How many tyrants have tried to oppress the Church! How many cauldrons, furnaces, teeth of beasts, sharp swords! They have accomplished nothing. Where are those enemies? They are handed over to silence and forgetfulness. Where is the Church? It shines brighter than the sun. Their deeds are extinct, its deeds are immortal. If when they were few, the Christians were not conquered, how can you conquer them when the whole world is full of this holy religion? *Heaven and earth will pass, my words will not pass away.*[16] Therefore not moved by any danger and not hesitating at all, let us persevere in prayer. Let us all strive to placate the celestial anger provoked by the sins of mankind so that the Almighty will rise up and command the winds and bring about tranquility.

32. In the meantime, We lovingly grant the apostolic blessing as a testimony of the special benevolence We have to you all, venerable brothers, and the clergy and the entire people committed to the care of each of you.

Given in Rome at St. Peter's, 21 November 1873, in the 28th year of Our Pontificate.

✠

---

[16] Homily, ante exil., nos. 1 and 2.

ETSI NOS
Encyclical of Pope Leo XIII
On conditions in Italy
February 15, 1882

Focused on the state of the Church in Italy, this encyclical references secret societies as forces promoting secularism and opposing Catholic influence in public life. It criticized their efforts to weaken the Church's moral authority. Though Freemasonry is not named explicitly, the encyclical's critique of secret societies aligns with Leo XIII's stronger anti-Masonic stance in Humanum Genus *(1884) and* Dall'Alto Dell'Apostolico Seggio *(1890).*

To the Archbishops and Bishops and the Other Ordinaries of Italy. Venerable Brethren, Health and Apostolic Benediction.

Although the authority and extent of Our Apostolic duties cause Us to embrace the whole Christian Republic and each of the provinces which compose it with all the love and vigilance which is in Our power, it is Italy which, at the present moment, more especially attracts Our solicitude and Our thoughts. These thoughts and these solicitudes extend far above mere temporal concerns, for it is the eternal salvation of souls which occupies Us and causes Us anxiety - a business which demands all Our zeal, and obliges Us to concentrate it entirely on that object, in proportion as We see it exposed to greater and greater perils. If ever these perils were menacing in Italy they are surely so now, at a time when the condition of the Civil State itself disastrously imperils the freedom of religion. We are also still more affected by this since an intimate alliance unites Us to Italy, where God has placed the residence of His Vicar, the Chair of truth and the centre of Catholic Unity. On other occasions We have urged the nations to take heed, and Christians individually to realize, what duties are incumbent on them in such baleful circumstances. Nevertheless the evils continue to increase and We desire, Venerable Brethren, to point them out and commend them to your diligent attention, in order that, having recognized the tendency of public affairs, you may with greater vigilance strengthen the minds of your flocks, and surround them with every help, for fear lest that most precious treasure, the Catholic faith, should be torn from them.

2. A pernicious sect, of which the founders and chiefs neither hide nor even mask their desires, has established itself for some time back in Italy; after having declared war against Jesus Christ it is attempting to rob the people of their Christian institutions. As to the extent to which it has carried its audacity, it is the less necessary for Us to speak, Venerable Brethren, since the grave injuries and even ruin which morality and religion have to deplore lie patent before your eyes. In the midst of the populations of Italy, which have always been so constant and steadfast in the faith of their fathers, the liberty of the Church is wounded on all sides; everyday efforts are redoubled in order to efface from the public institutions that Christian stamp and character which has always, and with good reason, been the seal of the glories of Italy. Religious houses suppressed, the goods of the Church confiscated, marriages contracted in despite of the laws and without the rites of the Church, the position of the religious authorities as to the education of the young utterly ignored-in fine, a cruel and deplorable war without limit and without measure declared against the Apostolic See, a war on account of which the Church is weighed down by inexpressible suffering, and the Roman Pontiff finds himself reduced to extreme anguish. For, despoiled of his Civil Princedom, he has of necessity fallen into the hands of another Power.

3. More than this; Rome, the most august of Christian cities, is now a place laid open to all the enemies of the Church; profane novelties defile it; here and there, temples and schools devoted to heresy are to be found. It is even reported that this year it is about to receive the deputies and leaders of the sect which is most embittered against Catholicism, who have appointed this city as the place for their solemn meeting. The reasons which have determined

their choice of such a meeting place are no secret; they desire by this outrageous provocation to glut the hatred which they nourish against the Church, and to bring their incendiary torches within reach of the Roman Pontificate by attacking it in its very seat.

4. The Church, without doubt, will in the end be triumphant and will baffle the impious conspiracies of men; but it is none the less admitted and certain that their designs aim at nothing less than the destruction of the whole system of the Church with its Head, and the abolition, if it were possible, of all religion.

5. For those who pretend to be friends of the honour of Italy to dream of such prospects would seem a thing incredible, for the ruin of the Catholic faith in Italy would dry up the source of the most precious of goods. If, in truth, the Christian religion has created for the nations the best guarantees for their prosperity, the sanctity of right and the guardianship of justice; if by her influence she has everywhere subdued headlong and hasty passions, she, the companion and protectress of all honesty, of all nobility, of all greatness; if she has everywhere summoned all classes and every member of society to meet in a lasting peace and in perfect harmony, Italy has received a richer share of these benefits than any other nation.

6. It is, in truth, the shame of too many persons that they dare to denounce the Church as dangerous to public safety and prosperity, and to regard the Roman Pontificate as the enemy of the greatness of the name of Italy. But the records of the past give the lie to such slanders and to absurd calumnies of a similar kind. It is to the Church and the Roman Pontiffs that Italy especially owes gratitude for having spread her glories in all lands, for never having allowed her to succumb under the repeated incursions of having for generations preserved in many ways a lawful amount of just and proper liberty, and for having enriched her cities with numerous and immortal monuments of science and of art. In truth it is not the least glory of the Roman Pontiffs that they have maintained united in a common faith the various provinces of Italy, so different in customs and in genius, and have kept them from most disastrous disagreements.

Frequently, in times of trouble and calamity, the welfare of the State would have been in peril, had not the Roman Pontificate saved it by exercise of its life-giving power.

7. And its influence will not be less beneficial in the future if the malice of men does not interfere and hinder its efficacy or stifle its liberty. This beneficial force, which is peculiar to Catholic institutions, because it flows from them as a natural consequence, is unchangeable and unceasing. Even as, for the salvation of souls, the Catholic religion embraces all countries without any limitations of time or space, so does it always and everywhere stand forth and present itself as the true friend of the civil power.

8. These great advantages are being lost, and are being followed by grave evils; for the enemies of Christian wisdom, be their rival pretensions what they may, are leading society to its ruin. Nothing can be more efficacious than their doctrines in the way of kindling in men's minds the flames of violence and of stirring up the most pernicious passions. In the sphere of science they are repudiating the heavenly lights of faith; and when once this torch is put out, the mind of men is usually carried away by errors, no longer sees the truth, and begins quietly to sink into the lowest depths of a base and shameful materialism. In the sphere of morals they are disdainfully rejecting the eternal and unchangeable reasoning, and are despising God-the sovereign Legislator and supreme Avenger and when once these foundations are torn away no sufficient authority remains for law, and the regulation of life merely depends upon the good pleasure and free will of man. In society, the liberty without limit which they preach and pursue engenders license, and this license is very soon followed by the overthrow of order, the most fatal scourge of the public welfare. Of a truth, it is impossible to see society in a more pitiable or miserable state than in those places where such men and such doctrines as we have been describing have gained the upper hand even for a moment. Unless recent examples had furnished evidence it would have been difficult to believe that men, in a transport of furious and criminal boldness, could even have cast themselves into excesses of such a kind, and while retaining as if in mockery the name of liberty, could have given themselves over to

saturnalia of conflagrations and murders. If Italy has not, up to the present time, experienced a similar reign of terror, we must attribute it first to the especial protection of God; but the fact must be also recognized-to explain this preservation-that the people of Italy-the immense majority of whom are still faithful to the Catholic religion-have never been able to be subdued by the vicious and shameful doctrines We have denounced. And it must be confessed that if the ramparts erected by religion begin to give way, Italy also will fall into the same abyss, in which the greatest and most flourishing nations have in past times lain prostrate as victims. Similar doctrines involve similar consequences, and since the germs are infected with the same poisons, it cannot be but that they should produce the same fruits.

9. Moreover Italy would perhaps have to pay yet more dearly for her apostasy, because in her case perfidy and impiety would be aggravated by ingratitude. It is not by chance or human caprice that Italy has from the first been a sharer in the salvation won by JESUS CHRIST, and has contained within her bosom the Chair of Peter, and enjoyed throughout a long course of ages the incomparable and divine benefits of which the Catholic religion is the natural source. She ought then greatly to fear for herself the judgment threatened by the Apostle Paul to ungrateful nations: "The earth that drinketh in the rain which cometh often upon it, and bringeth forth herbs meet for them by whom it is tilled, receiveth blessing from God. But that which bringeth forth thorns and briars is reprobate, and very near unto a curse, whose end is to be burnt."[109]

10. May God avert so terrible a misfortune! May all give a serious consideration to the evils by which in part we are afflicted, and with which in part we are threatened by those who, devoted to the interests of political sects, not of the public, have sworn to wage a war to the death against the Church. Unhappy men, if they were wise, if they had a true love for their country, far from distrusting the Church, and striving, under the influence of injurious suspicions, to deprive her of her necessary liberty, they would do all in their

---

[109] Heb. vi. 7, 8.

power to defend and protect her, and would first of all make provision for the re-establishment of the Roman Pontiff in the possession of his rights. In fact the more injurious the war against the Apostolic See is to the Church, the more fatal it is in the cause of Italy. We have elsewhere expressed this thought: "Say that the State in Italy can never prosper nor become stable and tranquil unless provision be made for the dignity of the Roman See and the liberty of the Supreme Pontiff, as every consideration of right requires."

11. And, therefore, as We have nothing more at heart than the safety of Christian interests, and deeply moved as We are by the peril in which the people of Italy now stands, We exhort you, Venerable Brethren, more earnestly than ever to unite your care and loving efforts to Ours, that a remedy for so many evils may be found.

12. And first endeavour to make your people understand of what value the Catholic Faith is to them, and how they ought to defend it at every cost. But, since the enemies and assailants of the Catholic name employ a thousand devices and a thousand feints to seduce those who are not on their guard, it is of the first importance to unmask and drag into the light of day their secret machinations, so that Catholics, having their eyes opened to the real aims of these men, may feel their own courage redoubled, and may resolve openly and intrepidly to defend the Church, the Roman Pontiff, and their own salvation.

13. Up to the present time, whether through unfamiliarity with the new state of things, or through an imperfect understanding of the extent of the danger, the courage of many from whom much might have been expected, does not seem to have displayed itself with all the activity and vigour required for the defence of so great a cause.

14. But now that We have learned by experience in what times We live, nothing could be more fatal than to endure in cowardly inertness the malice of the wicked which never tires, and to leave the field open to them to persecute the Church to the full satisfaction of their hate.

15. More prudent than the children of light, they have been daring in their enterprises; inferior in numbers, but superior in cunning and in riches, they have soon succeeded

in lighting up amongst us a great conflagration of evils. May all the friends of Catholicity now, at least, understand that it is time to make some daring effort, and to rouse themselves at any cost from a languid carelessness, for one is never more easily overcome than in the sleep of cowardly security. Let them behold how the noble courage of their ancestors knew no fear and no repose; how by their indefatigable labours, and at the price of their blood, the Catholic Faith has grown and spread in the world.

16. Do you then, Venerable Brethren, awaken the sleeping, stimulate the hesitating; by your example and your authority train them all to fulfil with constancy and courage the duties which are the Christian life in action. And in order to maintain and develop this revived courage, means must be taken to promote the growth, multiplication, harmony, and fruitfulness of Associations the principal object of which should be to preserve and excite zeal for the Christian faith and other virtues. Such are the associations of young men and of workmen; such are the committees organized by Catholics, and meeting periodically; such are the institutions destined to relieve poverty, to protect the sanctification of festival days, to instruct the children of the poor, and several others of the same kind. And since it is of supreme importance to Christian interests that the Roman Pontiff should be, and should be clearly seen to be, free from all danger, from all vexations, and from all hindrance in the government of the Church, it is necessary, to attain this end, that action should be taken, petitions, and every possible means within the limits of the law should be adopted, and that none should rest until We have restored to Us, in reality and not in appearance only, that liberty on which, not only the welfare of the Church, but the prosperity of Italy and the peace of Christian nations depend by a necessary connection.

17. Then it is of very great importance that writings of a healthy character should be published and circulated far and wide. Those who, with a deadly hatred, dissent from the Church, are wont to contend by means of publications, and to make use of these as the arms best adapted for inflicting injury. Hence a most evil deluge of books, hence the turbulent and wicked journals whose malevolent attacks neither the

laws avail to bridle, nor modesty to restrain. Whatsoever in these latter years has been wrought by sedition and mobs, that they maintain to have been lawfully done; they dissimulate or corrupt the truth; they pursue the Church and the Supreme Pontiff with daily maledictions and false accusations; nor are there any opinions so absurd and pestiferous that they are not eager every where to disseminate them. The violence of this so great evil, which is daily spreading wider, must be diligently arrested; you must severely and gravely lead the people to be carefully on their guard, and to be willing most religiously to exercise a prudent choice in their reading. Moreover, writings must be opposed by writings, so that the same art which can effect most for the destruction, may in turn be applied to the salvation and benefit of mankind, and remedies be supplied from that source whence evil poisons are now obtained. And to this end it is to be wished that, at any rate in every province, there should be established some method of publicly demonstrating what and how great are the duties of all Christians towards the Church, by frequent, and, as far as possible, daily publications with this object. But in the first place, let there be kept in sight the conspicuous deserts of the Catholic religion in regard to all nations; let it be verbally explained how its influence, both in private and public affairs, is most benign and salutary; let it be shown of how great importance it is that the Church should promptly be established in that place of dignity in the State, which both its Divine grandeur and the public advantage of the nations absolutely required. For these reasons it is necessary that those who have devoted themselves to writing should observe further that they all keep the same end in view, that they should clearly ascertain what is most expedient and carry it out; they omit none of those things the knowledge of which seems useful and desirable; that, with gravity and moderation of speech, they reprove errors and vices; in such a way, however, that their reproof may be without bitterness, and with respect for the individuals; lastly that they use a plain and clear manner of speech, which the multitude can easily understand. But let all other persons, who truly and ex ammo desire that religion and society, defended by human intellect and literature, should flourish, let them study by their liberality to guard and protect these productions of literature and intellect; and let everyone, in proportion to his income, support them by his money and influence. For to those who devote themselves to writing we ought by all means to bring helps of this kind; without which their industry will either have no results, or uncertain and miserable ones.-And in all these things if any inconvenience falls upon our friends, if there is any conflict to be sustained, let them still dare to be brave, since to the Christian there can be no cause for endurance or labour more just than that of not suffering religion to be attacked by the wicked. For the Church has not brought forth or educated her sons with this idea, that, when time and necessity compel, she should expect no assistance from them, but rather that they should all prefer the salvation of souls and the well-being of religion to their own ease and their own private interests.

18. But your chief cares and thoughts, Venerable Brethren, must have for their object the due appointment of fitting ministers of God. For if it be the office of Bishops to use very much labour and zeal in properly training the whole of their youth, they ought to spend themselves far more on the clerics who are growing up as the hope of the Church, and are to be some day sharers in the most sacred duties. Indeed, grave reasons, common to all times, demand in priests many and great graces; but this time in which we live demands that they should be even more and greater. In truth the defence of the Catholic Faith, in which the industry of priests ought specially to be employed, and which is in these days so very necessary, demands no common nor ordinary learning, but that which is recondite and varies; which embraces not only sacred, but even philosophical studies, and is rich in the treatment of physical and historical discoveries. For the error which has to be eradicated is multiform, and saps all the foundations of Christian wisdom; and very often a battle has to be waged with adversaries well prepared, pertinacious in disputing, who astutely draw confirmation from every kind of science. Similarly, since in these days there is great and far extended corruption of morals, there is need in priests of singular excellence of virtue and constancy. They can by no means avoid associating with men; by the very duties of their

office, indeed, they are compelled to have intimate relations with the people; and that in the midst of cities where there is hardly any lust that has not permitted and unbridled license. From which it follows that virtue in the clergy ought at this time to be strong enough peacefully to guard itself, and both conquer all the blandishments of desire and securely overcome dangerous examples. Besides a paucity of clerics has everywhere followed the laws which have been enacted to the injury of the Church, so plainly, that it is necessary for those who by the grace of God are being trained to Holy Orders, to give double attention, and by increased diligence, zeal, and devotion to compensate for the sparse supply. And, indeed, they cannot do this advantageously unless they possess a soul resolute of purpose, mortified, incorrupt, ardent with charity, ever prompt and quick in undertaking labours for the salvation of men. But for such tasks a long and diligent preparation must be made; for one is not accustomed to such great things easily and quickly. And they indeed will pass their time in the priesthood holily and purely, who have exercised themselves in this way from their youth, and have so advanced in discipline that they seem not so much to have been instructed to those virtues, of which We have spoken, as to have been born to them.

19. For these reasons, Venerable Brethren, the Seminaries of clerics demand a very great portion of your zeal, care, and vigilance.

20. As to virtue and morals, it does not escape your wisdom with what precepts and instruction the youth of clerics must be surrounded. In graver studies Our Encyclical Letters, *Aeterni Patris*, have pointed out the best way and course. But since in such a condition of mental activity many things have been wisely and usefully discovered, which it is not fitting to ignore especially when wicked men are accustomed to turn, as new weapons, against divinely revealed truths, every addition of this kind which the day brings-take care, Venerable Brethren, as far as lies in your power, that the young clerics be not only better instructed in natural sciences, but also properly educated in those arts which have connection with the interpretation or authority of the Sacred Scriptures. Of this surely we are not ignorant, that

many things are needful for perfection in the highest studies, the means for which in the religious seminaries of Italy hostile laws are taking away or diminishing. But in this also the time demands that by their bounty and munificence Our children should strive to merit well of the Catholic religion. The pious and beneficent goodwill of our ancestors had admirably provided for necessities of this kind; and this the Church had been able by prudence and economy to accomplish, so that she had no necessity whatever to recommend to the charity of her children the care and preservation of sacred property. But her legitimate and sacred patrimony, which the attacks of former ages had spared, the tempest of our times has dissipated; so that there is again a reason why those who love the Catholic name should be induced to renew the liberality of their ancestors. Illustrious indeed are the proofs of munificence on the part of Frenchmen, Belgians, and others in a cause not very dissimilar from this munificence most worthy the admiration not only of contemporaries, but also of posterity. Nor do We doubt but that the Italian people, moved by the consideration of their common circumstances, will, in proportion to their means, act so as to show themselves worthy of their father, and will imitate the example of their brethren.

21. In these things, of which We have spoken, We have the greatest hope of consolation and security. But since in all designs, and especially in those which are undertaken for the sake of public safety, it is necessary to add always to human instruments the aid of Almighty God, in Whose power are the wills of individual men no less than the course and fortunes of Empires, therefore we must invoke God by instant prayers, and beseech Him to look upon Italy, which has been enriched and increased by so many of His benefits, and, having taken away every suspicion of peril, ever to preserve in her the Catholic Faith, which is the chief good. For this self same reason let us devoutly implore the Immaculate Virgin Mary, the great Mother of God, the prompter and helper of good counsels, together with her most holy spouse Joseph, the guardian and patron of Christian nations. And with like care we must beseech the great Apostles, Peter and Paul, to guard safely in the Italian people the fruit of their labour, and to

keep holy and inviolate amongst their latest posterity the Catholic name which they begot for our fathers with their own blood.

22. Confiding in the celestial patronage of all these, as a pledge of divine favours, and a proof of Our particular good will, We most lovingly in the Lord bestow on you all, Venerable Brethren, and on the flocks committed to your care, the Apostolic Benediction.

Given at Rome, at St. Peter's, on the 15th day of February, in the year of Our Lord 1882, and of Our Pontificate the fourth.

✠

HUMANUM GENUS
Encyclical of Pope Leo XIII
On Freemasonry
April 20, 1884

The most prominent and comprehensive papal condemnation of Freemasonry, Humanum Genus *accuses Freemasons of promoting naturalism, religious indifference, and the separation of church and state, presenting the situation as part of a broader conflict between the "Kingdom of God" and the "Kingdom of Satan." It reviews prior papal condemnations and calls for Catholics to actively oppose Freemasonry. A definitive statement on Freemasonry, widely referenced in later Church documents, it defines Freemasonry as a moral and spiritual threat and influences Catholic policy into the 20th century.*

To the Patriarchs, Primates, Archbishops, and Bishops of the Catholic World in Grace and Communion with the Apostolic See.

The race of man, after its miserable fall from God, the Creator and the Giver of heavenly gifts, "through the envy of the devil," separated into two diverse and opposite parts, of which the one steadfastly contends for truth and virtue, the other of those things which are contrary to virtue and to truth. The one is the kingdom of God on earth, namely, the true Church of Jesus Christ; and those who desire from their heart to be united with it, so as to gain salvation, must of necessity serve God and His only-begotten Son with their whole mind and with an entire will. The other is the kingdom of Satan, in whose possession and control are all whosoever follow the fatal example of their leader and of our first parents, those who refuse to obey the divine and eternal law, and who have many aims of their own in contempt of God, and many aims also against God.

2. This twofold kingdom St. Augustine keenly discerned and described after the manner of two cities, contrary in their

laws because striving for contrary objects; and with a subtle brevity he expressed the efficient cause of each in these words: "Two loves formed two cities: the love of self, reaching even to contempt of God, an earthly city; and the love of God, reaching to contempt of self, a heavenly one."[1]

At every period of time each has been in conflict with the other, with a variety and multiplicity of weapons and of warfare, although not always with equal ardour and assault. At this period, however, the partisans of evil seems to be combining together, and to be struggling with united vehemence, led on or assisted by that strongly organized and widespread association called the Freemasons. No longer making any secret of their purposes, they are now boldly rising up against God Himself. They are planning the destruction of holy Church publicly and openly, and this with the set purpose of utterly despoiling the nations of Christendom, if it were possible, of the blessings obtained for us through Jesus Christ our Saviour. Lamenting these evils, We are constrained by the charity which urges Our heart to cry out often to God: "For lo, Thy enemies have made a noise; and they that hate Thee have lifted up the head. They have taken a malicious counsel against Thy people, and they have consulted against Thy saints. They have said, 'come, and let us destroy them, so that they be not a nation.'"[2]

3. At so urgent a crisis, when so fierce and so pressing an onslaught is made upon the Christian name, it is Our office to point out the danger, to mark who are the adversaries, and to the best of Our power to make head against their plans and devices, that those may not perish whose salvation is committed to Us, and that the kingdom of Jesus Christ entrusted to Our charge may not stand and remain whole, but may be enlarged by an ever-increasing growth throughout the world.

4. The Roman Pontiffs Our predecessors, in their incessant watchfulness over the safety of the Christian people, were prompt in detecting the presence and the purpose of this capital enemy immediately it sprang into the

---

[1] *De civ. Dei*, 14, 28 (PL 41, 436).
[2] Ps. 82:24.

light instead of hiding as a dark conspiracy; and, moreover, they took occasion with true foresight to give, as it were on their guard, and not allow themselves to be caught by the devices and snares laid out to deceive them.

5. The first warning of the danger was given by Clement XII in the year 1738,[3] and his constitution was confirmed and renewed by Benedict XIV[4] Pius VII followed the same path;[5] and Leo XII, by his apostolic constitution, *Quo Graviora*,[6] put together the acts and decrees of former Pontiffs on this subject, and ratified and confirmed them forever. In the same sense spoke Pius VIII,[7] Gregory XVI,[8] and, many times over, Pius IX.[9]

6. For as soon as the constitution and the spirit of the masonic sect were clearly discovered by manifest signs of its actions, by the investigation of its causes, by publication of its laws, and of its rites and commentaries, with the addition often of the personal testimony of those who were in the secret, this apostolic see denounced the sect of the Freemasons, and publicly declared its constitution, as contrary to law and right, to be pernicious no less to Christiandom than to the State; and it forbade any one to enter the society, under the penalties which the Church is wont to inflict upon exceptionally guilty persons. The sectaries, indignant at this, thinking to elude or to weaken the force of these decrees, partly by contempt of them, and partly by calumny, accused the sovereign Pontiffs who had passed them either of exceeding the bounds of moderation in their decrees or of decreeing what was not just. This was the manner in which they endeavoured to elude the authority and the weight of the apostolic constitutions of Clement XII and

---

[3] Const. *In Eminenti*, April 24, 1738.
[4] Const. *Providas*, May 18, 1751.
[5] Const. *Ecclesiam a Jesu Christo*, Sept. 13, 1821.
[6] Const. given March 13, 1825.
[7] Encyc. *Traditi*, May 21, 1829.
[8] Encyc. *Mirari*, Augusr 15, 1832.
[9] Encyc. *Qui Pluribus*, Nov. 9, 1846; address *Multiplices inter*, Sept. 25, 1865, etc.

Benedict XIV, as well as of Pius VII and Pius IX.[10] Yet, in the very society itself, there were to be found men who unwillingly acknowledged that the Roman Pontiffs had acted within their right, according to the Catholic doctrine and discipline. The Pontiffs received the same assent, and in strong terms, from many princes and heads of governments, who made it their business either to delate the masonic society to the apostolic see, or of their own accord by special enactments to brand it as pernicious, as, for example, in Holland, Austria, Switzerland, Spain, Bavaria, Savoy, and other parts of Italy.

7. But, what is of highest importance, the course of events has demonstrated the prudence of Our predecessors. For their provident and paternal solicitude had not always and every where the result desired; and this, either because of the simulation and cunning of some who were active agents in the mischief, or else of the thoughtless levity of the rest who ought, in their own interest, to have given to the matter their diligent attention. In consequence, the sect of Freemasons grew with a rapidity beyond conception in the course of a century and a half, until it came to be able, by means of fraud or of audacity, to gain such entrance into every rank of the State as to seem to be almost its ruling power. This swift and formidable advance has brought upon the Church, upon the power of princes, upon the public well-being, precisely that grievous harm which Our predecessors had long before foreseen. Such a condition has been reached that henceforth there will be grave reason to fear, not indeed for the Church - for her foundation is much too firm to be overturned by the effort of men - but for those States in which prevails the power, either of the sect of which we are speaking or of other sects not dissimilar which lend themselves to it as disciples and subordinates.

8. For these reasons We no sooner came to the helm of the Church than We clearly saw and felt it to be Our duty to use Our authority to the very utmost against so vast an evil. We have several times already, as occasion served, attacked

---

[10] Clement XII (1730-40); Benedict XIV (1740-58); Pius VII (1800-23); Pius IX (1846-78).

certain chief points of teaching which showed in a special manner the perverse influence of Masonic opinions. Thus, in Our encyclical letter, *Quod Apostolici Muneris*, We endeavoured to refute the monstrous doctrines of the socialists and communists; afterwards, in another beginning "*Arcanum*," We took pains to defend and explain the true and genuine idea of domestic life, of which marriage is the spring and origin; and again, in that which begins "*Diuturnum*,"[11] We described the ideal of political government conformed to the principles of Christian wisdom, which is marvellously in harmony, on the one hand, with the natural order of things, and, in the other, with the well-being of both sovereign princes and of nations. It is now Our intention, following the example of Our predecessors, directly to treat of the masonic society itself, of its whole teaching, of its aims, and of its manner of thinking and acting, in order to bring more and more into the light its power for evil, and to do what We can to arrest the contagion of this fatal plague.

9. There are several organized bodies which, though differing in name, in ceremonial, in form and origin, are nevertheless so bound together by community of purpose and by the similarity of their main opinions, as to make in fact one thing with the sect of the Freemasons, which is a kind of center whence they all go forth, and whither they all return. Now, these no longer show a desire to remain concealed; for they hold their meetings in the daylight and before the public eye, and publish their own newspaper organs; and yet, when thoroughly understood, they are found still to retain the nature and the habits of secret societies. There are many things like mysteries which it is the fixed rule to hide with extreme care, not only from strangers, but from very many members, also; such as their secret and final designs, the names of the chief leaders, and certain secret and inner meetings, as well as their decisions, and the ways and means of carrying them out. This is, no doubt, the object of the manifold difference among the members as to right, office, and privilege, of the received distinction of orders and grades, and of that severe discipline which is maintained.

---

[11] See nos. 79, 81, 84.

Candidates are generally commanded to promise - nay, with a special oath, to swear - that they will never, to any person, at any time or in any way, make known the members, the passes, or the subjects discussed. Thus, with a fraudulent external appearance, and with a style of simulation which is always the same, the Freemasons, like the Manichees of old, strive, as far as possible, to conceal themselves, and to admit no witnesses but their own members. As a convenient manner of concealment, they assume the character of literary men and scholars associated for purposes of learning. They speak of their zeal for a more cultured refinement, and of their love for the poor; and they declare their one wish to be the amelioration of the condition of the masses, and to share with the largest possible number all the benefits of civil life. Were these purposes aimed at in real truth, they are by no means the whole of their object. Moreover, to be enrolled, it is necessary that the candidates promise and undertake to be thenceforward strictly obedient to their leaders and masters with the utmost submission and fidelity, and to be in readiness to do their bidding upon the slightest expression of their will; or, if disobedient, to submit to the direst penalties and death itself. As a fact, if any are judged to have betrayed the doings of the sect or to have resisted commands given, punishment is inflicted on them not infrequently, and with so much audacity and dexterity that the assassin very often escapes the detection and penalty of his crime.

10. But to simulate and wish to lie hid; to bind men like slaves in the very tightest bonds, and without giving any sufficient reason; to make use of men enslaved to the will of another for any arbitrary act ; to arm men's right hands for bloodshed after securing impunity for the crime - all this is an enormity from which nature recoils. Wherefore, reason and truth itself make it plain that the society of which we are speaking is in antagonism with justice and natural uprightness. And this becomes still plainer, inasmuch as other arguments, also, and those very manifest, prove that it is essentially opposed to natural virtue. For, no matter how great may be men's cleverness in concealing and their experience in lying, it is impossible to prevent the effects of any cause from showing, in some way, the intrinsic nature of the cause

whence they come. "A good tree cannot produce bad fruit, nor a bad tree produce good fruit."[12] Now, the masonic sect produces fruits that are pernicious and of the bitterest savour. For, from what We have above most clearly shown, that which is their ultimate purpose forces itself into view - namely, the utter overthrow of that whole religious and political order of the world which the Christian teaching has produced, and the substitution of a new state of things in accordance with their ideas, of which the foundations and laws shall be drawn from mere naturalism.

11. What We have said, and are about to say, must be understood of the sect of the Freemasons taken generically, and in so far as it comprises the associations kindred to it and confederated with it, but not of the individual members of them. There may be persons amongst these, and not a few who, although not free from the guilt of having entangled themselves in such associations, yet are neither themselves partners in their criminal acts nor aware of the ultimate object which they are endeavoring to attain. In the same way, some of the affiliated societies, perhaps, by no means approve of the extreme conclusions which they would, if consistent, embrace as necessarily following from their common principles, did not their very foulness strike them with horror. Some of these, again, are led by circumstances of times and places either to aim at smaller things than the others usually attempt or than they themselves would wish to attempt. They are not, however, for this reason, to be reckoned as alien to the masonic federation; for the masonic federation is to be judged not so much by the things which it has done, or brought to completion, as by the sum of its pronounced opinions.

12. Now, the fundamental doctrine of the naturalists, which they sufficiently make known by their very name, is that human nature and human reason ought in all things to be mistress and guide. Laying this down, they care little for duties to God, or pervert them by erroneous and vague opinions. For they deny that anything has been taught by God; they allow no dogma of religion or truth which cannot

---

[12] Matt. 7:18.

be understood by the human intelligence, nor any teacher who ought to be believed by reason of his authority. And since it is the special and exclusive duty of the Catholic Church fully to set forth in words truths divinely received, to teach, besides other divine helps to salvation, the authority of its office, and to defend the same with perfect purity, it is against the Church that the rage and attack of the enemies are principally directed.

13. In those matters which regard religion let it be seen how the sect of the Freemasons acts, especially where it is more free to act without restraint, and then let any one judge whether in fact it does not wish to carry out the policy of the naturalists. By a long and persevering labor, they endeavor to bring about this result - namely, that the teaching office and authority of the Church may become of no account in the civil State; and for this same reason they declare to the people and contend that Church and State ought to be altogether disunited. By this means they reject from the laws and from the commonwealth the wholesome influence of the Catholic religion; and they consequently imagine that States ought to be constituted without any regard for the laws and precepts of the Church.

14. Nor do they think it enough to disregard the Church - the best of guides - unless they also injure it by their hostility. Indeed, with them it is lawful to attack with impunity the very foundations of the Catholic religion, in speech, in writing, and in teaching; and even the rights of the Church are not spared, and the offices with which it is divinely invested are not safe. The least possible liberty to manage affairs is left to the Church; and this is done by laws not apparently very hostile, but in reality framed and fitted to hinder freedom of action. Moreover, We see exceptional and onerous laws imposed upon the clergy, to the end that they may be continually diminished in number and in necessary means. We see also the remnants of the possessions of the Church fettered by the strictest conditions, and subjected to the power and arbitrary will of the administrators of the State, and the religious orders rooted up and scattered.

15. But against the apostolic see and the Roman Pontiff the contention of these enemies has been for a long time

directed. The Pontiff was first, for specious reasons, thrust out from the bulwark of his liberty and of his right, the civil princedom; soon, he was unjustly driven into a condition which was unbearable because of the difficulties raised on all sides; and now the time has come when the partisans of the sects openly declare, what in secret among themselves they have for a long time plotted, that the sacred power of the Pontiffs must be abolished, and that the papacy itself, founded by divine right, must be utterly destroyed. If other proofs were wanting, this fact would be sufficiently disclosed by the testimony of men well informed, of whom some at other times, and others again recently, have declared it to be true of the Freemasons that they especially desire to assail the Church with irreconcilable hostility, and that they will never rest until they have destroyed whatever the supreme Pontiffs have established for the sake of religion.

16. If those who are admitted as members are not commanded to abjure by any form of words the Catholic doctrines, this omission, so far from being adverse to the designs of the Freemasons, is more useful for their purposes. First, in this way they easily deceive the simple-minded and the heedless, and can induce a far greater number to become members. Again, as all who offer themselves are received whatever may be their form of religion, they thereby teach the great error of this age-that a regard for religion should be held as an indifferent matter, and that all religions are alike. This manner of reasoning is calculated to bring about the ruin of all forms of religion, and especially of the Catholic religion, which, as it is the only one that is true, cannot, without great injustice, be regarded as merely equal to other religions.

17. But the naturalists go much further; for, having, in the highest things, entered upon a wholly erroneous course, they are carried headlong to extremes, either by reason of the weakness of human nature, or because God inflicts upon them the just punishment of their pride. Hence it happens that they no longer consider as certain and permanent those things which are fully understood by the natural light of reason, such as certainly are - the existence of God, the immaterial nature of the human soul, and its immortality. The sect of the

Freemasons, by a similar course of error, is exposed to these same dangers; for, although in a general way they may profess the existence of God, they themselves are witnesses that they do not all maintain this truth with the full assent of the mind or with a firm conviction. Neither do they conceal that this question about God is the greatest source and cause of discords among them; in fact, it is certain that a considerable contention about this same subject has existed among them very lately. But, indeed, the sect allows great liberty to its votaries, so that to each side is given the right to defend its own opinion, either that there is a God, or that there is none; and those who obstinately contend that there is no God are as easily initiated as those who contend that God exists, though, like the pantheists, they have false notions concerning Him: all which is nothing else than taking away the reality, while retaining some absurd representation of the divine nature.

18. When this greatest fundamental truth has been overturned or weakened, it follows that those truths, also, which are known by the teaching of nature must begin to fall - namely, that all things were made by the free will of God the Creator; that the world is governed by Providence; that souls do not die; that to this life of men upon the earth there will succeed another and an everlasting life.

19. When these truths are done away with, which are as the principles of nature and important for knowledge and for practical use, it is easy to see what will become of both public and private morality. We say nothing of those more heavenly virtues, which no one can exercise or even acquire without a special gift and grace of God; of which necessarily no trace can be found in those who reject as unknown the redemption of mankind, the grace of God, the sacraments, and the happiness to be obtained in heaven. We speak now of the duties which have their origin in natural probity. That God is the Creator of the world and its provident Ruler; that the eternal law commands the natural order to be maintained, and forbids that it be disturbed; that the last end of men is a destiny far above human things and beyond this sojourning upon the earth: these are the sources and these the principles of all justice and morality. If these be taken away, as the

naturalists and Freemasons desire, there will immediately be no knowledge as to what constitutes justice and injustice, or upon what principle morality is founded. And, in truth, the teaching of morality which alone finds favor with the sect of Freemasons, and in which they contend that youth should be instructed, is that which they call "civil," and "independent," and "free," namely, that which does not contain any religious belief. But, how insufficient such teaching is, how wanting in soundness, and how easily moved by every impulse of passion, is sufficiently proved by its sad fruits, which have already begun to appear. For, wherever, by removing Christian education, this teaching has begun more completely to rule, there goodness and integrity of morals have begun quickly to perish, monstrous and shameful opinions have grown up, and the audacity of evil deeds has risen to a high degree. All this is commonly complained of and deplored; and not a few of those who by no means wish to do so are compelled by abundant evidence to give not infrequently the same testimony.

20. Moreover, human nature was stained by original sin, and is therefore more disposed to vice than to virtue. For a virtuous life it is absolutely necessary to restrain the disorderly movements of the soul, and to make the passions obedient to reason. In this conflict human things must very often be despised, and the greatest labors and hardships must be undergone, in order that reason may always hold its sway. But the naturalists and Freemasons, having no faith in those things which we have learned by the revelation of God, deny that our first parents sinned, and consequently think that free will is not at all weakened and inclined to evil.[13] On the contrary, exaggerating rather the power and the excellence of nature, and placing therein alone the principle and rule of justice, they cannot even imagine that there is any need at all of a constant struggle and a perfect steadfastness to overcome the violence and rule of our passions.

Wherefore we see that men are publicly tempted by the

---

[13] Trid., sess. vi, *De justif.*, c. 1. Text of the Council of Trent: *"tametsi in eis* (sc. Judaeis) *liberum arbitrium minime extinctum esset, viribus licet attenuatum et inclinatum"*.

many allurements of pleasure; that there are journals and pamphlets with neither moderation nor shame; that stage-plays are remarkable for license; that designs for works of art are shamelessly sought in the laws of a so called verism; that the contrivances of a soft and delicate life are most carefully devised; and that all the blandishments of pleasure are diligently sought out by which virtue may be lulled to sleep. Wickedly, also, but at the same time quite consistently, do those act who do away with the expectation of the joys of heaven, and bring down all happiness to the level of mortality, and, as it were, sink it in the earth. Of what We have said the following fact, astonishing not so much in itself as in its open expression, may serve as a confirmation. For, since generally no one is accustomed to obey crafty and clever men so submissively as those whose soul is weakened and broken down by the domination of the passions, there have been in the sect of the Freemasons some who have plainly determined and proposed that, artfully and of set purpose, the multitude should be satiated with a boundless license of vice, as, when this had been done, it would easily come under their power and authority for any acts of daring.

21. What refers to domestic life in the teaching of the naturalists is almost all contained in the following declarations: that marriage belongs to the genus of commercial contracts, which can rightly be revoked by the will of those who made them, and that the civil rulers of the State have power over the matrimonial bond; that in the education of youth nothing is to be taught in the matter of religion as of certain and fixed opinion; and each one must be left at liberty to follow, when he comes of age, whatever he may prefer. To these things the Freemasons fully assent; and not only assent, but have long endeavoured to make them into a law and institution. For in many countries, and those nominally Catholic, it is enacted that no marriages shall be considered lawful except those contracted by the civil rite; in other places the law permits divorce; and in others every effort is used to make it lawful as soon as may be. Thus, the time is quickly coming when marriages will be turned into another kind of contract - that is into changeable and uncertain unions which fancy may join together, and which

the same when changed may disunite.

With the greatest unanimity the sect of the Freemasons also endeavours to take to itself the education of youth. They think that they can easily mold to their opinions that soft and pliant age, and bend it whither they will; and that nothing can be more fitted than this to enable them to bring up the youth of the State after their own plan. Therefore, in the education and instruction of children they allow no share, either of teaching or of discipline, to the ministers of the Church; and in many places they have procured that the education of youth shall be exclusively in the hands of laymen, and that nothing which treats of the most important and most holy duties of men to God shall be introduced into the instructions on morals.

22. Then come their doctrines of politics, in which the naturalists lay down that all men have the same right, and are in every respect of equal and like condition; that each one is naturally free; that no one has the right to command another; that it is an act of violence to require men to obey any authority other than that which is obtained from themselves. According to this, therefore, all things belong to the free people; power is held by the command or permission of the people, so that, when the popular will changes, rulers may lawfully be deposed and the source of all rights and civil duties is either in the multitude or in the governing authority when this is constituted according to the latest doctrines. It is held also that the State should be without God; that in the various forms of religion there is no reason why one should have precedence of another; and that they are all to occupy the same place.

23. That these doctrines are equally acceptable to the Freemasons, and that they would wish to constitute States according to this example and model, is too well known to require proof. For some time past they have openly endeavoured to bring this about with all their strength and resources; and in this they prepare the way for not a few bolder men who are hurrying on even to worse things, in their endeavor to obtain equality and community of all goods by the destruction of every distinction of rank and property.

24. What, therefore, sect of the Freemasons is, and what

course it pursues, appears sufficiently from the summary We have briefly given. Their chief dogmas are so greatly and manifestly at variance with reason that nothing can be more perverse. To wish to destroy the religion and the Church which God Himself has established, and whose perpetuity He insures by His protection, and to bring back after a lapse of eighteen centuries the manners and customs of the pagans, is signal folly and audacious impiety. Neither is it less horrible nor more tolerable that they should repudiate the benefits which Jesus Christ so mercifully obtained, not only for individuals, but also for the family and for civil society, benefits which, even according to the judgment and testimony of enemies of Christianity, are very great. In this insane and wicked endeavor we may almost see the implacable hatred and spirit of revenge with which Satan himself is inflamed against Jesus Christ. So also the studious endeavour of the Freemasons to destroy the chief foundations of justice and honesty, and to co-operate with those who would wish, as if they were mere animals, to do what they please, tends only to the ignominious and disgraceful ruin of the human race.

The evil, too, is increased by the dangers which threaten both domestic and civil society. As We have elsewhere shown,[14] in marriage, according to the belief of almost every nation, there is something sacred and religious; and the law of God has determined that marriages shall not be dissolved. If they are deprived of their sacred character, and made dissoluble, trouble and confusion in the family will be the result, the wife being deprived of her dignity and the children left without protection as to their interests and well being.-To have in public matters no care for religion, and in the arrangement and administration of civil affairs to have no more regard for God than if He did not exist, is a rashness unknown to the very pagans; for in their heart and soul the notion of a divinity and the need of public religion were so firmly fixed that they would have thought it easier to have city without foundation than a city without God. Human society, indeed for which by nature we are formed, has been

---

[14] See *Arcanum*, no. 81.

constituted by God the Author of nature; and from Him, as from their principle and source, flow in all their strength and permanence the countless benefits with which society abounds. As we are each of us admonished by the very voice of nature to worship God in piety and holiness, as the Giver unto us of life and of all that is good therein, so also and for the same reason, nations and States are bound to worship Him; and therefore it is clear that those who would absolve society from all religious duty act not only unjustly but also with ignorance and folly.

25. As men are by the will of God born for civil union and society, and as the power to rule is so necessary a bond of society that, if it be taken away, society must at once be broken up, it follows that from Him who is the Author of society has come also the authority to rule; so that whosoever rules, he is the minister of God. Wherefore, as the end and nature of human society so requires, it is right to obey the just commands of lawful authority, as it is right to obey God who ruleth all things; and it is most untrue that the people have it in their power to cast aside their obedience whensoever they please.

26. In like manner, no one doubts that all men are equal one to another, so far as regards their common origin and nature, or the last end which each one has to attain, or the rights and duties which are thence derived. But, as the abilities of all are not equal, as one differs from another in the powers of mind or body, and as there are very many dissimilarities of manner, disposition, and character, it is most repugnant to reason to endeavor to confine all within the same measure, and to extend complete equality to the institutions of civic life. Just as a perfect condition of the body results from the conjunction and composition of its various members, which, though differing in form and purpose, make, by their union and the distribution of each one to its proper place, a combination beautiful to behole, firm in strength, and necessary for use; so, in the commonwealth, there is an almost infinite dissimilarity of men, as parts of the whole. If they are to be all equal, and each is to follow his own will, the State will appear most deformed; but if, with a distinction of degrees of dignity, of pursuits and

employments, all aptly conspire for the common good, they will present the image of a State both well constituted and conformable to nature.

27. Now, from the disturbing errors which We have described the greatest dangers to States are to be feared. For, the fear of God and reverence for divine laws being taken away, the authority of rulers despised, sedition permitted and approved, and the popular passions urged on to lawlessness, with no restraint save that of punishment, a change and overthrow of all things will necessarily follow. Yea, this change and overthrow is deliberately planned and put forward by many associations of communists and socialists; and to their undertakings the sect of Freemasons is not hostile, but greatly favours their designs, and holds in common with them their chief opinions. And if these men do not at once and everywhere endeavour to carry out their extreme views, it is not to be attributed to their teaching and their will, but to the virtue of that divine religion which cannot be destroyed; and also because the sounder part of men, refusing to be enslaved to secret societies, vigorously resist their insane attempts.

28. Would that all men would judge of the tree by its fruit, and would acknowledge the seed and origin of the evils which press upon us, and of the dangers that are impending! We have to deal with a deceitful and crafty enemy, who, gratifying the ears of people and of princes, has ensnared them by smooth speeches and by adulation. Ingratiating themselves with rulers under a pretense of friendship, the Freemasons have endeavoured to make them their allies and powerful helpers for the destruction of the Christian name; and that they might more strongly urge them on, they have, with determined calumny, accused the Church of invidiously contending with rulers in matters that affect their authority and sovereign power. Having, by these artifices, insured their own safety and audacity, they have begun to exercise great weight in the government of States; but nevertheless they are prepared to shake the foundations of empires, to harass the rulers of the State, to accuse, and to cast them out, as often as they appear to govern otherwise than they themselves could have wished. In like manner, they have by flattery deluded

the people. Proclaiming with a loud voice liberty and public prosperity, and saying that it was owing to the Church and to sovereigns that the multitude were not drawn out of their unjust servitude and poverty, they have imposed upon the people, and, exciting them by a thirst for novelty, they have urged them to assail both the Church and the civil power. Nevertheless, the expectation of the benefits which was hoped for is greater than the reality; indeed, the common people, more oppressed than they were before, are deprived in their misery of that solace which, if things had been arranged in a Christian manner, they would have had with ease and in abundance. But, whoever strive against the order which Divine Providence has constituted pay usually the penalty of their pride, and meet with affliction and misery where they rashly hoped to find all things prosperous and in conformity with their desires.

29. The Church, if she directs men to render obedience chiefly and above all to God the sovereign Lord, is wrongly and falsely believed either to be envious of the civil power or to arrogate to herself something of the rights of sovereigns. On the contrary, she teaches that what is rightly due to the civil power must be rendered to it with a conviction and consciousness of duty. In teaching that from God Himself comes the right of ruling, she adds a great dignity to civil authority, and on small help towards obtaining the obedience and good will of the citizens. The friend of peace and sustainer of concord, she embraces all with maternal love, and, intent only upon giving help to mortal man, she teaches that to justice must be joined clemency, equity to authority, and moderation to lawgiving; that no one's right must be violated; that order and public tranquility are to be maintained; and that the poverty of those are in need is, as far as possible, to be relieved by public and private charity. "But for this reason," to use the words of St. Augustine, "men think, or would have it believed, that Christian teaching is not suited to the good of the State; for they wish the State to be founded not on solid virtue, but on the impunity of vice."[15] Knowing these things, both princes and people would act

---

[15] *Epistola* 137, *ad Volusianum*, c. v, n. 20 (PL 33 525).

with political wisdom, and according to the needs of general safety, if, instead of joining with Freemasons to destroy the Church, they joined with the Church in repelling their attacks.

30. Whatever the future may be, in this grave and widespread evil it is Our duty, venerable brethren, to endeavour to find a remedy. And because We know that Our best and firmest hope of a remedy is in the power of that divine religion which the Freemasons hate in proportion to their fear of it, We think it to be of chief importance to call that most saving power to Our aid against the common enemy. Therefore, whatsoever the Roman Pontiffs Our predecessors have decreed for the purpose of opposing the undertakings and endeavours of the masonic sect, and whatsoever they have enacted to enter or withdraw men from societies of this kind, We ratify and confirm it all by our apostolic authority: and trusting greatly to the good will of Christians, We pray and beseech each one, for the sake of his eternal salvation, to be most conscientiously careful not in the least to depart from what the apostolic see has commanded in this matter.

31. We pray and beseech you, venerable brethren, to join your efforts with Ours, and earnestly to strive for the extirpation of this foul plague, which is creeping through the veins of the body politic. You have to defend the glory of God and the salvation of your neighbour; and with the object of your strife before you, neither courage nor strength will be wanting. It will be for your prudence to judge by what means you can best overcome the difficulties and obstacles you meet with. But, as it befits the authority of Our office that We Ourselves should point out some suitable way of proceeding, We wish it to be your rule first of all to tear away the mask from Freemasonry, and to let it be seen as it really is; and by sermons and pastoral letters to instruct the people as to the artifices used by societies of this kind in seducing men and enticing them into their ranks, and as to the depravity of their opinions and the wickedness of their acts. As Our predecessors have many times repeated, let no man think that he may for any reason whatsoever join the masonic sect, if he values his Catholic name and his eternal salvation as he ought to value them. Let no one be deceived by a pretense of

honesty. It may seem to some that Freemasons demand nothing that is openly contrary to religion and morality; but, as the whole principle and object of the sect lies in what is vicious and criminal, to join with these men or in any way to help them cannot be lawful.

32. Further, by assiduous teaching and exhortation, the multitude must be drawn to learn diligently the precepts of religion; for which purpose we earnestly advise that by opportune writings and sermons they be taught the elements of those sacred truths in which Christian philosophy is contained. The result of this will be that the minds of men will be made sound by instruction, and will be protected against many forms of error and inducements to wickedness, especially in the present unbounded freedom of writing and insatiable eagerness for learning.

33. Great, indeed, is the work; but in it the clergy will share your labours, if, through your care, they are fitted for it by learning and a well-turned life. This good and great work requires to be helped also by the industry of those amongst the laity in whom a love of religion and of country is joined to learning and goodness of life. By uniting the efforts of both clergy and laity, strive, venerable brethren, to make men thoroughly know and love the Church; for, the greater their knowledge and love of the Church, the more will they be turned away from clandestine societies.

34. Wherefore, not without cause do We use this occasion to state again what We have stated elsewhere, namely, that the Third Order of St. Francis, whose discipline We a little while ago prudently mitigated,[16] should be

---

[16] The text here refers to the encyclical letter *Auspicato Concessum* (Sept. 17, 1882), in which Pope Leo XIII had recently glorified St. Francis of Assisi on the occasion of the seventh centenary of his birth. In this encyclical, the Pope had presented the Third Order of St. Francis as a Christian answer to the social problems of the times. The constitution *Misericors Dei Filius* (June 23, 1883) expressly recalled that the neglect in which Christian virtues are held is the main cause of the evils that threaten societies. In confirming the rule of the Third Order and adapting it to the needs of modern times, Pope Leo XIII had intended to bring back the largest possible number of souls to the practice of these virtues.

studiously promoted and sustained; for the whole object of this Order, as constituted by its founder, is to invite men to an imitation of Jesus Christ, to a love of the Church, and to the observance of all Christian virtues; and therefore it ought to be of great influence in suppressing the contagion of wicked societies. Let, therefore, this holy sodality be strengthened by a daily increase. Amongst the many benefits to be expected from it will be the great benefit of drawing the minds of men to liberty, fraternity, and equality of right; not such as the Freemasons absurdly imagine, but such as Jesus Christ obtained for the human race and St. Francis aspired to: the liberty, We mean, of *sons of God*, through which we may be free from slavery to Satan or to our passions, both of them most wicked masters; the fraternity whose origin is in God, the common Creator and Father of all; the equality which, founded on justice and charity, does not take away all distinctions among men, but, out of the varieties of life, of duties, and of pursuits, forms that union and that harmony which naturally tend to the benefit and dignity of society.

35. In the third place, there is a matter wisely instituted by our forefathers, but in course of time laid aside, which may now be used as a pattern and form of something similar. We mean the associations of guilds of workmen, for the protection, under the guidance of religion, both of their temporal interests and of their morality. If our ancestors, by long use and experience, felt the benefit of these guilds, our age perhaps will feel it the more by reason of the opportunity which they will give of crushing the power of the sects. Those who support themselves by the labour of their hands, besides being, by their very condition, most worthy above all others of charity and consolation, are also especially exposed to the allurements of men whose ways lie in fraud and deceit. Therefore, they ought to be helped with the greatest possible kindness, and to be invited to join associations that are good, lest they be drawn away to others that are evil. For this reason, We greatly wish, for the salvation of the people, that, under the auspices and patronage of the bishops, and at convenient times, these gilds may be generally restored. To Our great delight, sodalities of this kind and also associations of masters have in many places already been established,

having, each class of them, for their object to help the honest workman, to protect and guard his children and family, and to promote in them piety, Christian knowledge, and a moral life. And in this matter We cannot omit mentioning that exemplary society, named after its founder, St. Vincent, which has deserved so well of the lower classes. Its acts and its aims are well known. Its whole object is to give relief to the poor and miserable. This it does with singular prudence and modesty; and the less it wishes to be seen, the better is it fitted for the exercise of Christian charity, and for the relief of suffering.

36. In the fourth place, in order more easily to attain what We wish, to your fidelity and watchfulness We commend in a special manner the young, as being the hope of human society. Devote the greatest part of your care to their instruction; and do not think that any precaution can be great enough in keeping them from masters and schools whence the pestilent breath of the sects is to be feared. Under your guidance, let parents, religious instructors, and priests having the cure of souls use every opportunity, in their Christian teaching, of warning their children and pupils of the infamous nature of these societies, so that they may learn in good time to beware of the various and fraudulent artifices by which their promoters are accustomed to ensnare people. And those who instruct the young in religious knowledge will act wisely if they induce all of them to resolve and to undertake never to bind themselves to any society without the knowledge of their parents, or the advice of their parish priest or director.

37. We well know, however, that our united labors will by no means suffice to pluck up these pernicious seeds from the Lord's field, unless the Heavenly Master of the vineyard shall mercifully help us in our endeavours. We must, therefore, with great and anxious care, implore of Him the help which the greatness of the danger and of the need requires. The sect of the Freemasons shows itself insolent and proud of its success, and seems as if it would put no bounds to its pertinacity. Its followers, joined together by a wicked compact and by secret counsels, give help one to another, and excite one another to an audacity for evil things. So vehement an attack demands an equal defence-namely, that all good

men should form the widest possible association of action and of prayer. We beseech them, therefore, with united hearts, to stand together and unmoved against the advancing force of the sects; and in mourning and supplication to stretch out their hands to God, praying that the Christian name may flourish and prosper, that the Church may enjoy its needed liberty, that those who have gone astray may return to a right mind, that error at length may give place to truth, and vice to virtue. Let us take our helper and intercessor the Virgin Mary, Mother of God, so that she, who from the moment of her conception overcame Satan may show her power over these evil sects, in which is revived the contumacious spirit of the demon, together with his unsubdued perfidy and deceit. Let us beseech Michael, the prince of the heavenly angels, who drove out the infernal foe; and Joseph, the spouse of the most holy Virgin, and heavenly patron of the Catholic Church; and the great Apostles, Peter and Paul, the fathers and victorious champions of the Christian faith. By their patronage, and by perseverance in united prayer, we hope that God will mercifully and opportunely succor the human race, which is encompassed by so many dangers.

38. As a pledge of heavenly gifts and of Our benevolence, We lovingly grant in the Lord, to you, venerable brethren, and to the clergy and all the people committed to your watchful care, Our apostolic benediction.

Given at St. Peter's in Rome, the twentieth day of April, 1884, the sixth year of Our pontificate.

✠

DALL'ALTO DELL'APOSTOLICO SEGGIO
Encyclical of Pope Leo XIII
On Freemasonry in Italy
October 15, 1890

This encyclical focuses on Freemasonry in Italy, accusing it of undermining the Church's authority and promoting anti-clerical policies. It reiterates the call for Catholics to resist Masonic influence in public and private life and addresses the specific context of Italian Freemasonry's role in the post-unification secular state.

To the Bishops, the Clergy, and the People of Italy.

Venerable Brethren and Beloved Children, Health and Apostolic Benediction.

From the height of the Apostolic Throne, where Divine Providence has placed Us to watch over the salvation of all nations, We look upon Italy in whose bosom, by an act of singular predilection, God has established the See of His Vicar, and from which come to Us at the present time many and most bitter sorrows. — It is not any personal offense that saddens Us, nor the privations and sacrifices imposed upon Us by the present condition of things, nor the outrages and scoffs which an insolent press has full power to hurl every day against Us. If only Our person were concerned, and not the ruin to which Italy threatened in its faith is hastening, We should bear these offenses without complaint, rejoicing even to repeat what one of Our most illustrious Predecessors said of himself: "If the captivity of my country did not every moment for each day increase, as to the contempt and scorn of myself I should joyfully be silent."[1] — But, besides the independence and dignity of the Holy See, the religion itself and the salvation of a whole nation are concerned, of a nation

---

[1] St. Gregory the Great: Letter to the Emperor Maurice, Reg.

which from the earliest times opened its bosom to the Catholic Faith and has ever jealously preserved it. Incredible it seems, but it is true; to such a pass have we come, that we have to fear for this Italy of ours the loss even of the faith. — Many times have We sounded the alarm, to give warning of the danger; but We do not therefore think that We have done enough. In face of the continued and fiercer assaults that are made, We hear the voice of duty calling upon Us more powerfully than before to speak to you again, Venerable Brethren, to your Clergy, and to the whole Italian people. As the enemy makes no truce, so neither you nor We must remain silent or inert. By the Divine mercy We have been constituted guardians and defenders of the religion of the people entrusted to Our care, Pastors and watchful sentinels of the flock of Christ; and for this flock We must be ready, if need be, to sacrifice everything, even life itself.

2. We shall not say anything new; for facts have not changed from what they were, and We have had at other times to speak of them when occasion was given. — But We now intend to recapitulate theese facts in some way, and to group them into one picture, so as to draw out for general instruction the consequences which flow from them. The facts are incontestable which have happened in the clear light of day; not separated one from another, but so connected together as in their series to reveal with fullest evidence a system of which they are the actual operation and development. The system is not new; but the audacity, the fury, and the rapidity with which it is now carried out, are new. It is the plan of the sects that is now unfolding itself in Italy, especially in what relates to the Catholic religion and the Church, with the final and avowed purpose, if it were possible, of reducing it to nothing. — It is needless now to put the Masonic sects upon their trial. They are already judged; their ends, their means, their doctrines, and their action, are all known with indisputable certainty. Possessed by the spirit of Satan, whose instrument they are, they burn like him with a deadly and implacable hatred of Jesus Christ and of His work; and they endeavor by every means to overthrow and fetter it. This war is at present waged more than elsewhere in Italy, in which the Catholic religion has taken deeper root; and above all in

Rome, the center of Catholic unity, and the See of the Universal Pastor and Teacher of the Church.

3. It is well to trace from the beginning the different phases of this warfare.

4. The war began by the overthrow of the civil power of the Popes, the downfall of which, according to the secret intentions of the real leaders, afterwards openly avowed, was, under a political pretext, to be the means of enslaving at least, if not of destroying the supreme spiritual power of the Roman Pontiffs. — That no doubt might remain as to the true object of this warfare, there followed quickly the suppression of the Religious Orders; and thereby a great reduction in the number of evangelical laborers for the propagation of the faith amongst the heathens, and for the sacred ministry and religious service of Catholic countries. — Later, the obligation of military service was extended to ecclesiastics, with the necessary result that many and grave obstacles were put to the recruiting and due formation even of the secular Clergy. Hands were laid upon ecclesiastical property, partly by absolute confiscation, and partly by charging it with enormous burdens, so as to impoverish the Clergy and the Church, and to deprive the Church of what is necessary for its temporal support and for carrying on institutions and works in aid of its divine apostolate. This the sectaries themselves have openly declared. To lessen the influence of the Clergy and of clerical bodies, one only efficacious means must be employed: to strip them all their goods, and to reduce them to absolute poverty. So also the action of the State is of itself all directed to efface from the nation its religious and Christian character. From the laws, and from the whole of official life, every religious inspiration and idea is systematically banished, when not directly assailed. Every public manifestation of faith and of Catholic piety is either forbidden or, under vain pretenses, in a thousand ways impeded.-From the family are taken away its foundation and religious constitution by the proclaiming of civil marriage, as it is called; and also by the entirely lay education which is now demanded, from the first elements to the higher teaching of the universities, so that the rising generations, as far as this can be effected by the State, have to grow up without any idea

of religion, and without the first essential notions of their duties towards God. This is to put the ax to the root. No more universal and efficacious means could be imagined of withdrawing society, and families, and individuals, from the influence of the Church and of the faith. To lay Clericalism (or Catholicism) waste in its foundations and in its very sources of life, namely, in the school and in the family: such is the authentic declaration of Masonic writers.

5. It will be said that this does not happen in Italy only, but is a system of government which States generally follow. — We answer, that this does not refute, but confirms what We are saying as to the designs and action of Freemasonry in Italy. Yes, this system is adopted and carried out wherever Freemasonry uses its impious and wicked action; and, as its action is widespread, so is this anti-Christian system widely applied. But the application becomes more speedy and general, and is pushed more to extremes, in countries where the government is more under the control of the sect and better promotes its interest.-Unfortunately, at the present time the new Italy is of the number of these countries. Not today only has it become subject to the wicked and evil influence of the sects; but for some time past they have tyrannized over it as they liked, with absolute dominion and power. Here the direction of public affairs, in what concerns religion, is wholly in conformity with the aspirations of the sects; and for accomplishing their aspirations, they find avowed supporters and ready instruments in those who hold the public power. Laws adverse to the Church and measures hostile to it are first proposed, decided, and resolved, in the secret meetings of the sect; and if anything presents even the least appearance of hostility or harm to the Church, it is at once received with favor and put forward. — Amongst the most recent facts We may mention the approval of the new penal code, in which what was most obstinately demanded, in spite of all reasons to the contrary, were the articles against the Clergy, which form for them an exceptional law, and even condemn as criminal certain actions which are sacred duties of their ministry. — The law as to pious works, by which all charitable property, accumulated by the piety and religion of our ancestors under the protection and guardianship of the

Church, was withdrawn altogether from the Church's action and control, had been for some years put forward in the meetings of the sect, precisely because it would inflict a new outrage on the Church, lessen its social influence, and suppress at once a great number of bequests made for divine worship. — Then came that eminently sectarian work, the erection of the monument to the renowned apostate of Nola, which, with the aid and favor of the government, was promoted, determined, and carried out by means of Freemasonry, whose most authorized spokesmen were not ashamed to acknowledge its purpose and to declare its meaning. Its purpose was to insult the Papacy; its meaning that, instead of the Catholic Faith, must now be substituted the most absolute freedom of examination, of criticism, of thought, and of conscience: and what is meant by such language in the mouth of the sects is well known. — The seal was put by the most explicit declarations made by the head of the government, which were to the following effect: — That the true and real conflict, which the government has the merit of understanding, is the conflict between faith and the Church on one side and free examination and reason on the other. That the Church may try to act as it has done before, to enchain anew reason and free-thought, and to prevail; but the government in this conflict declares itself openly in favor of reason as against faith, and takes upon itself the task of making the Italian State the evident expression of this reason and liberty: a sad task, which has just now been boldly reaffirmed on a like occasion.

6. In the light of such facts and such declarations as these, it is more than ever clear that the ruling idea which, as far as religion is concerned, controls the course of public affairs in Italy, is the realization of the Masonic program. We see how much has already been realized; we know how much still remains to be done; and we can foresee with certainty that, so long as the destinies of Italy are in the hands of sectarian rulers or of men subject to the sects, the realization of the program will be pressed on, more or less rapidly according to circumstances, unto its complete development. — The action of the sects is at present directed to attain the following objects, according to the votes and resolutions

passed in their most important assemblies, — votes and resolutions inspired throughout by a deadly hatred of the Church. The abolition in the schools of every kind of religious instruction, and the founding of institutions in which even girls are to be withdrawn from all clerical influence whatever it may be; because the State, which ought to be absolutely atheistic, has the inalienable right and duty to form the heart and the spirit of its citizens, and no school should exist apart from its inspiration and control. — The rigorous application of all laws now in force, which aim at securing the absolute independence of civil society from clerical influence. — The strict observance of laws suppressing religious corporations, and the employment of means to make them effectual. — The regulation of all ecclesiastical property, starting from the principle that its ownership belongs to the State, and its administration to the civil power. — The exclusion of every Catholic or clerical element from all public administrations, from pious works, hospitals, and schools, from the councils which govern the destinies of the country, from academical and other unions, from companies, committees, and families, — an exclusion from everything, everywhere, and forever. Instead, the Masonic influence is to make itself felt in all the circumstances of social life, and to become master and controller of everything. — Hereby the way will be smoothed towards the abolition of the Papacy; Italy will thus be free from its implacable and deadly enemy; and Rome, which in the past was the center of universal Theocracy will in the future be the center of universal secularization, whence the Magna Charta of human liberty is to be proclaimed in the face of the whole world. Such are the authentic declarations, aspirations, and resolutions, of Freemasons or of their assemblies.

7. Without exaggeration, this is the present condition and the future prospect of religion in Italy. To shrink from seeing the gravity of this would be a fatal error. To recognize it as it is, to confront it with evangelical prudence and fortitude, to infer the duties which it imposes on all Catholics, and upon us especially who as Pastors have to watch over them and guide them to salvation, is to enter into the views of

Providence, to do a work of wisdom and pastoral zeal. — As far as We are concerned, the Apostolic office lays upon Us the duty of protesting loudly once more against all that has been done, is doing, or is attempted in Italy to the harm of religion. Defending and guarding the sacred rights of the Church and of the Pontificate, We openly repel and denounce to the whole Catholic world the outrages which the Church and the Pontificate are continually receiving, especially in Rome, and which hamper Us in the government of the Catholic Church, and add difficulty and indignity to Our condition. We are determined not to omit anything on Our part which can serve to maintain the faith lively and vigorous amidst the Italian people, and to protect it against the assaults of its enemies. We, therefore, make appeal, Venerable Brethren, to your zeal and your great love for souls, in order that, possessed with a sense of the gravity of the danger which they incur, you may apply the proper remedies and do all you can to dispel this danger.

8. No means must be neglected that are in your power. All the resources of speech, every expedient in action, all the immense treasures of help and grace which the Church places in your hands, must be made use of, for the formation of a Clergy learned and full of the spirit of Jesus Christ, for the Christian education of youth, for the extirpation of evil doctrines, for the defense of Catholic truths, and for the maintenance of the Christian character and spirit of family life.

9. As to the Catholic people, before everything else it is necessary that they should be instructed as to the true state of things in Italy with regard to religion, the essentially religious character of the conflict in Italy against the Pontiff, and the real object constantly aimed at, so that they may see by the evidence of facts the many ways in which their religion is conspired against, and may be convinced of the risk they run of being robbed and spoiled of the inestimable treasure of the faith. — With this conviction in their minds, and having at the same time a certainty that without faith it is impossible to please God and to be saved, they will understand that what is now at stake is the greatest, not to say the only interest, which every one on earth is bound before all things, at the cost of

any sacrifice, to put out of danger, under penalty of everlasting misery. They will, moreover, easily understand that, in this time of open and raging conflict, it would be disgraceful for them to desert the field and hide themselves. Their duty is to remain at their post, and openly to show themselves to be true Catholics by their belief and by actions in conformity with their faith. This they must do for the honor of their faith, and the glory of the Sovereign Leader whose banner they follow; and that they may escape that great misfortune of being disowned at the last day, and of not being recognized as His by the Supreme Judge who has declared that whosoever is not with Him is against Him. — Without ostentation or timidity, let them give proof of that true courage which arises from the consciousness of fulfilling a sacred duty before God and men. To this frank profession of faith Catholics must unite a perfect docility and filial love towards the Church, a sincere respect for their Bishops, and an absolute devotion and obedience to the Roman Pontiff. In a word, they will recognize how necessary it is to cease from everything that is the work of the sects, or that receives impulse or favor from them, as being undoubtedly infected by the anti-Christian spirit; and they will, on the contrary, devote themselves with activity, courage and constancy, to Catholic works, and to the associations and institutions which the Church has blessed, and which the Bishops and the Roman Pontiff encourage and sustain.-Moreover, seeing that the chief instrument employed by our enemies is the press, which in great part receives from them its inspiration and support, it is important that Catholics should oppose the evil press by a press that is good, for the defense of truth, out of love for religion, and to uphold the rights of the Church. While the Catholic press is occupied in laying bare the perfidious designs of the sects, in helping and seconding the action of the sacred Pastors, and in defending and promoting Catholic works, it is the duty of the faithful efficaciously to support this press,-both by refusing or ceasing to favor in any way the evil press; and also directly, by concurring, as far as each one can, in helping it to live and thrive: and in this matter We think that hitherto enough has not been done in Italy.- Lastly, the teaching addressed by Us to all Catholics, especially in the Encyclicals "Humanum genus" and "Sapientiae Christianae," should be particularly applied to the Catholics of Italy, and be impressed upon them. If they have anything to suffer or to sacrifice through remaining faithful to these duties, let them take courage in the thought that the Kingdom of Heaven suffereth violence and is gained only by doing violence to ourselves; and that he who loves himself and what is his own more than Jesus Christ, is not worthy of Him. The example of the many invincible champions who, throughout all time, have generously sacrificed everything for the faith, and the special helps of grace which make the yoke of Jesus Christ sweet and His burden light, ought to animate powerfully their courage and to sustain them in the glorious contest.

10. So far We have considered only the religious side of the present state of things in Italy, inasmuch as this is for Us the most essential, and the subject which eminently concerns Us by reason of the Apostolic office which We hold. But it is worthwhile to consider also the social and political side, so that Italians may see that not only the love of religion, but also the noblest and sincerest love of country should stir them to resist the impious attempts of the sects. — As a convincing proof of this, it suffices to take note of the kind of future, in the social and political order, which is being prepared for Italy by men whose object is — and they make no secret of it — to wage an unrelenting war against Catholicism and the Papacy.

11. Already the test of the past speaks eloquently for itself. — What Italy has become in this first Period of its new life. as to public and private morality, internal safety, order and peace, national wealth and prosperity, all this is known to you by facts, Venerable Brethren, better than We could describe it in words. The very men whose interest it would be to hide all this, are constrained by truth to admit it. We will only say that, under present conditions, though a sad but real necessity, things could not be otherwise: the Masonic sect, with all its boast of a spirit of beneficence and philanthropy, can only exercise an evil influence — an influence which is evil because it attacks and endeavors to destroy the religion of Christ, the true benefactress of mankind.

12. All know with what salutary effect and in how many ways the influence of religion penetrates society. It is beyond dispute that sound public and private morality gives honor and strength to States. But it is equally certain that, without religion there is no true morality, either public or private. — From the family, solidly based on its natural foundations, comes the life, the growth, and the energy of society. But without religion, and without morality, the domestic partnership has no stability, and the family bonds grow weak and waste away. — The prosperity of peoples and of nations comes from God and from His blessings. If a people does not attribute its prosperity to Him, but rises up against Him, and in the pride of its heart tacitly tells Him that it has no need of Him, its prosperity is but a semblance, certain to disappear so soon as it shall please the Lord to confound the proud insolence of His enemies. — It is religion which, penetrating to the depth of each one's conscience, makes him feel the force of duty and urges him to fulfill it. It is religion which gives to rulers feelings of justice and love towards their subjects; which makes subjects faithful and sincerely devoted to their rulers; which makes upright and good legislators, just and incorruptible magistrates, brave and heroic soldiers, conscientious and diligent administrators. It is religion which produces concord and affection between husband and wife, love and reverence between parents and their children; which makes the poor respect the property of others, and causes the rich to make a right use of their wealth. From this fidelity to duty, and this respect for the rights of others come the order, the tranquillity, and the peace, which form so large a part of the prosperity of a people and of a State. Take away religion, and with it all these immensely precious benefits would disappear from society.

13. For Italy, moreover, the loss would be sensible. — All its glories and greatness, which for a long time gave to it the first place among the most cultured nations, are inseparable from religion, which has either produced or inspired them, or certainly has given to them favor, help, and increase. Its communes tell us of its public liberties: of its military glories we read in its many memorable enterprises against the enemies of the Christian name. Its sciences are

seen in its universities which, founded, fostered, and privileged by the Church, have been their home and theater. Its arts are shown in the numberless monuments of every kind with which Italy is profusely covered. Of its institutions for the relief of suffering, for the destitute, and the working-classes we have evidence in its many foundations of Christian charity, in the many asylums established for every kind of need and misfortune, and in the associations and corporations which have grown up under the protection of religion. The virtue and the strength of religion are immortal because religion is from God. It has treasures of help and most efficacious remedies, which can be wonderfully adapted to the needs of every time and epoch. What religion has known how to do and has done in former times, it can do also now with a virtue ever fresh and vigorous. To take away religion from Italy, is to dry up at once the most abundant source of inestimable help and benefits.

14. Moreover, one of the greatest and most formidable dangers of society at the present day, is the agitation of the Socialists, who threaten to uplift it from its foundations. From this great danger Italy is not free; and although other nations may be more infested than Italy by this spirit of subversion and disorder, it is not therefore less true that even here this spirit is widely spreading and increasing every day in strength. So criminal is its nature, so great the power of its organization and the audacity of its designs, that there is need of uniting all conservative forces, if we are to arrest its progress and successfully to prevent its triumph. Of these forces the first, and above all the chief one, is that which can be supplied by religion and the Church: without this, the strictest laws, the severest tribunals, and even the force of arms, will prove useless or insufficient. As, in old times, material force was of no avail against the hordes of barbarians, but only the power of the Christian religion, which entering into their souls quenched their ferocity, civilized their manners, and made them docile to the voice of truth and to the law of the gospel; so against the fury of lawless multitudes there will be no effectual defense without the salutary power of religion. It is only this power which, casting into their minds the light of truth, and instilling into

their hearts the holy moral precepts of Jesus Christ, can make them listen to the voice of conscience and of duty, and, before restraining their hand, restrain their minds and allay the violence of passion. — To assail religion, is therefore to deprive Italy of its most powerful ally against an enemy that becomes every day more formidable.

15. But this is not all. — As, in the social order, the war against religion is becoming most disastrous and destructive to Italy, so, in the political order, the enmity against the Holy See and the Roman Pontiff is for Italy a source of the greatest evils. Even as to this, demonstration is not needed; it is enough, for the full expression of our thought, to state in few words its conclusions. The war against the Pope is for Italy, internally, a cause of profound division between official Italy and the great part of Italians who are truly Catholic: and every division is a weakness. This war deprives our country of the support and co-operation of the party which is the most frankly conservative; it keeps up in the bosom of the nation a religious conflict which has never yet brought any public good, but ever bears within itself the fatal germs of evil and of most heavy chastisement.-Externally, the conflict with the Holy See, besides depriving Italy of the prestige and splendor which it would most certainly have by living in peace with the Pontificate, draws upon it the hostility of the Catholics of the whole world, is a cause of immense sacrifices, and may on any occasion furnish its enemies with a weapon to be used against it.

16. Such is the so-called welfare and greatness prepared for Italy by those who, having its destinies in their hands, do all they can, in accordance with the impious aspiration of the sects, to overthrow the Catholic religion and the Papacy.

17. Suppose, instead of this, that all connection and connivance with the sects were given up; that religion and the Church, as the greatest social power, were allowed real liberty and full exercise of their rights. — What a happy change would come over the destinies of Italy! The evils and the dangers which we have lamented, as the result of the war against religion and the Church, would cease with the termination of the conflict; and further, we should see once more flourish on the chosen soil of Catholic Italy the

greatness and glory which religion and the Church have ever abundantly produced. From their divine power would spring up spontaneously a reformation of public and private morality; family ties would be strengthened; and under religious influences, the feeling of duty and of fidelity in its fulfillment would be awakened in all ranks of the people to a new life. — The social questions which now so greatly occupy men's minds would find their way to the best and most complete solution, by the practical application of the gospel precepts of charity and justice. Popular liberty, not allowed to degenerate into license, would be directed only to good ends, and would become truly worthy of man. The sciences, through that truth of which the Church is mistress, would rise speedily to a higher excellence; and so also would the arts, through the powerful inspiration which religion derives from above, and which it knows how to transfuse into the minds of men. — Peace being made with the Church, religious unity and civil concord would be greatly strengthened; the separation between Italy and Catholics faithful to the Church would cease, and Italy would thus acquire a powerful element of order and stability. The just demands of the Roman Pontiff being satisfied, and his sovereign rights acknowledged, he would be restored to a condition of true and effective independence; and Catholics of other parts of the world, who, not through external influence of ignorance of what they want, but through a feeling of faith and sense of duty, all raise their voice in defense of the dignity and liberty of the supreme Pastor of their souls, would no longer have reason to regard Italy as the enemy of the Pontiff. — On the contrary, Italy would gain greater respect and esteem from other nations by living in harmony with the Apostolic See; for not only has this See conferred special benefits on Italians by its presence in the midst of them, but also, by the constant diffusion of the treasures of faith from this center of benediction and salvation, it has made the Italian name great and respected among all nations. Italy reconciled with the Pontiff, and faithful to its religion, would be able worthily to emulate the glory of its early times; and from whatever real progress there is in the present age it would receive a new impulse to advance in its glorious path. Rome, preeminently the Catholic city, destined by God to be the center of the religion of Christ and the See of His Vicar, has had in this the cause of its stability and greatness throughout the eventful changes of the many ages that are past. Placed again under the peaceful and paternal scepter of the Roman Pontiff, it would again become what Providence and the course of ages made it — not dwarfed to the condition of a capital of one kingdom, nor divided between two different and sovereign powers in a dualism contrary to its whole history; but the worthy capital of the Catholic world, great with all the majesty of Religion and of the supreme Priesthood, a teacher and an example to the nations of morality and of civilization.

18. These are not vain illusions, Venerable Brethren, but hopes resting upon the most solid and true foundation. The assertion which for some time has been commonly repeated, that Catholics and the Pontiff are the enemies of Italy, and in alliance, so to speak, with those who would overturn everything, is a gratuitous insult and a shameless calumny, artfully spread abroad by the sects to disguise their wicked designs, and to enable them to continue without obstacle their hateful work of stripping Italy of its Catholic character. The truth which is seen most clearly from what we have thus far said, is that Catholics are Italy's best friends. By keeping altogether aloof from the sects, by renouncing their spirit and their works, by striving in every way that Italy may not lose the faith, but preserve it in all its vigor-may not fight against the Church, but be its faithful daughter, — may not assail the Pontificate, but be reconciled to it, — Catholics give proof by all this of their strong and real love for the religion of their ancestors and for their country. — Do all that you can, Venerable Brethren, to spread the light of truth among the people so that they may come at last to understand where their welfare and their true interest are to be found; and may be convinced that only from fidelity to religion and from peace with the Church and with the Roman Pontiff, can they hope to obtain for Italy a future worthy of its glorious past. — To this We would call the attention, not of those affiliated to the sects, whose deliberate purpose it is to establish the new settlement of the Italian Peninsula upon the ruins of the

Catholic Religion; but of others who, without welcoming such malevolent designs, help these men in their work by supporting their policy; and especially of young men, who are so liable to go astray through inexperience and the predominance of mere sentiment. We would that everyone should become convinced that the course which is now followed cannot be otherwise than fatal to Italy; and, in once more making known this danger, We are moved only by a consciousness of duty and by love of our country.

19. But, for the enlightening of men's minds, we must above all ask for special help from heaven. Therefore, to our united action, Venerable Brethren, we must join prayer; and let it be a prayer that is general, constant, and fervent: a prayer that will offer gentle violence to the heart of God. and render Him merciful to Italy our country, so that He may avert from it every calamity, especially that which would be the most terrible — the loss of faith. — Let us take as our mediatrix with God the most glorious VIRGIN MARY, the invincible Queen of the Rosary, Who has such great power over the forces of hell, and has so many times made Italy feel the effects of Her maternal love. — Let us also with confidence have recourse to the holy Apostles PETER and PAUL, who subjected this blessed land to the faith, sanctified it by their labors, and bathed it in their blood.

20. As a pledge meanwhile of the help which We ask, and in token of Our most special affection, receive the Apostolic Benediction, which from the depth of Our heart We grant to you, Venerable Brethren, to your Clergy, and to the Italian people.

Given in Rome, at St. Peter's, on the 15th of October, 1890, the thirteenth year of Our Pontificate.

✠

AU MILIEU DES SOLLICITUDES
Letter of Pope Leo XIII
On the Church and State in France
February 16, 1892

This lesser-known letter addresses the spread of Freemasonry in France, warning against its influence on politics and education. It echoes themes from Humanum Genus *about the dangers of Masonic naturalism and religious indifferentism and targets a specific national context where Freemasonry was a driving force behind anti-clerical legislation, such as the French Third Republic's secularization laws.*

To Our Venerable Brothers the Archbishops, Bishops, Clergy and Faithful of France.
To the Bishops and Faithful of France,

Amid the cares of the universal Church We have many times, in the course of Our Pontificate, been pleased to testify Our affection for France and her noble people, and in one of Our Encyclicals, still within the memory of all, We endeavored solemnly to express the innermost feelings of Our soul on this subject. It is precisely this affection that has caused Us to watch with deep interest and then to revolve in Our mind the succession of events, sometimes sad, sometimes consoling, which, of late years, has taken place in your midst.

2. Again, at present, when contemplating the depths of the vast conspiracy that certain men have formed for the annihilation of Christianity in France and the animosity with which they pursue the realization of their design, trampling under foot the most elementary notions of liberty and justice for the sentiment of the greater part of the nation, and of respect for the inalienable rights of the Catholic Church, how can We but be stricken with deepest grief? And when We behold, one after another, the dire consequences of these

sinful attacks which conspire to ruin morals, religion, and even political interests, wisely understood, how express the bitterness that overwhelms Us and the apprehensions that beset Us?

3. On the other hand, We feel greatly consoled when We see this same French people increasing its zeal and affection for the Holy See in proportion as that See is abandoned — We should rather say warred with upon earth. Moved by deeply religious and patriotic sentiments, representatives of all the social classes have repeatedly come to Us from France, happy to aid the Church in her incessant needs and eager to ask us for light and counsel, so as to be sure that amid present tribulations they would in nowise deviate from the teachings of the Head of the Faithful. And We, in Our turn, either in writing or by word of mouth, have openly told Our sons what they had a right to demand of their Father, and, far from discouraging them, we have strongly exhorted them to increase their love and efforts in defense of the Catholic faith and likewise of their native land: two duties of paramount importance, and from which, in this life, no man can exempt himself.

4. Now We deem it opportune, nay, even necessary, once again to raise Our voice entreating still more earnestly, We shall not say Catholics only, but all upright and intelligent Frenchmen, utterly to disregard all germs of political strife in order to devote their efforts solely to the pacification of their country. All understand the value of this pacification; all continue to desire it more and more. And We who crave it more than any one, since We represent on earth the God of peace, urge by these present Letters all righteous souls, all generous hearts, to assist Us in making it stable and fruitful.

5. First of all, let us take as a starting-point a well-known truth admitted by all men of good sense and loudly proclaimed by the history of all peoples; namely, that religion, and religion only, can create the social bond; that it alone maintains the peace of a nation on a solid foundation. When different families, without giving up the rights and duties of domestic society, unite under the inspiration of nature, in order to constitute themselves members of another larger family circle called civil society, their object is not only

to find therein the means of providing for their material welfare, but, above all, to draw thence the boon of moral improvement. Otherwise society would rise but little above the level of an aggregation of beings devoid of reason, and whose whole life would consist in the satisfaction of sensual instincts. Moreover, without this moral improvement it would be difficult to demonstrate that civil society was an advantage rather than a detriment to man, as man.

6. Now, morality, in man, by the mere fact that it should establish harmony among so many dissimilar rights and duties, since it enters as an element into every human act, necessarily supposes God, and with God, religion, that sacred bond whose privilege is to unite, anteriorly to all other bonds, man to God. Indeed, the idea of morality signifies, above all, an order of dependence in regard to truth which is the light of the mind; in regard to good which is the object of the will; and without truth and good there is no morality worthy of the name. And what is the principal and essential truth, that from which all truth is derived? It is God. What, therefore, is the supreme good from which all other good proceeds? God. Finally, who is the creator and guardian of our reason, our will, our whole being, as well as the end of our life? God; always God. Since, therefore, religion is the interior and exterior expression of the dependence which, in justice, we owe to God. there follows a grave obligation. All citizens are bound to unite in maintaining in the nation true religious sentiment, and to defend it in case of need, if ever, despite the protestations of nature and of history, an atheistical school should set about banishing God from society, thereby surely annihilating the moral sense even in the depths of the human conscience. Among men who have not lost all notion of integrity there can exist no difference of opinion on this point.

7. In French Catholics the religious sentiment should be even deeper and more universal because they have the happiness of belonging to the true religion. If, indeed, religious beliefs were, always and everywhere, given as a basis of the morality of human actions and the existence of all wellordained society, it is evident that the Catholic religion, by the mere fact that it is the true Church of Jesus Christ, possesses, more than any other, the efficacy required

for the regulation of life in society and in the individual. Would you have a brilliant example of this? France herself furnishes the same.... In proportion as France progressed in the Christian faith she was seen to rise gradually to the moral greatness which she attained as a political and military power. To the natural generosity of her heart Christian charity came and added an abundant source of new energy; her wonderful activity received still greater impetus from contact with the light that guides and is the pledge of constancy, the Christian faith, which, by the hand of France, traced such glorious pages in the history of mankind. And even to-day does not her faith continue to add new glories to those of the past? We behold France, inexhaustible in her genius and resources, multiplying works of charity at home; we admire her enterprises in foreign lands where, by means of her gold and the labors of her missionaries who work even at the price of their blood, she simultaneously propagates her own renown and the benefits of the Catholic religion. No Frenchman, whatever his convictions in other respects, would dare to renounce glory such as this, for to do so would be to deny his native land.

8. Now the history of a nation reveals in an incontestable way the generating and preserving element of its moral greatness, and should this element ever be missing, neither a superabundance of gold nor even force of arms could save it from moral decadence and perhaps death. Who then but understands that for all Frenchmen professing the Catholic religion the great anxiety should be to insure its preservation, and that with all the more devotedness since in their midst the sects are making Christianity an object of implacable hostility. Therefore, on this ground, they can afford neither indolence of action nor party divisions; the one would bespeak cowardice unworthy of a Christian, the other would bring about disastrous weakness.

9. And now, before going any further, We must indicate a craftily circulated calumny making most odious imputations against Catholics, and even against the Holy See itself. It is maintained that that vigor of action inculcated in Catholics for the defense of their faith has for a secret motive much less the safeguarding of their religious interests than

the ambition of securing to the Church political domination over the State. Truly this is the revival of a very ancient calumny, as its invention belongs to the first enemies of Christianity. Was it not first of all formulated against the adorable person of the Redeemer? Yes, when He illuminated souls by His preaching and alleviated the corporal or spiritual sufferings of the unfortunate with the treasures of His divine bounty, he was accused of having political ends in view. "We have found this man perverting our nation, and forbidding to give tribute to Caesar, and saying that he is Christ, the king.[1] If thou release this man, thou are not Caesar's friend. For whomsoever maketh himself a king, speaketh against Caesar.... We have no king but Caesar."[2]

10. It was these threatening calumnies which drew from Pilate the sentence of death against Him whom he had repeatedly declared innocent. And the authors of these lies, or of others of equal strength, omitted nothing that would aid their emissaries in propagating them far and wide; and thus did St. Justin, martyr, rebuke the Jews of his time: "Far from repenting when you had learned of His resurrection from the dead, you sent to Jerusalem shrewdly chosen men to announce that a heresy and an impious sect had been started by a certain seducer called Jesus of Galilee."[3]

11. In so audaciously defaming Christianity its enemies know well what they did; their plan was to raise against its propagation a formidable adversary, the Roman Empire. The calumny made headway; and in their credulity the pagans called the first Christians "useless creatures, dangerous citizens, factionists, enemies of the Empire and the Emperors."[4] But in vain did the apologists of Christianity by their writings, and Christians by their splendid conduct, endeavor to demonstrate the absurdity and criminality of these qualifications: they were not heeded. Their very name was equivalent to a declaration of war; and Christians, by the mere fact of their being such, and for no other reason, were

---

[1] Lk 23.2.

[2] Jn 19. 12-15.

[3] Dialog. cum Tryphone.

[4] Tertull. In Apolog.; Minutius Felix, In Octavio.

forced to choose between apostasy and martyrdom, being allowed no alternative. During the following centuries the same grievances and the same severity prevailed to a greater or less extent, whenever governments were unreasonably jealous of their power and maliciously disposed against the Church. They never failed to call public attention to the pretended encroachment of the Church upon the State, in order to furnish the State with some apparent right to violently attack the Catholic religion.

12. We have expressly recalled some features of the past that Catholics might not be dismayed by the present. Substantially the struggle is ever the same: Jesus Christ is always exposed to the contradictions of the world, and the same means are always used by modern enemies of Christianity, means old in principle and scarcely modified in form; but the same means of defense are also clearly indicated to Christians of the present day by our apologists, our doctors and our martyrs. What they have done it is incumbent upon us to do in our turn. Let us therefore place above all else the glory of God and of His Church; let us work for her with an assiduity at once constant and effective, and leave all care of success to Jesus Christ, who tells us: "In the world you shall have distress: but have confidence, I have overcome the world."[5]

13. To attain this We have already remarked that a great union is necessary, and if it is to be realized, it is indispensable that all preoccupation capable of diminishing its strength and efficacy must be abandoned. Here We intend alluding principally to the political differences among the French in regard to the actual republic — a question We would treat with the clearness which the gravity of the subject demands, beginning with the principles and descending thence to practical results.

14. Various political governments have succeeded one another in France during the last century, each having its own distinctive form: the Empire, the Monarchy, and the Republic. By giving one's self up to abstractions, one could at length conclude which is the best of these forms,

---

[5] Jn 16.33.

considered in themselves; and in all truth it may be affirmed that each of them is good, provided it lead straight to its end — that is to say, to the common good for which social authority is constituted; and finally, it may be added that, from a relative point of view, such and such a form of government may be preferable because of being better adapted to the character and customs of such or such a nation. In this order of speculative ideas, Catholics, like all other citizens, are free to prefer one form of government to another precisely because no one of these social forms is, in itself, opposed to the principles of sound reason nor to the maxims of Christian doctrine. What amply justifies the wisdom of the Church is that in her relations with political powers she makes abstraction of the forms which differentiate them and treats with them concerning the great religious interests of nations, knowing that hers is the duty to undertake their tutelage above all other interests. Our preceding Encyclicals have already exposed these principles, but it was nevertheless necessary to recall them for the development of the subject which occupies us to-day.

15. In descending from the domain of abstractions to that of facts, we must beware of denying the principles just established: they remain fixed. However, becoming incarnated in facts, they are clothed with a contingent character, determined by the center in which their application is produced. Otherwise said, if every political form is good by itself and may be applied to the government of nations, the fact still remains that political power is not found in all nations under the same form; each has its own. This form springs from a combination of historical or national, though always human, circumstances which, in a nation, give rise to its traditional and even fundamental laws, and by these is determined the particular form of government, the basis of transmission of supreme power.

16. It were useless to recall that all individuals are bound to accept these governments and not to attempt their overthrow or a change in their form. Hence it is that the Church, the guardian of the truest and highest idea of political sovereignty, since she has derived it from God, has always condemned men who rebelled against legitimate authority

and disapproved their doctrines. And that too at the very time when the custodians of power used it against her, thereby depriving themselves of the strongest support given their authority and of efficacious means of obtaining from the people obedience to their laws. And apropos of this subject, We cannot lay too great stress upon the precepts given to the first Christians by the Prince of the apostles in the midst of persecutions: "Honor all men: love the brotherhood: fear God: honor the king";[6] and those of St. Paul: "I desire, therefore, first of all, that supplications, prayers, intercessions, and thanksgivings be made for all men: For kings and for all who are in high station, that we may lead a quiet and peaceable life, in all piety and chastity. For this is good and acceptable in the sight of God, our Savior."[7]

17. However, here it must be carefully observed that whatever be the form of civil power in a nation, it cannot be considered so definitive as to have the right to remain immutable, even though such were the intention of those who, in the beginning, determined it.... Only the Church of Jesus Christ has been able to preserve, and surely will preserve unto the consummation of time, her form of government. Founded by Him who was, who is, and who will be forever,[8] she has received from Him, since her very origin, all that she requires for the pursuing of her divine mission across the changeable ocean of human affairs. And, far from wishing to transform her essential constitution, she has not the power even to relinquish the conditions of true liberty and sovereign independence with which Providence has endowed her in the general interest of souls... But, in regard to purely human societies, it is an oft-repeated historical fact that time, that great transformer of all things here below, operates great changes in their political institutions. On some occasions it limits itself to modifying something in the form of the established government; or, again, it will go so far as to substitute other forms for the primitive ones-forms totally different, even as regards the mode of transmitting sovereign

---

[6] I Pt 2.17.

[7] I Tm 2.1-3.

[8] Heb 13.8.

power.

18. And how are these political changes of which We speak produced? They sometimes follow in the wake of violent crises, too often of a bloody character, in the midst of which preexisting governments totally disappear; then anarchy holds sway, and soon public order is shaken to its very foundations and finally overthrown. From that time onward a social need obtrudes itself upon the nation; it must provide for itself without delay. Is it not its privilege — or, better still, its duty — to defend itself against a state of affairs troubling it so deeply, and to re-establish public peace in the tranquillity of order? Now, this social need justifies the creation and the existence of new governments, whatever form they take; since, in the hypothesis wherein we reason, these new governments are a requisite to public order, all public order being impossible without a government. Thence it follows that, in similar junctures, all the novelty is limited to the political form of civil power, or to its mode of transmission; it in no wise affects the power considered in itself. This continues to be immutable and worthy of respect, as, considered in its nature, it is constituted to provide for the common good, the supreme end which gives human society its origin. To put it otherwise, in all hypotheses, civil power, considered as such, is from God, always from God: "For there is no power but from God."[9]

19. Consequently, when new governments representing this immutable power are constituted, their acceptance is not only permissible but even obligatory, being imposed by the need of the social good which has made and which upholds them. This is all the more imperative because an insurrection stirs up hatred among citizens, provokes civil war, and may throw a nation into chaos and anarchy, and this great duty of respect and dependence will endure as long as the exigencies of the common good shall demand it, since this good is, after God, the first and last law in society.

20. Thus the wisdom of the Church explains itself in the maintenance of her relations with the numerous governments which have succeeded one another in France in less than a

---

[9] Rom. 13.1. 10. Enarrat, in Psalm. CXXIV, n. 7, fin.

century, each change causing violent shocks. Such a line of conduct would be the surest and most salutary for all Frenchmen in their civil relations with the republic, which is the actual government of their nation. Far be it from them to encourage the political dissensions which divide them; all their efforts should be combined to preserve and elevate the moral greatness of their native land.

21. But a difficulty presents itself. "This Republic," it is said, "is animated by such anti-Christian sentiments that honest men, Catholics particularly, could not conscientiously accept it." This, more than anything else, has given rise to dissensions, and in fact aggravated them.... These regrettable differences would have been avoided if the very considerable distinction between constituted power and legislation had been carefully kept in view. In so much does legislation differ from political power and its form, that under a system of government most excellent in form legislation could be detestable; while quite the opposite under a regime most imperfect in form, might be found excellent legislation. It were an easy task to prove this truth, history in hand, but what would be the use? All are convinced of it. And who, better than the Church, is in position to know it — she who has striven to maintain habitual relations with all political governments? Assuredly she, better than any other power, could tell the consolation or sorrow occasioned her by the laws of the various governments by which nations have been ruled from the Roman Empire down to the present.

22. If the distinction just established has its major importance, it is likewise manifestly reasonable: Legislation is the work of men invested with power, and who, in fact, govern the nation; therefore it follows that, practically, the quality of the laws depends more upon the quality of these men than upon the power. The laws will be good or bad accordingly as the minds of the legislators are imbued with good or bad principles, and as they allow themselves to be guided by political prudence or by passion.

23. That several years ago different important acts of legislation in France proceeded from a tendency hostile to religion, and therefore to the interests of the nation, is admitted by all, and unfortunately confirmed by the evidence

of facts. We Ourselves, in obedience to a sacred duty, made earnest appeals to him who was then at the head of the republic, but these tendencies continued to exist; the evil grew, and it was not surprising that the members of the French Episcopate chosen by the Holy Ghost to rule over their respective illustrious churches should even quite recently have considered it an obligation publicly to express their grief concerning the condition of affairs in France in regard to the Catholic religion. Poor France! God alone can measure the abyss of evil into which she will sink if this legislation, instead of improving, will stubbornly continue in a course which must end in plucking from the minds and hearts of Frenchmen the religion which has made them so great.

24. And here is precisely the ground on which, political dissensions aside, upright men should unite as one to combat, by all lawful and honest means, these progressive abuses of legislation. The respect due to constituted power cannot prohibit this: unlimited respect and obedience cannot be yielded to all legislative measures, of no matter what kind, enacted by this same power. Let it not be forgotten that law is a precept ordained according to reason and promulgated for the good of the community by those who, for this end, have been entrusted with power. . . Accordingly, such points in legislation as are hostile to religion and to God should never be approved; to the contrary, it is a duty to disapprove them. It was this that St. Augustine, the great Bishop of Hippo, brought out so strongly in his eloquent reasoning: "Sometimes the powerful ones of earth are good and fear God; at other times they fear Him not. Julian was an emperor unfaithful to God, an apostate, a pervert, an idolator. Christian soldiers served this faithless emperor, but as soon as there was question of the cause of Jesus Christ they recognized only Him who was in heaven. Julian commanded them to honor idols and offer them incense, but they put God above the prince. However, when he made them form into ranks and march against a hostile nation, they obeyed instantly. They distinguished the eternal from the temporal master and still in view of the eternal Master they submitted to such a temporal master."

25. We know that, by a lamentable abuse of his reason, and still more so of his will, the atheist denies these principles. But, in a word, atheism is so monstrous an error that it could never, be it said to the honor of humanity, annihilate in it the consciousness of God's claims and substitute them with idolatry of the State.

26. The principles which should regulate our conduct towards God and towards human governments being thus defined, no unprejudiced man can censure French Catholics if, sparing themselves neither fatigue nor sacrifice, they labor to preserve a condition essential to their country's salvation, one which embodies so many glorious traditions registered by history, and which every Frenchmen is in duty bound not to forget.

27. Before closing Our Letter, We wish to touch upon two points bearing an affinity to each other and which, because so closely connected with religious interests, have stirred up some division among Catholics — One of them is the Concordat, which for so many years has facilitated in France the harmony between the government of the Church and that of the State. On the observance of this solemn, bilateral compact, always faithfully kept by the Holy See, the enemies of the Catholic religion do not themselves agree-The more violent among them desire its abolition, that the State may be entirely free to molest the Church of Jesus Christ — On the contrary, others, being more astute, wish, or rather claim to wish, the preservation of the Concordat: not because they agree that the State should fulfill toward the Church the subscribed engagements, but solely that the State may be benefited by the concessions made by the Church; as if one could, at will, separate engagements entered into from concessions obtained, when both of these things form a substantial part of one whole. For them the Concordat would amount to no more than a chain forged to fetter the liberty of the Church, that holy liberty to which she has a divine and inalienable right. Of these two opinions which will prevail? We know not. We desired to recall them only to recommend Catholics not to provoke a secession by interfering in a matter with which it is the business of the Holy See to deal.

28. We shall not hold to the same language on another

point, concerning the principle of the separation of the State and Church, which is equivalent to the separation of human legislation from Christian and divine legislation. We do not care to interrupt Ourselves here in order to demonstrate the absurdity of such a separation; each one will understand for himself. As soon as the State refuses to give to God what belongs to God, by a necessary consequence it refuses to give to citizens that to which, as men, they have a right; as, whether agreeable or not to accept, it cannot be denied that man's rights spring from his duty toward God. Whence if follows that the State, by missing in this connection the principal object of its institution, finally becomes false to itself by denying that which is the reason of its own existence. These superior truths are so clearly proclaimed by the voice of even natural reason, that they force themselves upon all who are not blinded by the violence of passion; therefore Catholics cannot be too careful in defending themselves against such a separation. In fact, to wish that the State would separate itself from the Church would be to wish, by a logical sequence, that the Church be reduced to the liberty of living according to the law common to all citizens....It is true that in certain countries this state of affairs exists. It is a condition which, if it have numerous and serious inconveniences, also offers some advantages — above all when, by a fortunate inconsistency, the legislator is inspired by Christian principles — and, though these advantages cannot justify the false principle of separation nor authorize its defense, they nevertheless render worthy of toleration a situation which, practically, might be worse.

29. But in France, a nation Catholic in her traditions and by the present faith of the great majority of her sons, the Church should not be placed in the precarious position to which she must submit among other peoples; and the better that Catholics understand the aim of the enemies who desire this separation, the less will they favor it. To these enemies, and they say it clearly enough, this separation means that political legislation be entirely independent of religious legislation; nay, more, that Power be absolutely indifferent to the interests of Christian society, that is to say, of the Church; in fact, that it deny her very existence. But they make a

reservation formulated thus: As soon as the Church, utilizing the resources which common law accords to the least among Frenchmen, will, by redoubling her native activity, cause her work to prosper, then the State intervening, can and will put French Catholics outside the common law itself... In a word: the ideal of these men would be a return to paganism: the State would recognize the Church only when it would be pleased to persecute her.

30. We have explained, Venerable Brethren, in an abridged though clear way, some if not all the points upon which French Catholics and all intelligent men should be at peace and unity, so as to remedy, in so far as still remains possible, the evils with which France is afflicted, and to elevate its moral greatness. The points in question are: Religion and country, political power and legislation, the conduct to be observed in regard to this power and legislation, the Concordat, the separation of Church and State....We cherish the hope and the confidence that the elucidation of these points will dissipate the prejudices of many honest, well-meaning men, facilitate the pacification of minds, and thereby cement the union of all Catholics for the sustaining of the great cause of Christ, who loves the Franks.

31. How consoling to Our heart to encourage you all in this way and to behold you all responding with docility to Our appeal! You, Venerable Brethren, by your authority and with the enlightened zeal for Church and Fatherland which so distinguishes you, will give able support to this peace-making work. We delight in the hope that those who are in power will appreciate Our words, which aim at the happiness and prosperity of France.

32. Meanwhile, as a pledge of Our paternal affection, we bestow upon you, Venerable Brethren, upon your clergy and also upon all the Catholics of France, the apostolic blessing.

Given at Rome, the 16th day of February, 1892, in the fourteenth year of Our Pontificate.

✠

CUSTODI DI QUELLA FEDE
Encyclical of Pope Leo XIII
On Freemasonry
December 8, 1892

Addressed to the Italian episcopate, this encyclical warned against the influence of Freemasonry in Italian society, particularly its role in promoting secular laws and anti-clerical policies. It urged Catholics to remain vigilant against Masonic activities. Issued concurrently with Inimica Vis, *it reinforced Leo XIII's focus on Freemasonry as a threat to the Christendom in Italy.*

To the Italian People.

Deplorable Conditions in Italy

Guardians of that faith to which the Christian nations owe their morality and civil redemption, We must dutifully discharge each one of Our supreme tasks. Therefore We must raise Our voice in loud protestations against the impious war which tries to take such a precious treasure away from you, beloved children. Already taught by long and sorrowful experience, you know well the terrible trials of this war, you who deplore it in your hearts as Catholics and as Italians. Can one be Italian in name and sentiment and not resent these continual offenses against divine beliefs? These beliefs are the most beautiful of our glories, for they gave to Italy its primacy over the other nations and to Rome the spiritual sceptre of the world. They likewise made the wonderful edifice of Christian civilization rise over the ruins of paganism and barbarism.

Can we be Catholic in mind and heart and gaze with dry eyes on that land where our wondrous Redeemer deigned to establish the seat of His kingdom? Now We see His teachings attacked and His reverence outraged, His Church embattled and His Vicar opposed. So many souls redeemed by His blood are now lost, the choicest portion of His flock, a people faithful to Him for nineteen centuries. How can We bear to look upon His chosen people exposed to a constant and ever-present danger of apostasy, pushed toward error and vice, material miseries, and moral degradation?

Threat of Masonry

2. This war is directed at the same time against the heavenly and the earthly kingdoms, against the faith of our ancestors and the culture which they handed on to us. It is thus doubly evil, being guilty of a divine offense no less than a human one. Is its chief source not that very masonic sect which We discussed at length in the encyclical *Humanum genus* of April 20, 1884, and in the more recent one of October 15, 1890, addressed to the bishops, the clergy and the Italian people? With these two letters We tore from the face of masonry the mask which it used to hide itself and We showed it in its crude deformity and dark fatal activity.

3. We shall restrict Ourselves now to its deplorable effects on Italy. For a long time now it has bored its way under the deceitful guise of a philanthropic society and redeemer of the Italian people. By way of conspiracies, corruptions, and violences, it has finally come to dominate Italy and even Rome. To what troubles, to what calamities has it opened the way in a little more than thirty years?

Troubles Caused by Masonry

4. Our country has seen and suffered great evils in such a short span of time, for the faith of our fathers has been made a sign for persecutions of every sort. The satanic intent of the persecutors has been to substitute naturalism for Christianity, the worship of reason for the worship of faith, so-called independent morality for Catholic morality, and material progress for spiritual progress. To the holy maxims and laws of the Gospel, they have opposed laws and maxims which can be called the code of revolution. They have also opposed an atheistic doctrine and a vile realism to school, science, and the Christian arts. Having invaded the temple of the Lord, they have squandered the booty of the Church's goods, the greatest part of the inheritance necessary for the ministers,

and reduced the number of priests by the conscription of clerics beyond the limits of extreme need. If the administration of the sacraments could not be impeded, they sought nonetheless to introduce and promote civil marriages and funerals. If they have not yet succeeded in seizing control of education and the direction of charitable institutions, they always aim with perseverance to laicize everything, which is to remove the mark of Christianity from it. If they could not silence the voice of the Catholic press, they made every effort to discredit and revile it.

Contradictions in the Masonic Program

5. In this battle against the Catholic religion, what partiality and contradictions there are! They closed monasteries and convents, but they let multiply at will masonic lodges and sectarian dens. They proclaimed the right of association, while the legal rights which all kinds of organizations use and abuse are denied to religious societies. They proclaim freedom of religion and reserve odious intolerance and vexations precisely for the religion of the Italians - which, for that reason, should be assured respect and a special protection. They made protests and great promises for the protection of the dignity and independence of the pope, but you see their daily contempt of Our person. All kinds of public shows find an open field; yet this or that Catholic demonstration is either prohibited or disturbed. They encourage schisms, apostasies, and revolts against legitimate superiors in the Church. Religious vows and especially religious obedience are rebuked as contrary to human dignity and freedom, while impious associations which bind their followers by wicked oaths and demand blind, absolute obedience in crime are allowed to flourish with impunity.

The Spirit of Masonry

6. We do not wish to exaggerate the masonic power by attributing to its direct and immediate action all the evils which presently preoccupy Us. However, you can clearly see its spirit in the facts which We have just recorded and in many others which We could recall. That spirit, which is the

implacable enemy of Christ and of the Church, tries all ways, uses all arts, and prevails upon all means. It seizes from the Church its first-born daughter and seizes from Christ His favored nation, the seat of His Vicar on earth and the center of Catholic unity. To see the evil and efficacious influence of this spirit on our affairs, We have more than a few fleeting indications and the series of facts which have succeeded themselves for thirty years. Proud of its successes, the sect herself has spoken out and told us all its past accomplishments and future goals. It regards the public powers as its instruments, wining or not, which is to say that the impious sect boasts as one of its principal works the religious persecution which has troubled and is troubling our Italy. Though often executed by other hands, this persecution is inspired and promoted by masonry, in an immediate or mediate, direct or indirect manner, by flattery or threats, seduction or revolution.

Social Evils of Masonry

7. The road is very short from religious to social ruin. The heart of man is no longer raised to heavenly hopes and loves; capable and needing the infinite, it throws itself insatiably on the goods of this earth. Inevitably there is a perpetual struggle of avid passions to enjoy, become rich, and rise. Then we encounter a large and inexhaustible source of grudges, discords, corruptions, and crimes. In our Italy there was no lack of moral and social disorders before the present events-but what a sorrowful spectacle we see in our days! That loving respect which forms domestic harmony is substantially diminished; paternal authority is too often unrecognized by children and parents alike. Disagreements are frequent, divorce common. Civil discords and resentful anger between the various orders increase every day in the cities. New generations which grew up in a spirit of misunderstood freedom are unleashed in the cities, generations which do not respect anything from above or below. The cities teem with incitements to vice, precocious crimes, and public scandals. The state should be content with the high and noble office of recognizing, protecting, and helping divine and human rights in their harmonious

universality. Now, however, the state believes itself almost a judge and disowns these rights or restricts them at will. Finally, the general social order is undermined at its foundations. Books and journals, schools and universities, clubs and theaters, monuments and political discourse, photographs and the fine arts, everything conspires to pervert minds and corrupt hearts. Meanwhile the oppressed and suffering people tremble and the anarchic sects arouse themselves. The working classes raise their heads and go to swell the ranks of socialism, communism, and anarchy. Characters exhaust themselves and many souls, no longer knowing how to suffer nobly nor how to redeem themselves manfully, take their lives with cowardly suicide.

8. Such are the fruits which the masonic sect has borne to us Italians. And after that it yearns to come before you, extolling its merits towards . Italy. It likewise yearns to give Us and all those who, heeding Our words, remain faithful to Jesus Christ, the calumnious title of enemies of the state. The facts reveal the merits of this guilty sect toward our peninsula, "merits" which bear repeating. The facts say that masonic patriotism is no less than sectarian egotism which yearns to dominate everything, particularly the modern states which unite and concentrate everything in their hands. The facts say that in the plans of masonry, the names of political independence, equality, civilization, and progress aimed to facilitate the independence of man from God in our country. From them, license of error and vice and union of faction at the expense of other citizens have grown. The easy and delicious enjoyment of life by the world's fortunate is nurtured in the same source. A people redeemed by divine blood have thus returned to divisions, corruptions, and the shames of paganism.

Evil Nature of Masonry

9. That does not surprise Us. - After nineteen centuries of Christian civilization, this sect tries to overthrow the Catholic Church and to cut off its divine sources. It absolutely denies the supernatural, repudiating every revelation and all the means of salvation which revelation shows us. Through its plans and works, it bases itself solely and entirely on such

a weak and corrupt nature as ours. Such a sect cannot be anything other than the height of pride, greed, and sensuality. Now, pride oppresses, greed plunders, and sensuality corrupts. When these three concupiscences are brought to the extreme, the oppressions, greed, and seductive corruptions spread slowly. They take on boundless dimensions and become the oppression, plundering and source of corruption of an entire people.

10. Let Us then show you masonry as an enemy of God, Church, and country. Recognize it as such once and for all, and with all the weapons which reason, conscience, and faith put in your hands, defend yourselves from such a proud foe. Let no one be taken in by its attractive appearance or allured by its promises; do not be seduced by its enticements or frightened by its threats. Remember that Christianity and masonry are essentially irreconcilable, such that to join one is to divorce the other. You can no longer ignore such incompatibility between Catholic and mason, beloved children: you have been warned openly by Our predecessors, and We have loudly repeated the warning.

Christian Response to Masonry

11. Those who, by some supreme misfortune, have given their name to one of these societies of perdition should know that they are strictly bound to separate themselves from it. Otherwise they must remain separated from Christian communion and lose their soul now and for eternity. Parents, teachers, godparents, and whoever has care of others should also know that a rigorous duty binds them to keep their wards from this guilty sect or to draw them from it if they have already entered.

12. In a matter of such importance and where the seduction is so easy in these times, it is urgent that the Christian watch himself from the beginning. He should fear the least danger, avoid every occasion, and take the greatest precautions. Use all the prudence of the serpent, while keeping in your heart the simplicity of the dove, according to the evangelical counsel. Fathers and mothers should be wary of inviting strangers into their homes or admitting them to domestic intimacy, at least insofar as their faith is not

sufficiently known. They should try to first ascertain that an astute recruiter of the sect does not hide himself in the guise of a friend, teacher, doctor or other benefactor. Oh, in how many families has the wolf penetrated in sheep's clothing!

Masonic Threat to Groups

13. It is beautiful to see the varied groups which arise everywhere today in every order of social life: worker groups, groups of mutual aid and social security, organizations to promote science, arts, letters, and other similar things. When they are inspired by a good moral and religious spirit, these groups certainly prove to be useful and proper. But because the masonic poison has penetrated and continues to penetrate here also, especially here, any groups that remove themselves from religious influence should be generally suspect. They can easily be directed and more or less dominated by masons, becoming the sowing-ground and the apprenticeship of the sect in addition to providing assistance to it.

14. Women should not join philanthropic societies whose nature and purpose are not well-known without first seeking advice from wise and experienced people. That talkative philanthropy which is opposed to Christian charity with such pomp is often the passport for masonic business.

15. Everyone should avoid familiarity or friendship with anyone suspected of belonging to masonry or to affiliated groups. Know them by their fruits and avoid them. Every familiarity should be avoided, not only with those impious libertines who openly promote the character of the sect, but also with those who hide under the mask of universal tolerance, respect for all religions, and the craving to reconcile the maxims of the Gospel with those of the revolution. These men seek to reconcile Christ and Belial, the Church of God and the state without God.

16. Every Christian should shun books and journals which distill the poison of impiety and which stir up the fire of unrestrained desires or sensual passions. Groups and reading clubs where the masonic spirit stalks its prey should be likewise shunned.

The Offensive Against Masonry

17. In addition, since we are dealing with a sect which has pervaded everything, it is not enough to remain on the defensive. We must courageously go out into the battlefield and confront it. That is what you will do, beloved children, opposing press to press, school to school, organization to organization, congress to congress, action to action.

18. Masonry has taken control of the public schools, leaving private schools, paternal schools, and those directed by zealous ecclesiastics and religious of both sexes to compete in the education of Christian youth. Christian parents especially should not entrust the education of their children to uncertain schools. Masonry has confiscated the inheritance of public charity; fill the void, then, with the treasure of private relief. It has placed pious works in the hands of its followers, so you should entrust those that depend on you to Catholic institutions. It opens and maintains houses of vice, leaving you to do what is possible to open and maintain shelters for honesty in danger. An anti-Christian press in religious and secular matters militates at its expense, so that your effort and money are required by the Catholic press. Masonry establishes societies of mutual help and credit unions for its partisans; you should do the same not only for your brothers but for all the indigent. This will show that true and sincere charity is the daughter of the One who makes the sun to rise and the rain to fall on the just man and sinner alike.

19. May this struggle between good and evil extend to everything, and may good prevail. Masonry holds frequent meetings to plan new ways to combat the Church, and you should hold them frequently to better agree on the means and order of defense. It multiplies its lodges, so that you should multiply Catholic clubs and parochial groups, promote charitable associations and prayer organizations, and maintain and increase the splendor of the temple of God. The sect, having nothing to fear, today shows its face to the light of day. You Italian Catholics should also make open profession of your faith and follow the example of your glorious ancestors who confessed their faith bravely before tyrants, torture, and death. What more? Does the sect try to enslave the Church and to put it at the feet of the state as a

humble servant? You must then demand and claim for it the freedom and independence due it before the law. Does masonry seek to tear apart Catholic unity, sowing discord even in the clergy itself, arousing quarrels, fomenting strife, and inciting insubordination, revolt, and schism? By tightening the sacred bond of charity and obedience, you can thwart its plans, bring to naught its efforts, and disappoint its hopes. Be all of one heart and one mind, like the first Christians. Gathered around the See of Peter and united to your pastors, protect the supreme interests of church and papacy, which are just as much the supreme interests of Italy and of all the Christian world. The Apostolic See has always been the inspirer and jealous guardian of Italian glory. Therefore, be Italians and Catholics, free and non-sectarian, faithful to the nation as well as to Christ and His visible Vicar. An anti-Christian and antipapal Italy would truly be opposed to the divine plan, and thus condemned to perish.

20. Beloved children, faith and state speak to you at this time through Us. Listen to their cry, arise together and fight manfully the battles of the Lord. May the number, boldness, and strength of the enemy not frighten you, because God is stronger than they; if God is for you, who can be against you?

21. Redouble your prayers so that God might be with you in a greater abundance of grace, fighting and triumphing with you. Accompany your prayers with the practice of the Christian virtues, especially charity toward the needy. Seek God's mercies with humility and perseverance, renewing every day the promises of your baptism.

22. As a pledge of these things and as a sign of Our paternal love, We bestow on you Our apostolic blessing, beloved children.

Given in Rome at Saint Peter's, the eighth day of December, 1892, in the fifteenth year of Our pontificate.

✠

INIMICA VIS
Encyclical of Pope Leo XIII
On Freemasonry
December 8, 1892

Inimica Vis *reaffirms the Church's opposition to Freemasonry, emphasizing its dangers to faith and society. It urges bishops to educate the faithful about the "artifices" of Freemasonry and its incompatibility with Catholicism. This encyclical continued Leo XIII's strong anti-Masonic stance, reinforcing the call to action against the organization.*

To the Bishops of Italy.

The enemy forces, inspired by the evil spirit, ever wage war on the Christian name. They join forces in this endeavor with certain groups of men whose purpose is to subvert divinely revealed truths and to rend the very fabric of Christian society with disastrous dissent. Indeed, how much damage these cohorts, as it were, have inflicted on the Church is well-known. And yet, the spirit of all previous groups hostile to Catholic institutions has come to life again in that group called the Masonic sect, which, strong in manpower and resources, is the leader in a war against anything sacred.

Condemnation of Masonic Sect

2. Our predecessors in the Roman pontificate have in the course of a century and a half outlawed this group not once, but repeatedly. We too, in accordance with Our duty, have condemned it strongly to Christian people, so that they might beware of its wiles and bravely repel its impious assaults. Moreover, lest cowardice and sloth overtake us imperceptively, We have deliberately endeavored to reveal the secrets of this pernicious sect and the means by which it labors for the destruction of the Catholic enterprise.

Catholicism Endangered

3. Now, though, a certain thoughtless indifference on the part of many Italians has resulted in their not recognizing the magnitude and extent of the peril. And so the faith of our ancestors, the salvation won for mankind by Jesus Christ, and, consequently the great benefits of Christian civilization are endangered. Indeed, fearing nothing and yielding to no one, the Masonic sect proceeds with greater boldness day by day: with its poisonous infection it pervades entire communities and strives to entangle itself in all the institutions of our country in its conspiracy to forcefully deprive the Italian people of their Catholic faith, the origin and source of their greatest blessings.

4. This is the reason for the endless artifices they employ in their assault on the divinely inspired faith; this is the reason why the legitimate liberty of the Church is treated with contempt and beset with legal oppression. They believe that the Church does not possess the nature and essence of a true society, that the State has priority over it, and that civil authority takes precedence over sacred authority. This false and destructive doctrine has been frequently condemned by the Holy See. Among many other ills, it has been responsible for the usurpation on the part of civil authorities of that to which they have no right and for their unscrupulous appropriation of what they have alienated from the Church. This is clear in the case of ecclesiastical benefices; they usurp the right to give or withhold the revenues of these according to their good pleasure.

Clergy Have Been Underestimated

5. Likewise, in a manner no less insidious, they plan to soften the opposition of the lower clergy with their promises. Their purpose in this endeavor can easily be detected, especially since the very authors of this undertaking do not take sufficient pains to conceal what they intend. They wish to win over the clergy by cajolery; once the novelties have confused them, they will withdraw their obedience to legitimate authority. And yet in this matter they seem to have underestimated the virtue of our clergy, who for so many years have given manifest examples of their moderation and

loyalty. We have every reason to be confident that, with God's help, they will continue their devotion to duty no matter what circumstances may arise.

Those Already Misled

6. This summary indicates both the extent of the activity of the Masonic sect and the goal of its endeavors. What compounds this harmful situation, however, and causes Us deep anxiety is that far too many of our compatriots, driven by hope of their personal advantage or by perverse ambition, have given their names or support to the sect. This being so, We commend first and foremost to your efforts the eternal salvation of those whom we have just mentioned: may your zeal never waver in constantly and insistently recalling them from their error and certain destruction. To be sure, the task of extricating those who have fallen into the snares of the Masons is laborious, and its outcome is doubtful, if we consider the cleverness of the sect: still the recovery of no one should ever be despaired of since the force of apostolic charity is truly marvellous.

7. Next, we must heal those who have erred in this respect out of faint-heartedness, that is, those who, not because of a debased nature but because of weakness of spirit and lack of discretion, have allowed themselves to be drawn into supporting the Masonic enterprises. Sufficiently weighty are the words of Our predecessor Felix III in this regard. "An error which is not resisted is approved; a truth which is not defended is suppressed.... He who does not oppose an evident crime is open to the suspicion of secret complicity." By reminding them of the examples of their forefathers, the broken spirits of these men must be reanimated with that courage which is the guardian of duty and dignity alike, so that they may be ashamed and regret their cowardly actions. For surely our whole life is involved in a constant battle in which our salvation itself is at stake; nothing is more disgraceful for a Christian than cowardice.

8. It is likewise necessary to strengthen those who fall because of ignorance. By this we mean those, not few in number, who, deceived by appearances and allured by various enticements, allow themselves without

understanding it to be enrolled in the Masonic order. In these cases We hope that with divine inspiration they will be able some day to repudiate their error and perceive the truth, especially if you try to remove the false outward appearance of the sect and reveal its hidden designs. Indeed these can no longer be considered hidden since their very accomplices have themselves disclosed them in many ways. Why, within the last few months, the designs of the Masons have been publicly proclaimed throughout Italy, even to the point of ostentation! They wish to see the religion founded by God reudiated and all affairs, private as well as public, regulated by the principles of naturalism alone; this is what, in their impiety and stupidity, they call the restoration of civil society. And yet the State will plunge headlong into ruin if Christians are not willing to be vigilant and not willing to labor to support its well-being!

Course of Action

9. But in the presence of such audacious evils, it is not sufficient merely to be aware of the wiles of this vile sect: we must also war against it, using those very arms furnished by the divine faith which once prevailed against paganism. Therefore, it is your task to inflame souls by persuasion, exhortation and example; nourish in the clergy and our people a zeal for religion and salvation which is active, resolute, and intrepid. These qualities frequently distinguish Catholic peoples of other nations in similar situations. It is commonly claimed that the ancient ardor of spirit in protecting their ancestral faith has grown cold among the Italian people. Nor is this perhaps false; especially since if the dispositions of both sides be inspected, those who wage war on religion seem to show more energy than those who repel it. But for those who seek salvation there can be no middle ground between laborious struggle and destruction. Therefore, in the case of the weak and sluggish, courage must be stirred up through your efforts; in the case of the strong, it must be kept active; with all trace of dissent wiped out, under your leadership and command, the result will be that all alike, with united minds and common discipline, may undertake the battle in a spirited manner.

10. Because of the gravity of the matter and the necessity of repelling the danger, We have decided to address the Italian people in a letter which We are including along with this one; propagate it as widely as possible and, where needed, interpret it to your people. In this manner, with the blessing of God, we can hope that spirits may be aroused through the contemplation of the threatening evils and betake themselves without delay to the remedies which We have pointed out.

11. As a presage of divine gifts and testimony of Our benevolence We affectionately accord to you, Venerable Brethren, and the people entrusted to your care, the apostolic blessing.

Given in Rome at St. Peter's, 8 December 1892, in the 15th year of Our Pontificate.

PRAECLARA GRATULATIONIS PUBLICAE
Apostolic Letter of Pope Leo XIII
The Reunion of Christendom
June 20, 1894

Praeclara Gratulationis Publicae *commemorates Pope Leo XIII's episcopal jubilee. In it he calls for the reunion of the Orthodox and Protestant denominations with Rome. By warning against "enemies" of Christian unity, he alludes to Freemasons, who promote religious indifferentism and undermine the authority of the Church. In Praeclara, Leo XIII writes of those who "strive to destroy the foundation of Christian truth" and "scatter seeds of discord," themes that echo his descriptions of Masonic influence in other documents.*

To Our Venerable Brethren, all Patriarchs, Primates, Archbishops and Bishops of the Catholic World in Grace and Communion with the Apostolic See, Venerable Brethren, Health and Apostolic Benediction,

The splendid tokens of public rejoicing which have come to Us from all sides in the whole course of last year, to commemorate Our Episcopal Jubilee, and which were lately crowned by the remarkable devotion of the Spanish Nation, have afforded Us special joy, inasmuch as the Unity of the Church and the admirable adhesion of her members to the Sovereign Pontiff have shone forth in this perfect agreement of concurring sentiments. During those days it seemed as if the Catholic world, forgetful of everything else, had centered its gaze and all its thoughts upon the Vatican.

The special missions sent by Kings and Princes, the many Pilgrimages, the letters We received so full of affectionate feeling, the Sacred Services—everything clearly brought out the fact that all Catholics are of one mind and of one heart in their veneration for the Apostolic See. And this was all the more pleasing and agreeable to Us, that it is entirely in conformity with Our intent and with Our endeavors. For, indeed, well acquainted with Our times, and mindful of the duties of Our Ministry, We have constantly sought during the whole course of Our Pontificate and striven, as far as it was possible, by teaching and action, to bind every Nation and people more closely to Us, and make manifest everywhere the salutary influence of the See of Rome. Therefore, do We most earnestly offer thanks in the first place to the goodness of God, by whose help and bounty We have been preserved to attain Our great age; and then, next, to all the Princes and Rulers, to the Bishops and Clergy, and to as many as have co-operated by such repeated tokens of Piety and Reverence to Honor Our Character and Office, while affording Us personally such seasonable consolation.

A great deal, however, has been wanting to the entire fullness of that consolation. Amidst these very manifestations of public joy and Reverence Our thoughts went out towards the immense multitude of those who are strangers to the gladness that filled all Catholic hearts: some because they lie in absolute ignorance of the Gospel; others because they dissent from the Catholic belief, though they bear the name of Christians.

This thought has been, and is, a source of deep concern to Us; for it is impossible to think of such a large portion of mankind deviating, as it were, from the right path, as they move away from Us, and not experience a sentiment of innermost grief.

But since We hold upon this earth the place of God Almighty, Who will have all men to be saved and to come to the knowledge of the Truth, and now that Our advanced age and the bitterness of anxious cares urge Us on towards the end common to every mortal, We feel drawn to follow the example of Our Redeemer and Master, Jesus Christ, Who, when about to return to Heaven, implored of God, His Father, in earnest Prayer, that His Disciples and followers should be of one mind and of one heart: I pray . . . that they all may be one, as Thou Father in Me, and I in Thee: that they also may be one in Us. And as this Divine Prayer and Supplication does not include only the souls who then believed in Jesus Christ, but also every one of those who were henceforth to believe in Him, this Prayer holds out to Us no indifferent reason for confidently expressing Our hopes, and for making all possible endeavors in order that the men of every race and clime should be called and moved to embrace the Unity of Divine Faith.

Pressed on to Our intent by Charity, that hastens fastest there where the need is greatest, We direct Our first thoughts to those most unfortunate of all nations who have never received the light of the Gospel, or who, after having possessed it, have lost it through neglect or the vicissitudes of time: Hence do they ignore God, and live in the depths of error. Now, as all salvation comes from Jesus Christ–for there is no other Name under Heaven given to men whereby we must be saved–Our ardent desire is that the most Holy Name of Jesus should rapidly pervade and fill every land.

And here, indeed, is a duty which the Church, faithful to the Divine Mission entrusted to her, has never neglected. What has been the object of her labors for more than nineteen centuries? Is there any other work she has undertaken with greater zeal and constancy than that of bringing the nations of the earth to the Truth and Principles of Christianity? Today, as ever, by Our Authority, the Heralds of the Gospel constantly cross the seas to reach the farthest corners of the earth; and We Pray God daily that in His goodness He may deign to increase the number of His Ministers who are really worthy of this Apostolate, and who are ready to Sacrifice their convenience, their health, and their very life, if need be, in order to extend the frontiers of the Kingdom of Christ.

Do Thou, above all, O Savior and Father of mankind, Christ Jesus, hasten and do not delay to bring about what Thou didst once promise to do–that when lifted up from the earth Thou wouldst draw all things to Thyself. Come, then, at last, and manifest Thyself to the immense multitude of souls who have not felt, as yet, the ineffable Blessings which Thou hast earned for men with Thy Blood; rouse those who are sitting in darkness and in the shadow of death, that, enlightened by the rays of Thy Wisdom and Virtue, in Thee and by Thee "they may be made perfect in one."

As We consider the Mystery of this Unity We see before Us all the countries which have long since passed, by the

Mercy of God, from timeworn error to the wisdom of the Gospel. Nor could We, indeed, recall anything more pleasing or better calculated to extol the work of Divine Providence that the memory of the days of yore, when the Faith that had come down from Heaven was looked upon as the common inheritance of one and all; when civilized nations, separated by distance, character and habits, in spite of frequent disagreements and warfare on other points, were united by Christian Faith in all that concerned Religion. The recollection of that time causes Us to regret all the more deeply that as the ages rolled by the waves of suspicion and hatred arose, and great and flourishing nations were dragged away, in an evil hour, from the bosom of the Roman Church. In spite of that, however, We trust in the Mercy of God's Almighty Power, in Him Who alone can fix the hour of His benefits and Who has Power to incline man's will as He pleases; and We turn to those same nations, exhorting and beseeching them with Fatherly love to put an end to their dissensions and return again to Unity.

First of all, then, We cast an affectionate look upon the East, from whence in the beginning came forth the salvation of the world. Yes, and the yearning desire of Our heart bids us conceive and hope that the day is not far distant when the Eastern Churches, so illustrious in their ancient faith and glorious past, will return to the fold they have abandoned. We hope it all the more, that the distance separating them from Us is not so great: nay, with some few exceptions, we agree so entirely on other heads that, in defense of the Catholic Faith, we often have recourse to reasons and testimony borrowed from the teaching, the Rites, and Customs of the East.

The Principal subject of contention is the Primacy of the Roman Pontiff. But let them look back to the early years of their existence, let them consider the sentiments entertained by their forefathers, and examine what the oldest Traditions testify, and it will, indeed, become evident to them that Christ's Divine Utterance, Thou art Peter, and upon this rock I will build My Church, has undoubtedly been realized in the Roman Pontiffs. Many of these latter in the first gates of the Church were chosen from the East, and foremost among them

Anacletus, Evaristus, Anicetus, Eleutherius, Zosimus, and Agatho; and of these a great number, after Governing the Church in Wisdom and Sanctity, Consecrated their Ministry with the shedding of their blood. The time, the reasons, the promoters of the unfortunate division, are well known. Before the day when man separated what God had joined together, the name of the Apostolic See was held in Reverence by all the nations of the Christian world: and the East, like the West, agreed without hesitation in its obedience to the Pontiff of Rome, as the Legitimate Successor of St. Peter, and, therefore, the Vicar of Christ here on earth.

And, accordingly, if we refer to the beginning of the dissension, we shall see that Photius himself was careful to send his advocates to Rome on the matters that concerned him; and Pope Nicholas I sent his Legates to Constantinople from the Eternal City, without the slightest opposition, "in order to examine the case of Ignatius the Patriarch with all diligence, and to bring back to the Apostolic See a full and accurate report"; so that the history of the whole negotiation is a manifest Confirmation of the Primacy of the Roman See with which the dissension then began. Finally, in two great Councils, the second of Lyons and that of Florence, Latins and Greeks, as is notorious, easily agreed, and all unanimously proclaimed as Dogma the Supreme Power of the Roman Pontiffs.

We have recalled those things intentionally, for they constitute an invitation to peace and reconciliation; and with all the more reason that in Our own days it would seem as if there were a more conciliatory spirit towards Catholics on the part of the Eastern Churches, and even some degree of kindly feeling. To mention an instance, those sentiments were lately made manifest when some of Our faithful travelled to the East on a Holy Enterprise, and received so many proofs of courtesy and good-will.

Therefore, Our mouth is open to you, to you all of Greek or other Oriental Rites who are separated from the Catholic Church, We earnestly desire that each and every one of you should meditate upon the words, so full of gravity and love, addressed by Bessarion to your forefathers: "What answer shall we give to God when He comes to ask why we have separated from our Brethren: to Him Who, to unite us and bring us into One Fold, came down from Heaven, was Incarnate, and was Crucified? What will our defense be in the eyes of posterity? Oh, my Venerable Fathers, we must not suffer this to be, we must not entertain this thought, we must not thus so ill provide for ourselves and for our Brethren."

Weigh carefully in your minds and before God the nature of Our request. It is not for any human motive, but impelled by Divine Charity and a desire for the salvation of all, that We advise the reconciliation and union with the Church of Rome; and We mean a perfect and complete union, such as could not subsist in any way if nothing else was brought about but a certain kind of agreement in the Tenets of Belief and an intercourse of Fraternal love. The True Union between Christians is that which Jesus Christ, the Author of the Church, instituted and desired, and which consists in a Unity of Faith and Unity of Government.

Nor is there any reason for you to fear on that account that We or any of Our Successors will ever diminish your rights, the privileges of your Patriarchs, or the established Ritual of any one of your Churches. It has been and always will be the intent and Tradition of the Apostolic See, to make a large allowance, in all that is right and good, for the primitive Traditions and special customs of every nation. On the contrary, if you re-establish Union with Us, you will see how, by God's bounty, the glory and dignity of your Churches will be remarkably increased. May God, then, in His goodness, hear the Prayer that you yourselves address to Him: "Make the schisms of the Churches cease," and "Assemble those who are dispersed, bring back those who err, and unite them to Thy Holy Catholic and Apostolic Church." May you thus return to that one Holy Faith which has been handed down both to Us and to you from time immemorial; which your forefathers preserved untainted, and which was enhanced by the rival splendor of the Virtues, the great genius, and the sublime learning of St. Athanasius and St. Basil, St. Gregory of Nazianzum and St. John Chrysostom, the two Saints who bore the name of Cyril, and so many other great men whose glory belongs as a common inheritance to the East and to the West.

Suffer that We should address you more particularly, nations of the Slavonic race, you whose glorious name and deeds are attested by many an ancient record. You know full well how much the Slavs are indebted to the merits of St. Cyril and St. Methodius, to whose memory We Ourselves have rendered due honor only a few years ago. Their virtues and their labors were to great numbers of your race the source of civilization and salvation. And hence the admirable interchange, which existed for so long between the Slavonic nations and the Pontiffs of Rome, of favors on the one side and of filial devotion on the other. If in unhappy times many of your forefathers were separated from the Faith of Rome, consider now what priceless benefits a return of Unity would bring to you. The Church is anxious to welcome you also to her arms, that she may give you manifold aids to salvation, prosperity, and grandeur.

With no less affection do We now look upon the nations who, at a more recent date, were separated from the Roman Church by an extraordinary revolution of things and circumstances. Let them forget the various events of times gone by, let them raise their thoughts far above all that is human, and seeking only truth and salvation, reflect within their hearts upon the Church as it was constituted by Christ. If they will but compare that Church with their own communions, and consider what the actual state of Religion is in these, they will easily acknowledge that, forgetful of their early history, they have drifted away, on many and important points, into the novelty of various errors; nor will they deny that of what may be called the Patrimony of Truth, which the authors of those innovations carried away with them in their desertion, there now scarcely remains to them any article of belief that is really certain and supported by Authority.

Nay, more, things have already come to such a pass that many do not even hesitate to root up the very Foundation upon which alone rests all Religion, and the hope of men, to wit, the Divine Nature of Jesus Christ, Our Savior. And again, whereas formerly they used to assert that the books of the Old and the New Testament were written under the inspiration of God, they now deny them that Authority; this, indeed, was an inevitable consequence when they granted to all the right of private interpretation. Hence, too, the acceptance of individual conscience as the sole guide and rule of conduct to the exclusion of any other: hence those conflicting opinions and numerous sects that fall away so often into the doctrines of Naturalism and Rationalism.

Therefore it is, that having lost all hope of an agreement in their persuasions, they now proclaim and recommend a union of brotherly love. And rightly, too, no doubt, for we should all be united by the bond of mutual Charity. Our Lord Jesus Christ enjoined it most emphatically, and wished that this love of one another should be the mark of His Disciples. But how can hearts be united in perfect Charity where minds do not agree in Faith?

It is on this account that many of those We allude to men of sound judgment and seeking after Truth, have looked to the Catholic Church for the sure way of salvation; for they clearly understand that they could never be united to Jesus Christ, as their Head if they were not members of His Body, which is the Church; nor really acquire the True Christian Faith if they rejected the Legitimate teaching confided to Peter and his Successors. Such men as these have recognized in the Church of Rome the Form and Image of the True Church, which is clearly made manifest by the Marks that God, her Author, placed upon her: and not a few who were possessed with penetrating judgment and a special talent for historical research, have shown forth in their remarkable writings the uninterrupted succession of the Church. of Rome from the Apostles, the integrity of her Doctrine, and the consistency of her Rule and Discipline.

With the example of such men before you, Our heart appeals to you even more than Our words: to you, Our Brethren, who for three centuries and more differ from Us on Christian Faith; and to you all likewise, who in later times, for any reason whatsoever, have turned away from Us: Let us all meet in the Unity of Faith and of the Knowledge of the Son of God. Suffer that We should invite you to the Unity which has ever existed in the Catholic Church and can never fail; suffer that We should lovingly hold out Our hand to you. The Church, as the common mother of all, has long been calling you back to her; the Catholics of the world await you with brotherly love, that you may render Holy Worship to God together with us, united in perfect Charity Worship to God together with us, united in perfect charity by the profession of one Gospel, One Faith and One Hope.

To complete the harmony of this most desired unity, it remains for Us to address all those throughout the world whose salvation has long been the object of Our thoughts and watchful cares; We mean Catholics, whom the profession of the Roman Faith, while it renders them obedient to the Apostolic See, preserves in Union with Jesus Christ. There is no need to exhort them to True and Holy Unity, since through the Divine Goodness they already possess it; nevertheless, they must be admonished, lest under pressure of the growing perils on all sides around them, through negligence or indolence they should lose this great Blessing of God. For this purpose, let them take this Rule of thought and action, as the occasion may require, from those instructions which at other times We have addressed to Catholic people, either collectively or individually; and above all, let them lay down for themselves as a Supreme Law, to yield obedience in all things to the teaching and Authority of the Church, in no narrow or mistrustful spirit, but with their whole soul and promptitude of will.

On this account let them consider how injurious to Christian Unity is that error, which in various forms of opinion has oft-times obscured, nay, even destroyed the True Character and idea of the Church. For by the Will and Ordinance of God, its Founder, it is a Society perfect in its kind, whose Office and Mission it is to school mankind in the Precepts and Teachings of the Gospel, and by safeguarding the integrity of Morals and the exercise of Christian Virtue, to lead men to that happiness which is held out to every one in Heaven. And since it is, as we have said, a perfect Society, therefore it is endowed with a living Power and efficacy which is not derived from any external source, but in virtue of the Ordinance of God and its own Constitution, inherent in its very nature; for the same reason it has an inborn Power of making Laws, and Justice requires that in its exercise it should be dependent on no one; it must likewise have

Praeclara Gratulationis Publicae

freedom in other matters appertaining to its rights.

But this freedom is not of a kind to occasion rivalry or envy, for the Church does not covet Power, nor is she urged on by any selfish desire; but this one thing she does wish, this only does she seek, to preserve amongst men the duties which Virtue imposes, and by this means and in this way to provide for their everlasting welfare. Therefore is she wont to be yielding and indulgent as a mother; yes, it not infrequently happens that in making large concessions to the exigencies of States, she refrains from the exercise of her own rights, as the compacts often concluded with civil governments abundantly testify.

Nothing is more foreign to her disposition than to encroach on the rights of civil power; but the civil power in its turn must respect the rights of the Church, and beware of arrogating them in any degree to itself. Now, what is the ruling spirit of the times when actual events and circumstances are taken into account? No other than this: it has been the fashion to regard the Church with suspicion, to despise and hate and spitefully calumniate her; and, more intolerable still, men strive with might and main to bring her under the sway of civil governments. Hence it is that her property has been plundered and her liberty curtailed: hence again, that the training of her Priesthood has been beset with difficulties; that laws of exceptional rigor have been passed against her Clergy; that Religious Orders, those excellent safeguards of Christianity, have been suppressed and placed under a ban; in a word, the principles and practice of the regalists have been renewed with increased virulence.

Such a policy is a violation of the most Sacred Rights of the Church, and it breeds enormous evils to States, for the very reason that it is in open conflict with the Purposes of God. When God, in His most Wise Providence, placed over human society both temporal and Spiritual Authority, He intended them to remain distinct indeed, but by no means disconnected and at war with each other. On the contrary, both the Will of God and the common weal of human society imperatively require that the civil power should be in accord with the Ecclesiastical in its Rule and Administration.

Hence the State has its own peculiar rights and duties,

the Church likewise has hers; but it is necessary that each should be united with the other in the bonds of concord. Thus will it come about that the close mutual relations of Church and State will be freed from the present turmoil, which for manifold reasons is ill-advised and most distressing to all well-disposed persons; furthermore, it will be brought to pass that, without confusion or separation of the peculiar interests of each, the people will render to Caesar the things that are Caesar's, and to God the things that are God's.

There is likewise a great danger threatening unity on the part of that association which goes by the name of Freemasons, whose fatal influence for a long time past oppresses Catholic nations in particular. Favored by the agitations of the times, and waxing insolent in its power and resources and success, it strains every nerve to consolidate its sway and enlarge its sphere. It has already sallied forth from its hiding-places, where it hatched its plots, into the throng of cities, and as if to defy the Almighty, has set up its throne in this very city of Rome, the Capital of the Catholic world. But what is most disastrous is, that wherever it has set its foot it penetrates into all ranks and departments of the commonwealth, in the hope of obtaining at last supreme control. This is, indeed, a great calamity: for its depraved principles and iniquitous designs are well known. Under the pretence of vindicating the rights of man and of reconstituting society, it attacks Christianity; it rejects revealed Doctrine, denounces practices of Piety, the Divine Sacraments, and every Sacred thing as superstition; it strives to eliminate the Christian Character from Marriage and the family and the education of youth, and from every form of instruction, whether public or private, and to root out from the minds of men all respect for Authority, whether human or Divine. On its own part, it preaches the worship of nature, and maintains that by the principles of nature are truth and probity and justice to be measured and regulated. In this way, as is quite evident, man is being driven to adopt customs and habits of life akin to those of the heathen, only more corrupt in proportion as the incentives to sin are more numerous.

Although We have spoken on this subject in the strongest terms before, yet We are led by Our Apostolic watchfulness to urge it once more, and We repeat Our warning again and again, that in face of such an eminent peril, no precaution, howsoever great, can be looked upon as sufficient. May God in His Mercy bring to naught their impious designs; nevertheless, let all Christians know and understand that the shameful yoke of Freemasonry must be shaken off once and for all; and let them be the first to shake it off who are most galled by its oppression–the men of Italy and of France. With what weapons and by what method this may best be done We Ourselves have already pointed out: the victory cannot be doubtful to those who trust in that Leader Whose Divine Words still remain in all their force: I have overcome the world.

Were this twofold danger averted, and government and States restored to the Unity of Faith, it is wonderful what efficacious remedies for evils and abundant store of benefits would ensue. We will touch upon the principal ones.

The first regards the Dignity and Office of the Church. She would receive that Honor which is her due and she would go on her way, free from envy and strong in her liberty, as the Minister of Gospel Truth and Grace to the notable welfare of States. For as she has been given by God as a Teacher and Guide to the human race, she can contribute assistance which is peculiarly adapted to direct even the most radical transformations of time to the common good, to solve the most complicated questions, and to promote uprightness and justice, which are the most solid foundations of the commonwealth.

Moreover there would be a marked increase of union among the nations, a thing most desirable to ward off the horrors of war.

We behold the condition of Europe. For many years past peace has been rather an appearance than a realty. Possessed with mutual suspicions, almost all the nations are vying with one another in equipping themselves with military armaments. Inexperienced youths are removed from paternal direction and control, to be thrown amid the dangers of the soldier's life; robust young men are taken from agriculture or ennobling studies or trade of the arts to be put under arms. Hence the treasures of States are exhausted by the enormous expenditure, the national resources are frittered away, and private fortunes impaired; and this, as it were, armed peace, which now prevails, cannot last much longer. Can this be the normal condition of human society? Yet we cannot escape from this situation, and obtain True Peace, except by the aid of Jesus Christ. For to repress ambition and covetousness and envy–the chief instigators of war–nothing is more fitted than the Christian Virtues and, in particular, the Virtue of Justice; for, by its exercise, both the law of nations and the faith of treaties may be maintained inviolate, and the bonds of brotherhood continue unbroken, if men are but convinced that Justice exalteth a nation.

As in its external relations, so in the internal life of the State itself, the Christian Virtues will provide a guarantee of the commonweal much more sure and stronger far than any which laws or armies can afford. For there is no one who does not see that the dangers to public security and order are daily on the increase, since seditious societies continue to conspire for the overthrow and ruin of States, as the frequency of their atrocious outrages testifies.

There are two questions, forsooth–the one called the social, and the other the political question–which are discussed with the greatest vehemence. Both of them, without doubt, are of the last importance, and, though praiseworthy efforts have been put forth, in studies and measures and experiments for their wise and just solution, yet nothing could contribute more to this purpose than that the minds of men in general should be imbued with right sentiments of duty from the internal principle of Christian Faith. We treated expressly of the social question in this sense a short time ago, from the standpoint of principles drawn from the Gospel and natural reason.

As regards the political question, which aims at reconciling liberty with Authority–two things which many confound in theory, and separate too widely in practice–most efficient aid may be derived from the Christian Philosophy. For, when this point has been settled and recognized by common agreement, that, whatsoever the form of government, the Authority is from God, reason at once perceives that in some there is a Legitimate right to command, in others the corresponding duty to obey, and that without prejudice to their dignity, since obedience is rendered to God rather than to man; and God has denounced the most rigorous judgment against those in Authority, if they fail to represent Him with uprightness and justice. Then the liberty of the individual can afford ground of suspicion or envy to no one; since, without injury to any, his conduct will be guided by Truth and rectitude and whatever is allied to public order. Lastly, if it be considered what influence is possessed by the Church, the mother of and peacemaker between rulers and peoples, whose mission it is to help them both with her Authority and Counsel, then it will be most manifest how much it concerns the commonweal that all nations should resolve to unite in the same belief and the same profession of the Christian Faith.

With these thoughts in Our mind and ancient yearnings in Our heart, We see from afar what would be the new order of things that would arise upon the earth, and nothing could be sweeter to Us than the contemplation of the benefits that would flow from it. It can hardly be imagined what immediate and rapid progress would be made all over the earth, in all manner of greatness and prosperity, with the establishment of tranquility and peace, the promotion of studies, the founding and the multiplying on Christian lines according to Our directions, of associations for the cultivators of soil, for workmen and tradesmen, through whose agency rapacious usury would be put down, and a large field opened up for useful labors.

And these abundant benefits would not be confined within the limits of civilized nations, but, like an overcharged river, would flow far and wide. It must be remembered, as we observed at the outset, that an immense number of races have been waiting, all through the long ages, to receive the light of Truth and civilization. Most certainly, the counsels of God with regard to the eternal salvation of peoples are far removed above the understanding of man; yet if miserable superstition still prevails in so many parts of the world, the blame must be attributed in no small measure to Religious dissensions. For, as far as it is given to human reason to judge from the nature of events, this seems without doubt to be the mission assigned by God to Europe, to go on by degrees carrying Christian civilization to every portion of the earth. The beginnings and first growth of this great work, which sprang from the labors of former centuries, were rapidly receiving large development, when all of a sudden the discord of the sixteenth century broke out. Christendom was torn with quarrels and dissensions, Europe exhausted with contests and wars, and the Sacred Mission felt the baneful influence of the times. While the causes of dissension still remain, what wonder is it that so large a portion of mankind is held enthralled with barbarous customs and insane rites?

Let us one and all, then, for the sake of the common welfare, labor with equal assiduity to restore the ancient concord. In order to bring about this concord, and spread abroad the benefits of the Christian Revelation, the present is the most seasonable time; for never before have the sentiments of human brotherhood penetrated so deeply into the souls of men, and never in any age has man been seen to seek out his fellowmen more eagerly in order to know them better and to help them. Immense tracts of land and sea are traversed with incredible rapidity, and thus extraordinary advantages are afforded not only for commerce and scientific investigations but also for the propagation of the Word of God from the rising of the sun to the going down of the same.

We are well aware of the long labors involved in the restoration of that order of things which We desire; and it may be that there are those who consider that We are far too sanguine and look for things that are rather to be wished for than expected. But we unhesitatingly place all Our hope and confidence in the Savior of mankind, Jesus Christ, well remembering what great things have been achieved in times past by the folly of the Cross and its preaching, to the astonishment and confusion of the wisdom of the world. We beg of Princes and Rulers of States, appealing to their statesmanship and earnest solicitude for the people, to weigh Our Counsels in the balance of Truth and second them with their Authority and favor. If only a portion of the looked-for results should come about, it will cause no inconsiderable boon in the general decadence, when the intolerable evils of the present day bring with them the dread of further evils in days to come.

The last years of the past century left Europe worn out with disasters and panic-stricken with the turmoils of revolution. And why should not our present century, which is now hastening to its close, by a reversion of circumstances bequeath to mankind the pledges of concord, with the prospects of the great benefits which are bound up in the Unity of the Christian Faith?

May God, Who is rich in Mercy, and in Whose Power are the times and moments, grant Our wishes and desires, and in His great Goodness, hasten the fulfillment of that Divine Promise of Jesus Christ: There will be One Fold and One Shepherd.

As a pledge of these Heavenly Gifts, and in witness of Our good will to you, Venerable Brothers, and to the Clergy and people committed to each of you, We most lovingly grant in the Lord the Apostolic Benediction.

✠

Annum Ingressi
Apostolic Letter of Pope Leo XIII
March 18, 1902

This letter reflects on Leo XIII's pontificate and reiterates concerns about secret societies for their role in promoting secularism and undermining Christian principles in public institutions. While not a major condemnation like Humanum Genus, *it maintains the Church's consistent opposition to Freemasonry.*

Venerable Brothers, Health and Apostolic Benediction.

HAVING come to the twenty-fifth year of our Apostolic Ministry, and being astonished ourselves at the length of the way which we have traveled amidst painful and continual cares, we are naturally inspired to lift our thoughts to the ever blessed God, who, with so many other favors, has deigned to accord us a Pontificate the length of which has scarcely been surpassed in history. To the Father of all mankind, therefore; to Him who holds in His hands the mysterious secret of life, ascends, as an imperious need of the heart, the canticle of our thanksgiving. Assuredly the eye of man cannot pierce all the depths of the designs of God in thus prolonging our old age beyond the limits of hope: here we can only be silent and adore. But there is one thing which we do well understand; namely, that as it has pleased Him, and still pleases Him, to preserve our existence, a great duty is incumbent on us — to live for the good and the development of His immaculate spouse, the holy Church; and far from losing courage in the midst of cares and pains, to consecrate to Him the remainder of our strength unto our last sigh.

After paying a just tribute of gratitude to our Heavenly Father, to whom be honor and glory for all eternity, it is most agreeable to us to turn our thoughts and address our words to you, Venerable Brothers, who, called by the Holy Ghost to govern the appointed portions of the flock of Jesus Christ,

Annum Ingressi

share thereby with us in the struggle and triumph, the sorrows and joys, of the ministry of pastors. No, they shall never fade from our memory, those frequent and striking testimonials of religious veneration which you have lavished upon us during the course of our Pontificate, and which you still multiply with emulation full of tenderness in the present circumstances. Intimately united with you already by our duty and our paternal love, we are more closely drawn by those proofs of your devotedness, so dear to our heart, less for what was personal in them in our regard than for the inviolable attachment which they denote to this Apostolic See, centre and mainstay of all the Sees of Catholicity. If it has always been necessary, that, according to the different grades of the ecclesiastical hierarchy, all the children of the Church should be sedulously united by the bonds of mutual charity and by the pursuit of the same objects, so as to form but one heart and one soul, this union is become in our day more indispensable than ever. For who can ignore the vast conspiracy of hostile forces which aims today at destroying and making disappear the great work of Jesus Christ, by endeavoring, with a fury which knows no limits, to rob man, in the intellectual order of the treasure of heavenly truth, and, in the social order, to obliterate the most holy, the most salutary Christian institutions. But by all this you yourselves are impressed every day. You who, more than once, have poured out to us your anxieties and anguish, deploring the multitude of prejudices, the false systems and errors which are disseminated with impunity amongst the masses of the people. What snares are set on every side for the souls of those who believe! What obstacles are multiplied to weaken, and if possible to destroy the beneficent action of the Church! And, meanwhile, as if to add derision to injustice, the Church herself is charged with having lost her pristine vigor, and with being powerless to stem the tide of overflowing passions which threaten to carry everything away.

We would wish, Venerable Brothers, to entertain you with subjects less sad, and more in harmony with the great and auspicious occasion which induces us to address you. But nothing suggests such tenor of discourse — neither the grievous trials of the Church which call with insistence for prompt remedies; nor the conditions of contemporary society which, already undermined from a moral and material point of view, tend toward a yet more gloomy future by the abandonment of the great Christian traditions; a law of Providence, confirmed by history, proving that the great religious principles cannot be renounced without shaking at the same time the foundations of order and social prosperity. In those circumstances, in order to allow souls to recover, to furnish them with a new provision of faith and courage, it appears to us opportune and useful to weigh attentively, in its origin, causes and various forms, the implacable war that is waged against the Church; and in denouncing its pernicious consequences to indicate a remedy. May our words, therefore, resound loudly, though they but recall truths already asserted; may they be hearkened to, not only by the children of Catholic unity, but also by those who differ from us, and even by the unhappy souls who have no longer any faith; for they are all children of one Father, all destined for the same supreme good: may our words, finally, be received as the testament which, at the short distance that separates us from eternity, we would wish to leave to the people as a presage of the salvation which we desire for all.

During the whole course of her history the Church of Christ has had to combat and suffer for truth and justice. Instituted by the Divine Redeemer Himself to establish throughout the world the Kingdom of God, she must, by the light of the Gospel law, lead fallen humanity to its immortal destinies; that is, to make it enter upon the possession of the blessings without end which God has promised us, and to which our unaided natural power could never rise — a heavenly mission, in the pursuit of which the Church could not fail to be opposed by the countless passions begotten of man's primal fall and consequent corruption — pride, cupidity, unbridled desire of material pleasures: against all the vices and disorders springing from those poisonous roots the Church has ever been the most potent means of restraint. Nor should we be astonished at the persecutions which have arisen, in consequence, since the Divine Master foretold them; and they must continue as long as this world endures. What words did He address to His disciples when sending them to carry the treasure of His doctrines to all nations? They are familiar to us all: "You will be persecuted from city to city: you will be hated and despised for My Name's sake: you will be dragged before the tribunals and condemned to extreme punishment." And wishing to encourage them for the hour of trial, He proposed Himself as their example: "If the world hate you, know ye that it hath hated Me before you." (St. John xv., 18.)

Certainly, no one, who takes a just and unbiased view of things, can explain the motive of this hatred. What offense was ever committed, what hostility deserved by the Divine Redeemer? Having come down amongst men through an impulse of Divine charity, He had taught a doctrine that was blameless, consoling, most efficacious to unite mankind in a brotherhood of peace and love; He had coveted neither earthly greatness nor honor; He had usurped no one's right; on the contrary, He was full of pity for the weak, the sick, the poor, the sinner and the oppressed: hence His life was but a passage to distribute with munificent hand His benefits amongst men. We must acknowledge, in consequence, that it was simply by an excess of human malice, so much the more deplorable because unjust, that, nevertheless, He became, in truth, according to the prophecy of Simeon, "a sign to be contradicted."

What wonder, then, if the Catholic Church, which continues His Divine mission, and is the incorruptible depositary of His truths, has inherited the same lot? The world is always consistent in its way. Near the sons of God are constantly present the satellites of that great adversary of the human race, who, a rebel from the beginning against the Most High, is named in the Gospel the prince of this world. It is on this account that the spirit of the world, in the presence of the law and of him who announces it in the name of God, swells with the measureless pride of an independence that ill befits it. Alas, how often, in more stormy epochs, with unheard-of cruelty and shameless injustice, and to the evident undoing of the whole social body, have the adversaries banded themselves together for the foolhardy enterprise of dissolving the work of God! And not succeeding with one manner of persecution, they adopted others. For three long centuries the Roman Empire, abusing its brute force, scattered the bodies of martyrs through all its provinces, and bathed with their blood every foot of ground in this sacred city of Rome; while heresy, acting in concert, whether hidden beneath a mask or with open effrontery, with sophistry and snare, endeavored to destroy at least the harmony and unity of faith. Then were set loose, like a devastating tempest, the hordes of barbarians from the north, and the Moslems from the south, leaving in their wake only ruins in a desert. So has been transmitted from age to age the melancholy heritage of hatred by which the Spouse of Christ has been overwhelmed. There followed a Cæsarism as suspicious as powerful, jealous of all other power, no matter what development it might itself have thence acquired, which incessantly attacked the Church, to usurp her rights and tread her liberties under foot. The heart bleeds to see this mother so often oppressed with anguish and woes unutterable. However, triumphing over every obstacle, over all violence and all tyrannies, she pitched her peaceful tents more and more widely; she saved from disaster the glorious patrimony of arts, history, science and letters; and imbuing deeply the whole body of society with the spirit of the Gospel, she created Christian civilization — that civilization to which the nations, subjected to its beneficent influence, owe the equity of their laws, the mildness of their manners, the protection of the weak, pity for the afflicted and the poor, respect for the rights and dignity of all men, and, thereby, as far as it is possible amidst the fluctuations of human affairs, that calm of social life which springs from the just and prudent alliance between justice and liberty.

Those proofs of the intrinsic excellence of the Church are as striking and sublime as they have been enduring. Nevertheless, as in the Middle Ages and during the first centuries, so in those nearer our own, we see the Church assailed more harshly, in a certain sense at least, and more distressingly than ever. Through a series of well-known historical causes, the pretended Reformation of the sixteenth century raised the standard of revolt; and, determining to strike straight into the heart of the Church, audaciously attacked the Papacy. It broke the precious link of the ancient unity of faith and authority, which, multiplying a hundredfold, power, prestige and glory, thanks to the harmonious pursuit of the same objects, united all nations under one staff and one shepherd. This unity being broken, a pernicious principle of disintegration was introduced amongst all ranks of Christians.

We do not, indeed, hereby pretend to affirm that from the beginning there was a set purpose of destroying the principle of Christianity in the heart of society; but by refusing, on the one hand, to acknowledge the supremacy of the Holy See, the effective cause and bond of unity, and by proclaiming, on the other, the principle of private judgment, the divine structure of faith was shaken to its deepest foundations and the way was opened to infinite variations, to doubts and denials of the most important things, to an extent which the innovators themselves had not foreseen. The way was opened. Then came the contemptuous and mocking philosophism of the eighteenth century, which advanced farther. It turned to ridicule the sacred canon of the Scriptures and rejected the entire system of revealed truths, with the purpose of being able ultimately to root out from the conscience of the people all religious belief and stifling within it the last breath of the spirit of Christianity. It is from this source that have flowed rationalism, pantheism, naturalism and materialism — poisonous and destructive systems which, under different appearances, renew the ancient errors triumphantly refuted by the Fathers and Doctors of the Church; so that the pride of modern times, by excessive confidence in its own lights, was stricken with blindness; and, like paganism, subsisted thenceforth on fancies, even concerning the attributes of the human soul and the immortal destinies which constitute our glorious heritage.

The struggle against the Church thus took on a more serious character than in the past, no less because of the vehemence of the assault than because of its universality. Contemporary unbelief does not confine itself to denying or doubting articles of faith. What it combats is the whole body of principles which sacred revelation and sound philosophy maintain; those fundamental and holy principles which teach man the supreme object of his earthly life, which keep him in the performance of his duty, which inspire his heart with courage and resignation, and which in promising him incorruptible justice and perfect happiness beyond the tomb, enable him to subject time to eternity, earth to heaven. But what takes the place of these principles which form the incomparable strength bestowed by faith? A frightful skepticism, which chills the heart and stifles in the conscience every magnanimous aspiration.

This system of practical atheism must necessarily cause, as in point of fact it does, a profound disorder in the domain of morals, for, as the greatest philosophers of antiquity have declared, religion is the chief foundation of justice and virtue. When the bonds are broken which unite man to God, who is the Sovereign Legislator and Universal Judge, a mere phantom of morality remains; a morality which is purely civic and, as it is termed, independent, which, abstracting from the Eternal Mind and the laws of God descends inevitably till it reaches the ultimate conclusion of making man a law unto himself. Incapable, in consequence, of rising on the wings of Christian hope to the goods of the world beyond, man will seek a material satisfaction in the comforts and enjoyments of life. There will be excited in him a thirst for pleasure, a desire of riches and an eager quest of rapid and unlimited wealth, even at the cost of justice. There will be enkindled in him every ambition and a feverish and frenzied desire to gratify them even in defiance of law, and he will be swayed by a contempt for right and for public authority, as well as by licentiousness of life which, when the condition becomes general, will mark the real decay of society.

Perhaps we may be accused of exaggerating the sad consequences of the disorders of which we speak. No; for the reality is before our eyes and warrants but too truly our forebodings. It is manifest that if there is not some betterment soon, the bases of society will crumble and drag down with them the great and eternal principles of law and morality.

It is in consequence of this condition of things that the social body, beginning with the family, is suffering such serious evils. For the lay State, forgetting its limitations and the essential object of the authority which it wields, has laid its hands on the marriage bond to profane it and has stripped it of its religious character; it has dared as much as it could in the matter of that natural right which parents possess to educate their children, and in many countries it has destroyed the stability of marriage by giving a legal sanction to the licentious institution of divorce. All know the result of these attacks. More than words can tell they have multiplied marriages which are prompted only by shameful passions, which are speedily dissolved and which, at times, bring about bloody tragedies, at others the most shocking infidelities. We say nothing of the innocent offspring of these unions, the children who are abandoned or whose morals are corrupted on one side by the bad example of the parents, on the other by the poison which the officially lay State constantly pours into their hearts.

Along with the family, the political and social order is also endangered by doctrines which ascribe a false origin to authority, and which have corrupted the genuine conception of government. For if sovereign authority is derived formally from the consent of the people and not from God, who is the supreme and Eternal Principle of all power, it loses in the eyes of the governed its most august characteristic and degenerates into an artificial sovereignty which rests on unstable and shifting bases, namely, the will of those from whom it is said to be derived. Do we not see the consequences of this error in the carrying out of our laws? Too often these laws instead of being sound reason formulated in writing are but the expression of the power of the greater number and the will of the predominant political party. It is thus that the mob is cajoled in seeking to satisfy its desires; that a loose rein is given to popular passion, even when it disturbs the laboriously acquired tranquillity of the State, when the disorder in the last extremity can only be quelled by violent measures and the shedding of blood.

Consequent upon the repudiation of those Christian principles which had contributed so efficaciously to unite the nations in the bonds of brotherhood, and to bring all humanity into one great family, there has arisen little by little in the international order, a system of jealous egoism, in consequence of which the nations now watch each other, if not with hate, at least with the suspicion of rivals. Hence, in their great undertakings they lose sight of the lofty principles of morality and justice and forget the protection which the feeble and the oppressed have a right to demand. In the desire by which they are actuated to increase their national riches, they regard only the opportunity which circumstances afford, the advantages of successful enterprises and the tempting bait of an accomplished fact, sure that no one will trouble them in the name of right or the respect which right can claim. Such are the fatal principles which have consecrated material power as the supreme law of the world and to them is to be imputed the limitless increase of military establishments, and that armed peace, which in many respects, is equivalent to a disastrous war.

This lamentable confusion in the realm of ideas has produced restlessness among the people, outbreaks and the general spirit of rebellion. From these have sprung the frequent popular agitations and disorders of our times which are only the preludes of much more terrible disorders in the future. The miserable condition, also, of a large part of the poorer classes, who assuredly merit our assistance, furnishes an admirable opportunity for the designs of scheming agitators, and especially of socialist factions, which hold out to the humbler classes the most extravagant promises and use them to carry out the most dreadful projects.

Those who start on a dangerous descent are soon hurled down in spite of themselves into the abyss. Prompted by an inexorable logic, a society of veritable criminals has been organized, which, at its very first appearance, has, by its savage character, startled the world. Thanks to the solidarity of its construction and its international ramifications, it has already attempted its wicked work, for it stands in fear of nothing and recoils before no danger. Repudiating all union with society, and cynically scoffing at law, religion and morality, its adepts have adopted the name of Anarchists, and propose to utterly subvert the actual conditions of society by making use of every means that a blind and savage passion can suggest. And as society draws its unity and its life from the authority which governs it, so it is against authority that anarchy directs its efforts. Who does not feel a thrill of horror, indignation and pity at the remembrance of the many victims that of late have fallen beneath its blows, Emperors, Empresses, Kings, Presidents of powerful republics, whose only crime was the sovereign power with which they were invested?

In presence of the immensity of the evils which overwhelm society and the perils which menace it, our duty compels us to again warn all men of good will, especially those who occupy exalted positions, and to conjure them as we now do, to devise what remedies the situation calls for and with prudent energy to apply them without delay.

First of all, it behooves them to inquire what remedies are needed, and to examine well their potency in the present needs. We have extolled liberty and its advantages to the skies, and have proclaimed it as a sovereign remedy and an incomparable instrument of peace and prosperity which will be most fruitful in good results. But facts have clearly shown us that it does not possess the power which is attributed to it. Economic conflicts, struggles of the classes are surging around us like a conflagration on all sides, and there is no promise of the dawn of the day of public tranquility. In point of fact, and there is no one who does not see it, liberty as it is now understood, that is to say, a liberty granted indiscriminately to truth and to error, to good and to evil, ends only in destroying all that is noble, generous and holy, and in opening the gates still wider to crime, to suicide and to a multitude of the most degrading passions.

The doctrine is also taught that the development of public instruction, by making the people more polished and more enlightened, would suffice as a check to unhealthy tendencies and to keep man in the ways of uprightness and probity. But a hard reality has made us feel every day more and more of how little avail is instruction without religion and morality. As a necessary consequence of inexperience, and of the promptings of bad passion, the mind of youth is enthralled by the perverse teachings of the day. It absorbs all the errors which an unbridled press does not hesitate to sow broadcast and which depraves the mind and the will of youth and foments in them that spirit of pride and insubordination which so often troubles the peace of families and cities.

So also was confidence reposed in the progress of

science. Indeed the century which has just closed has witnessed progress that was great, unexpected, stupendous. But is it true that it has given us all the fullness and healthfulness of fruitage that so many expected from it? Doubtless the discoveries of science have opened new horizons to the mind; it has widened the empire of man over the forces of matter and human life has been ameliorated in many ways through its instrumentality. Nevertheless, every one feels and many admit that the results have not corresponded to the hopes that were cherished. It cannot be denied, especially when we cast our eyes on the intellectual and moral status of the world as well as on the records of criminality, when we hear the dull murmurs which arise from the depths, or when we witness the predominance which might has won over right. Not to speak of the throngs who are a prey to every misery, a superficial glance at the condition of the world will suffice to convince us of the indefinable sorrow which weighs upon souls and the immense void which is in human hearts. Man may subject nature to his sway, but matter cannot give him what it has not, and to the questions which most deeply affect our gravest interests human science gives no reply. The thirst for truth, for good, for the infinite, which devours us, has not been slaked, nor have the joys and riches of earth, nor the increase of the comforts of life ever soothed the anguish which tortures the heart. Are we then to despise and fling aside the advantages which accrue from the study of science, from civilization and the wise and sweet use of our liberty? Assuredly not. On the contrary, we must hold them in the highest esteem, guard them and make them grow as a treasure of great price, for they are means which of their nature are good, designed by God Himself, and ordained by the Infinite Goodness and Wisdom for the use and advantage of the human race. But we must subordinate the use of them to the intentions of the Creator, and so employ them as never to eliminate the religious element in which their real advantage resides, for it is that which bestows on them a special value and renders them really fruitful. Such is the secret of the problem. When an organism perishes and corrupts, it is because it had ceased to be under the action of the causes which had given it its form and constitution. To make it healthy and flourishing again it is necessary to restore it to the vivifying action of those same causes. So society in its foolhardy effort to escape from God has rejected the divine order and revelation; and it is thus withdrawn from the salutary efficacy of Christianity which is manifestly the most solid guarantee of order, the strongest bond of fraternity and the inexhaustible source of public and private virtue.

This sacrilegious divorce has resulted in bringing about the trouble which now disturbs the world. Hence it is the pale of the Church which this lost society must reenter, if it wishes to recover its well-being, its repose and its salvation.

Just as Christianity cannot penetrate in the soul without making it better, so it cannot enter into public life without establishing order. With the idea of a God who governs all, who is infinitely wise, good and just, the idea of duty seizes upon the consciences of men. It assuages sorrow, it calms hatred, it engenders heroes. If it has transformed pagan society — and that transformation was a veritable resurrection — for barbarism disappeared in proportion as Christianity extended its sway, so, after the terrible shocks which unbelief has given to the world in our days, it will be able to put that world again on the true road, and bring back to order the states and peoples of modern times. But the return to Christianity will not be efficacious and complete if it does not restore the world to a sincere love of the one Holy Catholic and Apostolic Church. In the Catholic Church Christianity is incarnate. It identifies itself with that perfect, spiritual, and, in its own order, sovereign society, which is the mystical body of Jesus Christ and which has for its visible head the Roman Pontiff, successor of the Prince of the Apostles. It is the continuation of the mission of the Saviour, the daughter and the heiress of His redemption. It has preached the Gospel, and has defended it at the price of its blood, and strong in the Divine assistance, and of that immortality which have been promised it, it makes no terms with error, but remains faithful to the commands which it has received to carry the doctrine of Jesus Christ to the uttermost limits of the world and to the end of time and to protect it in its inviolable integrity. Legitimate dispensatrix of the teachings of the Gospel it does not reveal itself only as the consoler and redeemer of souls, but it is still more the internal source of justice and charity, and the propagator as well as the guardian of true liberty, and of that equality which alone is possible here below. In applying the doctrine of its Divine Founder, it maintains a wise equilibrium and marks the true limits between the rights and privileges of society. The equality which it proclaims does not destroy the distinction between the different social classes. It keeps them intact, as nature itself demands, in order to oppose the anarchy of reason emancipated from faith, and abandoned to its own devices. The liberty which it gives in no wise conflicts with the rights of truth, because those rights are superior to the demands of liberty. Nor does it infringe upon the rights of justice, because those rights are superior to the claims of mere numbers or power. Nor does it assail the rights of God because they are superior to the rights of humanity.

In the domestic circle, the Church is no less fruitful in good results. For not only does it oppose the nefarious machinations which incredulity resorts to in order to attack the life of the family, but it prepares and protects the union and stability of marriage, whose honor, fidelity and holiness it guards and develops. At the same time it sustains and cements the civil and political order by giving on one side most efficacious aid to authority, and on the other by showing itself favorable to the wise reforms and the just aspirations of the classes that are governed; by imposing respect for rulers and enjoining whatever obedience is due to them, and by defending unwaveringly the imprescriptible rights of the human conscience. And thus it is that the people who are subject to her influence have no fear of oppression because she checks in their efforts the rulers who seek to govern as tyrants.

Fully aware of this divine power, we, from the very beginning of our Pontificate, have endeavored to place in the clearest light the benevolent designs of the Church and to increase as far as possible, along with the treasures of her doctrine the field of her salutary action. Such has been the object of the principal acts of our Pontificate, notably in the Encyclicals on *Christian Philosophy*, on *Human Liberty*, on

Christian Marriage, on *Freemasonry*, on *The Powers of Government*, on *The Christian Constitution of States*, on *Socialism*, on the *Labor Question*, and the *Duties of Christian Citizens* and other analogous subjects. But the ardent desire of our soul has not been merely to illumine the mind. We have endeavored to move and to purify hearts by making use of all our powers to cause Christian virtue to flourish among the peoples. For that reason we have never ceased to bestow encouragement and counsel in order to elevate the minds of men to the goods of the world beyond; to enable them to subject the body to the soul; their earthly life to the heavenly one; man to God. Blessed by the Lord, our word has been able to increase and to strengthen the convictions of a great number of men; to throw light on their minds in the difficult questions of the day; to stimulate their zeal and to advance the various works which have been undertaken.

It is especially for the disinherited classes that these works have been inaugurated, and have continued to grow in every country, as is evident from the increase of Christian charity which has always found in the midst of the people its favorite field of action. If the harvest has not been more abundant, Venerable Brothers, let us adore God who is mysteriously just and beg Him, at the same time, to have pity on the blindness of so many souls, to whom unhappily the terrifying word of the Apostle may be addressed: "The god of this world has blinded the minds of unbelievers, that the light of the Gospel of the glory of Christ, who is the image of God, should not shine to them." II. Corinthians iv., 4.

The more the Catholic Church devotes itself to extend its zeal for the moral and material advancement of the peoples, the more the children of darkness arise in hatred against it and have recourse to every means in their power to tarnish its divine beauty and paralyze its action of life-giving reparation. How many false reasonings have they not made and how many calumnies have they not spread against it! Among their most perfidious devices is that which consists in repeating to the ignorant masses and to suspicious governments that the Church is opposed to the progress of science, that it is hostile to liberty, that the rights of the state are usurped by it and that politics is a field which it is constantly invading. Such are the mad accusations that have been a thousand times repudiated and a thousand times refuted by sound reason and by history and, in fact, by every man who has a heart for honesty and a mind for truth.

The Church the enemy of knowledge and instruction! Without doubt she is the vigilant guardian of revealed dogma, but it is this very vigilance which prompts her to protect science and to favor the wise cultivation of the mind. No! in submitting his mind to the revelation of the Word, who is the supreme truth from whom all truths must flow, man will in no wise contradict what reason discovers. On the contrary, the light which will come to him from the Divine Word will give more power and more clearness to the human intellect, because it will preserve it from a thousand uncertainties and errors. Besides, nineteen centuries of a glory achieved by Catholicism in all the branches of learning amply suffice to refute this calumny. It is to the Catholic Church that we must ascribe the merit of having propagated and defended Christian philosophy, without which the world would still be buried in the darkness of pagan superstitions and in the most abject barbarism. It has preserved and transmitted to all generations the precious treasure of literature and of the ancient sciences. It has opened the first schools for the people and crowded the universities which still exist, or whose glory is perpetuated even to our own days. It has inspired the loftiest, the purest and the most glorious literature, while it has gathered under its protection men whose genius in the arts has never been eclipsed.

The Church the enemy of liberty! Ah, how they travesty the idea of liberty which has for its object one of the most precious of God's gifts when they make use of its name to justify its abuse and excess! What do we mean by liberty? Does it mean the exemption from all laws; the deliverance from all restraint, and as a corollary, the right to take man's caprice as a guide in all our actions? Such liberty the Church certainly reproves, and good and honest men reprove it likewise. But do they mean by liberty the rational faculty to do good, magnanimously, without check or hindrance and according to the rules which eternal justice has established? That liberty which is the only liberty worthy of man, the only one useful to society, none favors or encourages or protects more than the Church. By the force of its doctrine and the efficaciousness of its action the Church has freed humanity from the yoke of slavery in preaching to the world the great law of equality and human fraternity. In every age it has defended the feeble and the oppressed against the arrogant domination of the strong. It has demanded liberty of Christian conscience while pouring out in torrents the blood of its martyrs; it has restored to the child and to the woman the dignity and the noble prerogatives of their nature in making them share by virtue the same right that reverence and justice which is their due, and it has largely contributed, both to introduce and maintain civil and political liberty in the heart of the nations.

The Church the usurper of the rights of the State! The Church invading the political domain! Why, the Church knows and teaches that her Divine Founder has commanded us to give to Cæsar what is Cæsar's and to God what is God's, and that He has thus sanctioned the immutable principle of an enduring distinction between those two powers which are both sovereign in their respective spheres, a distinction which is most pregnant in its consequences and eminently conducive to the development of Christian civilization. In its spirit of charity it is a stranger to every hostile design against the State. It aims only at making these two powers go side by side for the advancement of the same object, namely, for man and for human society, but by different ways and in conformity with the noble plan which has been assigned for its divine mission. Would to God that its action was received without mistrust and without suspicion. It could not fail to multiply the numberless benefits of which we have already spoken. To accuse the Church of ambitious views is only to repeat the ancient calumny, a calumny which its powerful enemies have more than once employed as a pretext to conceal their own purposes of oppression.

Far from oppressing the State, history clearly shows when it is read without prejudice, that the Church like its Divine Founder has been, on the contrary, most commonly the victim of oppression and injustice. The reason is that its power rests not on the force of arms but on the strength of thought and of truth.

It is therefore assuredly with malignant purpose that they hurl against the Church accusations like these. It is a pernicious and disloyal work, in the pursuit of which above all others a certain sect of darkness is engaged, a sect which human society these many years carries within itself and which like a deadly poison destroys its happiness, its fecundity and its life. Abiding personification of the revolution, it constitutes a sort of retrogressive society whose object is to exercise an occult suzerainty over the established order and whose whole purpose is to make war against God and against His Church. There is no need of naming it, for all will recognize in these traits the society of Freemasons, of which we have already spoken, expressly in our Encyclical, *Humanum Genus* of the 20th of April, 1884. While denouncing its destructive tendency, its erroneous teachings and its wicked purpose of embracing in its far-reaching grasp almost all nations, and uniting itself to other sects which its secret influences puts in motion, directing first and afterwards retaining its members by the advantages which it procures for them, bending governments to its will, sometimes by promises and sometimes by threats, it has succeeded in entering all classes of society, and forms an invisible and irresponsible state existing within the legitimate state. Full of the spirit of Satan who, according to the words of the Apostle, knows how to transform himself at need into an angel of light, it gives prominence to its humanitarian object, but it sacrifices everything to its sectarian purpose and protests that it has no political aim, while in reality it exercises the most profound action on the legislative and administrative life of the nations, and while loudly professing its respect for authority and even for religion, has for its ultimate purpose, as its own statutes declare, the destruction of all authority as well as of the priesthood, both of which it holds up as the enemies of liberty.

It becomes more evident day by day that it is to the inspiration and the assistance of this sect that we must attribute in great measure the continual troubles with which the Church is harassed, as well as the recrudescence of the attacks to which it has recently been subjected. For the simultaneousness of the assaults in the persecutions which have so suddenly burst upon us in these later times, like a storm from a clear sky, that is to say without any cause proportionate to the effect; the uniformity of means employed to inaugurate this persecution, namely, the press, public assemblies, theatrical productions; the employment in every country of the same arms, to wit, calumny and public uprisings, all this betrays clearly the identity of purpose and a programme drawn up by one and the same central direction. All this is only a simple episode of a prearranged plan carried out on a constantly widening field to multiply the ruins of which we speak. Thus they are endeavoring by every means in their power first to restrict and then to completely exclude religious instruction from the schools so as to make the rising generation unbelievers or indifferent to all religion; as they are endeavoring by the daily press to combat the morality of the Church, to ridicule its practices and its solemnities. It is only natural, consequently, that the Catholic priesthood, whose mission is to preach religion and to administer the sacraments, should be assailed with a special fierceness. In taking it as the object of their attacks this sect aims at diminishing in the eyes of the people its prestige and its authority. Already their audacity grows hour by hour in proportion as it flatters itself that it can do so with impunity. It puts a malignant interpretation on all the acts of the clergy, bases suspicion upon the slenderest proofs and overwhelms it with the vilest accusations. Thus new prejudices are added to those with which the clergy are already overwhelmed, such for example as their subjection to military service, which is such a great obstacle for the preparation for the priesthood, and the confiscation of the ecclesiastical patrimony which the pious generosity of the faithful had founded.

As regards the religious orders and religious congregations, the practice of the evangelical counsels made them the glory of society and the glory of religion. These very things rendered them more culpable in the eyes of the enemies of the Church and were the reasons why they were fiercely denounced and held up to contempt and hatred. It is a great grief for us to recall here the odious measures which were so undeserved and so strongly condemned by all honest men by which the members of religious orders were lately overwhelmed. Nothing was of avail to save them, neither the integrity of their life, which their enemies were unable to assail, nor the right which authorizes all natural associations entered into for an honorable purpose, nor the right of the constitutions which loudly proclaimed their freedom to enter into those organizations, nor the favor of the people who were so grateful for the precious services rendered in the arts, in the sciences and in agriculture, and for the charity which poured itself out upon the most numerous and poorest classes of society. And hence it is that these men and women who themselves had sprung from the people and who had spontaneously renounced all the joys of family to consecrate to the good of their fellowmen, in those peaceful associations, their youth, their talent, their strength and their lives, were treated as malefactors as if they had formed criminal associations, and have been excluded from the common and prescriptive rights at the very time when men are speaking loudest of liberty. We must not be astonished that the most beloved children are struck when the father himself, that is to say, the head of Catholicity, the Roman Pontiff, is no better treated. The facts are known to all. Stripped of the temporal sovereignty and consequently of that independence which is necessary to accomplish his universal and divine mission; forced in Rome itself to shut himself up in his own dwelling because the enemy has laid siege to him on every side, he has been compelled in spite of the derisive assurances of respect and of the precarious promises of liberty to an abnormal condition of existence which is unjust and unworthy of his exalted ministry. We know only too well the difficulties that are each instant created to thwart his intentions and to outrage his dignity. It only goes to prove what is every day more and more evident that it is the spiritual power of the head of the Church which little by little they aim at destroying when they attack the temporal power of the Papacy. Those who are the real authors of this spoliation have not hesitated to confess it.

Judging by the consequences which have followed, this action was not only impolitic, but was an attack on society itself; for the assaults that are made upon religion are so many blows struck at the very heart of society.

In making man a being destined to live in society, God in His providence has also founded the Church, which as the holy text expresses it, He has established on Mount Zion in order that it might be a light which, with its lifegiving rays, would cause the principle of life to penetrate into the various degrees of human society by giving it divinely inspired laws, by means of which society might establish itself in that order which would be most conducive to its welfare. Hence in proportion as society separates itself from the Church, which is an important element in its strength, by so much does it decline, or its woes are multiplied for the reason that they are separated whom God wished to bind together.

As for us, we never weary as often as the occasion presents itself to inculcate these great truths, and we desire to do so once again and in a very explicit manner on this extraordinary occasion. May God grant that the faithful will take courage from what we say and be guided to unite their efforts more efficaciously for the common good; that they may be more enlightened and that our adversaries may understand the injustice which they commit in persecuting the most loving mother and the most faithful benefactress of humanity.

We would not wish that the remembrance of these afflictions should diminish in the souls of the faithful that full and entire confidence which they ought to have in the Divine assistance. For God, in His own hour and in His mysterious ways, will bring about a certain victory. As for us, no matter how great the sadness which fills our heart, we do not fear for the immortal destiny of the Church. As we have said in the beginning, persecution is its heritage, because in trying and in purifying its children, God thereby obtains for them greater and more precious advantages. And in permitting the Church to undergo these trials He manifests the Divine assistance which He bestows upon it, for He provides new and unlooked for means of assuring the support and the development of His work, while revealing the futility of the powers which are leagued against it. Nineteen centuries of a life passed in the midst of the ebb and flow of all human vicissitudes teach us that the storms pass by without ever affecting the foundations of the Church. We are able all the more to remain unshaken in this confidence, as the present time affords indications which forbid depression. We cannot deny that the difficulties that confront us are extraordinary and formidable, but there are also facts before our eyes which give evidence, at the same time, that God is fulfilling His promises with admirable wisdom and goodness.

While so many powers conspire against the Church and while she is progressing on her way deprived of all human help and assistance, is she not in effect carrying on her gigantic work in the world and is she not extending her action in every clime and every nation? Expelled by Jesus Christ, the prince of this world can no longer exercise his proud dominion as heretofore; and although doubtless the efforts of Satan may cause us many a woe they will not achieve the object at which they aim. Already a supernatural tranquillity due to the Holy Ghost who provides for the Church and who abides in it reigns not only in the souls of the faithful but also throughout Christianity; a tranquillity whose serene development we witness everywhere, thanks to the union ever more and more close and affectionate with the Apostolic See; a union which is in marvelous contrast with the agitation, the dissension and the continual unrest of the various sects which disturb the peace of society. There exists also between bishops and clergy a union which is fruitful in numberless works of zeal and charity. It exists likewise between the clergy and laity who more closely knit together and more completely freed from human respect than ever before, are awakening to a new life and organizing with a generous emulation in defense of the sacred cause of religion. It is this union which we have so often recommended and which we recommend again, which we bless that it may develop still more and may rise like an impregnable wall against the fierce violence of the enemies of God.

There is nothing more natural than that like the branches which spring from the roots of the tree, these numberless associations which we see with joy flourish in our days in the bosom of the Church should arise, grow strong and multiply. There is no form of Christian piety which has been omitted whether there is question of Jesus Christ Himself, or His adorable mysteries, or His Divine Mother, or the saints whose wonderful virtues have illumined the world. Nor has any kind of charitable work been forgotten. On all sides there is a zealous endeavor to procure Christian instruction for youth; help for the sick; moral teaching for the people and assistance for the classes least favored in the goods of this world. With what remarkable rapidity this movement would propagate itself and what precious fruits it would bear if it were not opposed by the unjust and unfriendly efforts with which it finds itself so often in conflict.

God, who gives to the Church such great vitality in civilized countries where it has been established for so many centuries, consoles us besides with other hopes. These hopes we owe to the zeal of Catholic missionaries. Not permitting themselves to be discouraged by the perils which they face; by the privations which they endure; by the sacrifices of every kind which they accept, their numbers are increasing and they are gaining whole countries to the Gospel and to civilization. Nothing can diminish their courage, although after the manner of their Divine Master they receive only accusations and calumnies as the reward of their untiring labors.

Thus our sorrows are tempered by the sweetest consolations, and in the midst of the struggles and the difficulties which are our portion we have wherewith to refresh our souls and to inspire us with hope. This ought to suggest useful and wise reflections to those who view the world with intelligence, and who do not permit passions to blind them; for it proves that God has not made man independent in what regards the last end of life, and just as He has spoken to him in the past so He speaks again in our day by His Church which is visibly sustained by the Divine assistance and which shows clearly where salvation and truth can be found. Come what may, this eternal assistance will inspire our hearts with an incredible hope and persuade us that at the hour marked by Providence and in a future which is not remote, truth will scatter the mists in which men endeavor to shroud it and will shine forth more brilliantly than ever. The spirit of the Gospel will spread life anew in the heart of our corrupted society and in its perishing members.

In what concerns us, Venerable Brethren, in order to

hasten the day of divine mercy we shall not fail in our duty to do everything to defend and develop the Kingdom of God upon earth. As for you, your pastoral solicitude is too well known to us to exhort you to do the same. May the ardent flame which burns in your hearts be transmitted more and more to the hearts of all your priests. They are in immediate contact with the people. If full of the spirit of Jesus Christ and keeping themselves above political passion, they unite their action with yours they will succeed with the blessing of God in accomplishing marvels. By their word they will enlighten the multitude; by their sweetness of manners they will gain all hearts, and in succoring with charity their suffering brethren, they will help them little by little to better the condition in which they are placed.

The clergy will be firmly sustained by the active and intelligent cooperation of all men of good will. Thus the children who have tasted the sweetness of the Church will thank her for it in a worthy way, viz., by gathering around her to defend her honor and her glory. All can contribute to this work which will be so splendidly meritorious for them; literary and learned men, by defending her in books or in the daily press, which is such a powerful instrument now made use of by her enemies; fathers of families and teachers, by giving a Christian education to children; magistrates and representatives of the people, by showing themselves firm in the principles which they defend as well as by the integrity of their lives and in the profession of their faith without any vestige of human respect. Our age exacts lofty ideals, generous designs, and the exact observance of the laws. It is by a perfect submission to the directions of the Holy See that this discipline will be strengthened, for it is the best means of causing to disappear or at least of diminishing the evil which party opinions produce in fomenting divisions; and it will assist us in uniting all our efforts for attaining that higher end, namely, the triumph of Jesus Christ and His Church. Such is the duty of Catholics. As for her final triumph she depends upon Him who watches with wisdom and love over His immaculate spouse, and of whom it is written, "Jesus Christ, yesterday, today and forever." (Heb. xiii., 8.)

It is therefore to Him, that at this moment we should lift

our hearts in humble and ardent prayer, to Him who loving with an infinite love our erring humanity has wished to make Himself an expiatory victim by the sublimity of His martyrdom; to Him who seated although unseen in the mystical bark of His Church can alone still the tempest and command the waves to be calm and the furious winds to cease. Without doubt, Venerable Brethren, you with us will ask this Divine Master for the cessation of the evils which are overwhelming society, for the repeal of all hostile law; for the illumination of those who more perhaps through ignorance than through malice, hate and persecute the religion of Jesus Christ; and also for the drawing together of all men of good will in close and holy union.

May the triumph of truth and of justice be thus hastened in the world, and for the great family of men may better days dawn; days of tranquillity and of peace.

Meanwhile as a pledge of the most precious and Divine favor may the benediction which we give you with all our heart, descend upon you and all the faithful committed to your care.

Given at Rome, at St. Peter's, 19th March, 1902, in the twenty-fifth year of our Pontificate.

PASCENDI DOMINICI GREGIS
Encyclical of Pope Saint Pius X
On the Doctrine of the Modernists
September 8, 1907

This encyclical addresses modernism, which is the name Saint Pius X assigned to the ideologies of Freemasonry, such as religious indifferentism and rationalism. In fact, he defined the term as "the synthesis of all heresies." While not explicitly about Freemasonry, Pascendi Domini Gregis exposes Masonic ideological threats.

Venerable Brethren, Health and the Apostolic Blessing:

1. One of the primary obligations assigned by Christ to the office divinely committed to Us of feeding the Lord's flock is that of guarding with the greatest vigilance the deposit of the faith delivered to the saints, rejecting the profane novelties of words and the gainsaying of knowledge falsely so called. There has never been a time when this watchfulness of the supreme pastor was not necessary to the Catholic body, for owing to the efforts of the enemy of the human race, there have never been lacking "men speaking perverse things,"[1] "vain talkers and seducers,"[2] "erring and driving into error."[3] It must, however, be confessed that these latter days have witnessed a notable increase in the number of the enemies of the Cross of Christ, who, by arts entirely new and full of deceit, are striving to destroy the vital energy of the Church, and, as far as in them lies, utterly to subvert the very Kingdom of Christ. Wherefore We may no longer keep silence, lest We should seem to fail in Our most sacred duty, and lest the kindness that, in the hope of wiser counsels, We have hitherto shown them, should be set down to lack of diligence in the discharge of Our office.

---

[1] Acts 20:30.
[2] Titus 1:10.
[3] ii Tim. 3:13.

2. That We should act without delay in this matter is made imperative especially by the fact that the partisans of error are to be sought not only among the Church's open enemies; but, what is to be most dreaded and deplored, in her very bosom, and are the more mischievous the less they keep in the open. We allude, Venerable Brethren, to many who belong to the Catholic laity, and, what is much more sad, to the ranks of the priesthood itself, who, animated by a false zeal for the Church, lacking the solid safeguards of philosophy and theology, nay more, thoroughly imbued with the poisonous doctrines taught by the enemies of the Church, and lost to all sense of modesty, put themselves forward as reformers of the Church; and, forming more boldly into line of attack, assail all that is most sacred in the work of Christ, not sparing even the Person of the Divine Redeemer, whom, with sacrilegious audacity, they degrade to the condition of a simple and ordinary man.

3. Although they express their astonishment that We should number them amongst the enemies of the Church, no one will be reasonably surprised that We should do so, if, leaving out of account the internal disposition of the soul, of which God alone is the Judge, he considers their tenets, their manner of speech, and their action. Nor indeed would he be wrong in regarding them as the most pernicious of all the adversaries of the Church. For, as We have said, they put into operation their designs for her undoing, not from without but from within. Hence, the danger is present almost in the very veins and heart of the Church, whose injury is the more certain from the very fact that their knowledge of her is more intimate. Moreover, they lay the ax not to the branches and shoots, but to the very root, that is, to the faith and its deepest fibers. And once having struck at this root of immortality, they proceed to diffuse poison through the whole tree, so that there is no part of Catholic truth which they leave untouched, none that they do not strive to corrupt. Further, none is more skillful, none more astute than they, in the employment of a thousand noxious devices; for they play the double part of rationalist and Catholic, and this so craftily that they easily lead the unwary into error; and as audacity is their chief characteristic, there is no conclusion of any kind from which

they shrink or which they do not thrust forward with pertinacity and assurance To this must be added the fact, which indeed is well calculated to deceive souls, that they lead a life of the greatest activity, of assiduous and ardent application to every branch of learning, and that they possess, as a rule, a reputation for irreproachable morality. Finally, there is the fact which is all but fatal to the hope of cure that their very doctrines have given such a bent to their minds, that they disdain all authority and brook no restraint; and relying upon a false conscience, they attempt to ascribe to a love of truth that which is in reality the result of pride and obstinacy.

Once indeed We had hopes of recalling them to a better mind, and to this end We first of all treated them with kindness as Our children, then with severity; and at last We have had recourse, though with great reluctance, to public reproof. It is known to you, Venerable Brethren, how unavailing have been Our efforts. For a moment they have bowed their head, only to lift it more arrogantly than before. If it were a matter which concerned them alone, We might perhaps have overlooked it; but the security of the Catholic name is at stake. Wherefore We must interrupt a silence which it would be criminal to prolong, that We may point out to the whole Church, as they really are, men who are badly disguised.

4. It is one of the cleverest devices of the Modernists (as they are commonly and rightly called) to present their doctrines without order and systematic arrangement, in a scattered and disjointed manner, so as to make it appear as if their minds were in doubt or hesitation, whereas in reality they are quite fixed and steadfast. For this reason it will be of advantage, Venerable Brethren, to bring their teachings together here into one group, and to point out their interconnection, and thus to pass to an examination of the sources of the errors, and to prescribe remedies for averting the evil results.

5. To proceed in an orderly manner in this somewhat abstruse subject, it must first of all be noted that the Modernist sustains and includes within himself a manifold personality; he is a philosopher, a believer, a theologian, an

historian, a critic, an apologist, a reformer. These roles must be clearly distinguished one from another by all who would accurately understand their system and thoroughly grasp the principles and the outcome of their doctrines.

6. We begin, then, with the philosopher. Modernists place the foundation of religious philosophy in that doctrine which is commonly called Agnosticism. According to this teaching human reason is confined entirely within the field of phenomena, that is to say, to things that appear, and in the manner in which they appear: it has neither the right nor the power to overstep these limits. Hence it is incapable of lifting itself up to God, and of recognizing His existence, even by means of visible things. From this it is inferred that God can never be the direct object of science, and that, as regards history, He must not be considered as an historical subject. Given these premises, everyone will at once perceive what becomes of Natural Theology, of the motives of credibility, of external revelation. The modernists simply sweep them entirely aside; they include them in Intellectualism, which they denounce as a system which is ridiculous and long since defunct. Nor does the fact that the Church has formally condemned these portentous errors exercise the slightest restraint upon them. Yet the Vatican Council has defined, "If anyone says that the one true God, our Creator and Lord, cannot be known with certainty by the natural light of human reason by means of the things that are made, let him be anathema";[4] and also, "If anyone says that it is not possible or not expedient that man be taught, through the medium of divine revelation, about God and the worship to be paid Him, let him be anathema";[5] and finally, "If anyone says that divine revelation cannot be made credible by external signs, and that therefore men should be drawn to the faith only by their personal internal experience or by private inspiration, let him be anathema."[6] It may be asked, in what way do the Modernists contrive to make the transition from Agnosticism, which is a state of pure nescience, to scientific and historic

---

[4] De Revelatione, can. 1.

[5] Ibid., can. 2.

[6] De Fide, can. 3. 7. De Revelatione, can. 3.

Atheism, which is a doctrine of positive denial; and consequently, by what legitimate process of reasoning, they proceed from the fact of ignorance as to whether God has in fact intervened in the history of the human race or not, to explain this history, leaving God out altogether, as if He really had not intervened. Let him answer who can. Yet it is a fixed and established principle among them that both science and history must be atheistic: and within their boundaries there is room for nothing but phenomena; God and all that is divine are utterly excluded. We shall soon see clearly what, as a consequence of this most absurd teaching, must be held touching the most sacred Person of Christ, and the mysteries of His life and death, and of His Resurrection and Ascension into Heaven.

7. However, this Agnosticism is only the negative part of the system of the Modernists: the positive part consists in what they call vital immanence. Thus they advance from one to the other. Religion, whether natural or supernatural, must, like every other fact, admit of some explanation. But when natural theology has been destroyed, and the road to revelation closed by the rejection of the arguments of credibility, and all external revelation absolutely denied, it is clear that this explanation will be sought in vain outside of man himself. It must, therefore, be looked for in man; and since religion is a form of life, the explanation must certainly be found in the life of man. In this way is formulated the principle of religious immanence. Moreover, the first actuation, so to speak, of every vital phenomenon — and religion, as noted above, belongs to this category — is due to a certain need or impulsion; but speaking more particularly of life, it has its origin in a movement of the heart, which movement is called a sense. Therefore, as God is the object of religion, we must conclude that faith, which is the basis and foundation of all religion, must consist in a certain interior sense, originating in a need of the divine. This need of the divine, which is experienced only in special and favorable circumstances, cannot of itself appertain to the domain of consciousness, but is first latent beneath consciousness, or, to borrow a term from modern philosophy, in the subconsciousness, where also its root lies hidden and

undetected.

It may perhaps be asked how it is that this need of the divine which man experiences within himself resolves itself into religion? To this question the Modernist reply would be as follows: Science and history are confined within two boundaries, the one external, namely, the visible world, the other internal, which is consciousness. When one or other of these limits has been reached, there can be no further progress, for beyond is the unknowable. In presence of this unknowable, whether it is outside man and beyond the visible world of nature, or lies hidden within the subconsciousness, the need of the divine in a soul which is prone to religion excites — according to the principles of Fideism, without any previous advertence of the mind — a certain special sense, and this sense possesses, implied within itself both as its own object and as its intrinsic cause, the divine reality itself, and in a way unites man with God. It is this sense to which Modernists give the name of faith, and this is what they hold to be the beginning of religion.

8. But we have not yet reached the end of their philosophizing, or, to speak more accurately, of their folly. Modernists find in this sense not only faith, but in and with faith, as they understand it, they affirm that there is also to be found revelation. For, indeed, what more is needed to constitute a revelation? Is not that religious sense which is perceptible in the conscience, revelation, or at least the beginning of revelation? Nay, is it not God Himself manifesting Himself, indistinctly, it is true, in this same religious sense, to the soul? And they add: Since God is both the object and the cause of faith, this revelation is at the same time of God and from God, that is to say, God is both the Revealer and the Revealed.

From this, Venerable Brethren, springs that most absurd tenet of the Modernists, that every religion, according to the different aspect under which it is viewed, must be considered as both natural and supernatural. It is thus that they make consciousness and revelation synonymous. From this they derive the law laid down as the universal standard, according to which religious consciousness is to be put on an equal footing with revelation, and that to it all must submit, even the supreme authority of the Church, whether in the capacity of teacher, or in that of legislator in the province of sacred liturgy or discipline.

9. In all this process, from which, according to the Modernists, faith and revelation spring, one point is to be particularly noted, for it is of capital importance on account of the historicocritical corollaries which they deduce from it. The unknowable they speak of does not present itself to faith as something solitary and isolated; but on the contrary in close conjunction with some phenomenon, which, though it belongs to the realms of science or history, yet to some extent exceeds their limits. Such a phenomenon may be a fact of nature containing within itself something mysterious; or it may be a man, whose character, actions, and words cannot, apparently, be reconciled with the ordinary laws of history. Then faith, attracted by the unknowable which is united with the phenomenon, seizes upon the whole phenomenon, and, as it were, permeates it with its own life. From this two things follow. The first is a sort of transfiguration of the phenomenon, by its elevation above its own true conditions, an elevation by which it becomes more adapted to clothe itself with the form of the divine character which faith will bestow upon it. The second consequence is a certain disfiguration — so it may be called — of the same phenomenon, arising from the fact that faith attributes to it, when stripped of the circumstances of place and time, characteristics which it does not really possess; and this takes place especially in the case of the phenomena of the past, and the more fully in the measure of their antiquity. From these two principles the Modernists deduce two laws, which, when united with a third which they have already derived from agnosticism, constitute the foundation of historic criticism. An example may be sought in the Person of Christ. In the Person of Christ, they say, science and history encounter nothing that is not human. Therefore, in virtue of the first canon deduced from agnosticism, whatever there is in His history suggestive of the divine must be rejected. Then, according to the second canon, the historical Person of Christ was transfigured by faith; therefore everything that raises it above historical conditions must be removed. Lastly, the third

canon, which lays down that the Person of Christ has been disfigured by faith, requires that everything should be excluded, deeds and words and all else, that is not in strict keeping with His character, condition, and education, and with the place and time in which He lived. A method of reasoning which is passing strange, but in it we have the Modernist criticism.

10. It is thus that the religious sense, which through the agency of vital immanence emerges from the lurking-places of the subconsciousness, is the germ of all religion, and the explanation of everything that has been or ever will be in any religion. This sense, which was at first only rudimentary and almost formless, under the influence of that mysterious principle from which it originated, gradually matured with the progress of human life, of which, as has been said, it is a certain form. This, then, is the origin of all. even of supernatural religion. For religions are mere developments of this religious sense. Nor is the Catholic religion an exception; it is quite on a level with the rest; for it was engendered, by the process of vital immanence, and by no other way, in the consciousness of Christ, who was a man of the choicest nature, whose like has never been, nor will be. In hearing these things we shudder indeed at so great an audacity of assertion and so great a sacrilege. And yet, Venerable Brethren, these are not merely the foolish babblings of unbelievers. There are Catholics, yea, and priests too, who say these things openly; and they boast that they are going to reform the Church by these ravings! The question is no longer one of the old error which claimed for human nature a sort of right to the supernatural. It has gone far beyond that, and has reached the point when it is affirmed that our most holy religion, in the man Christ as in us, emanated from nature spontaneously and of itself. Nothing assuredly could be more utterly destructive of the whole supernatural order. For this reason the Vatican Council most justly decreed: "If anyone says that man cannot be raised by God to a knowledge and perfection which surpasses nature, but that he can and should, by his own efforts and by a constant development, attain finally to the possession of all truth and good, let him be

anathema."[7]

11. So far, Venerable Brethren, there has been no mention of the intellect. It also, according to the teaching of the Modernists, has its part in the act of faith. And it is of importance to see how. In that sense of which We have frequently spoken, since sense is not knowledge, they say God, indeed, presents Himself to man, but in a manner so confused and indistinct that He can hardly be perceived by the believer. It is therefore necessary that a certain light should be cast upon this sense so that God may clearly stand out in relief and be set apart from it. This is the task of the intellect, whose office it is to reflect and to analyze; and by means of it, man first transforms into mental pictures the vital phenomena which arise within him, and then expresses them in words. Hence the common saying of Modernists: that the religious man must think his faith. The mind then, encountering this sense, throws itself upon it, and works in it after the manner of a painter who restores to greater clearness the lines of a picture that have been dimmed with age. The simile is that of one of the leaders of Modernism. The operation of the mind in this work is a double one: first, by a natural and spontaneous act it expresses its concept in a simple, popular statement; then, on reflection and deeper consideration, or, as they say, by elaborating its thought, it expresses the idea in secondary propositions, which are derived from the first, but are more precise and distinct. These secondary propositions, if they finally receive the approval of the supreme magisterium of the Church, constitute dogma.

12. We have thus reached one of the principal points in the Modernist's system, namely, the origin and the nature of dogma. For they place the origin of dogma in those primitive and simple formulas, which, under a certain aspect, are necessary to faith; for revelation, to be truly such, requires the clear knowledge of God in the consciousness. But dogma itself, they apparently hold, strictly consists in the secondary formulas.

To ascertain the nature of dogma, we must first find the

---

[7] *De Revel.*, can. 3.

relation which exists between the religious formulas and the religious sense. This will be readily perceived by anyone who holds that these formulas have no other purpose than to furnish the believer with a means of giving to himself an account of his faith. These formulas therefore stand midway between the believer and his faith; in their relation to the faith they are the inadequate expression of its object, and are usually called symbols; in their relation to the believer they are mere instruments.

Hence it is quite impossible to maintain that they absolutely contain the truth: for, in so far as they are symbols, they are the images of truth, and so must be adapted to the religious sense in its relation to man; and as instruments, they are the vehicles of truth, and must therefore in their turn be adapted to man in his relation to the religious sense. But the object of the religious sense, as something contained in the absolute, possesses an infinite variety of aspects, of which now one, now another, may present itself. In like manner he who believes can avail himself of varying conditions. Consequently, the formulas which we call dogma must be subject to these vicissitudes, and are, therefore, liable to change. Thus the way is open to the intrinsic evolution of dogma. Here we have an immense structure of sophisms which ruin and wreck all religion.

13. Dogma is not only able, but ought to evolve and to be changed. This is strongly affirmed by the Modernists, and clearly flows from their principles. For among the chief points of their teaching is the following, which they deduce from the principle of vital immanence, namely, that religious formulas if they are to be really religious and not merely intellectual speculations, ought to be living and to live the life of the religious sense. This is not to be understood to mean that these formulas, especially if merely imaginative, were to be invented for the religious sense. Their origin matters nothing, any more than their number or quality. What is necessary is that the religious sense — with some modification when needful — should vitally assimilate them. In other words, it is necessary that the primitive formula be accepted and sanctioned by the heart; and similarly the subsequent work from which are brought forth the secondary

formulas must proceed under the guidance of the heart. Hence it comes that these formulas, in order to be living, should be, and should remain, adapted to the faith and to him who believes. Wherefore, if for any reason this adaptation should cease to exist, they lose their first meaning and accordingly need to be changed. In view of the fact that the character and lot of dogmatic formulas are so unstable, it is no wonder that Modernists should regard them so lightly and in such open disrespect, and have no consideration or praise for anything but the religious sense and for the religious life. In this way, with consummate audacity, they criticize the Church, as having strayed from the true path by failing to distinguish between the religious and moral sense of formulas and their surface meaning, and by clinging vainly and tenaciously to meaningless formulas, while religion itself is allowed to go to ruin. "Blind'- they are, and "leaders of the blind" puffed up with the proud name of science, they have reached that pitch of folly at which they pervert the eternal concept of truth and the true meaning of religion; in introducing a new system in which "they are seen to be under the sway of a blind and unchecked passion for novelty, thinking not at all of finding some solid foundation of truth, but despising the holy and apostolic traditions, they embrace other and vain, futile, uncertain doctrines, unapproved by the Church, on which, in the height of their vanity, they think they can base and maintain truth itself.

14. Thus far, Venerable Brethren, We have considered the Modernist as a philosopher. Now if We proceed to consider him as a believer, and seek to know how the believer, according to Modernism, is marked off from the philosopher, it must be observed that, although the philosopher recognizes the reality of the divine as the object of faith, still this reality is not to be found by him but in the heart of the believer, as an object of feeling and affirmation, and therefore confined within the sphere of phenomena; but the question as to whether in itself it exists outside that feeling and affirmation is one which the philosopher passes over and neglects. For the Modernist believer, on the contrary, it is an established and certain fact that the reality of the divine does really exist in itself and quite independently

of the person who believes in it. If you ask on what foundation this assertion of the believer rests, he answers: In the personal experience of the individual. On this head the Modernists differ from the Rationalists only to fall into the views of the Protestants and pseudo-mystics. The following is their manner of stating the question: In the religious sense one must recognize a kind of intuition of the heart which puts man in immediate contact with the reality of God, and infuses such a persuasion of God's existence and His action both within and without man as far to exceed any scientific conviction. They assert, therefore, the existence of a real experience, and one of a kind that surpasses all rational experience. If this experience is denied by some, like the Rationalists, they say that this arises from the fact that such persons are unwilling to put themselves in the moral state necessary to produce it. It is this experience which makes the person who acquires it to be properly and truly a believer.

How far this position is removed from that of Catholic teaching! We have already seen how its fallacies have been condemned by the Vatican Council. Later on, we shall see how these errors, combined with those which we have already mentioned, open wide the way to Atheism. Here it is well to note at once that, given this doctrine of experience united with that of symbolism, every religion, even that of paganism, must be held to be true. What is to prevent such experiences from being found in any religion? In fact, that they are so is maintained by not a few. On what grounds can Modernists deny the truth of an experience affirmed by a follower of Islam? Will they claim a monopoly of true experiences for Catholics alone? Indeed, Modernists do not deny, but actually maintain, some confusedly, others frankly, that all religions are true. That they cannot feel otherwise is obvious. For on what ground, according to their theories, could falsity be predicated of any religion whatsoever? Certainly it would be either on account of the falsity of the religious .sense or on account of the falsity of the formula pronounced by the mind. Now the religious sense, although it maybe more perfect or less perfect, is always one and the same; and the intellectual formula, in order to be true, has but to respond to the religious sense and to the believer, whatever be the intellectual capacity of the latter. In the conflict between different religions, the most that Modernists can maintain is that the Catholic has more truth because it is more vivid, and that it deserves with more reason the name of Christian because it corresponds more fully with the origins of Christianity. No one will find it unreasonable that these consequences flow from the premises. But what is most amazing is that there are Catholics and priests, who, We would fain believe, abhor such enormities, and yet act as if they fully approved of them. For they lavish such praise and bestow such public honor on the teachers of these errors as to convey the belief that their admiration is not meant merely for the persons, who are perhaps not devoid of a certain merit, but rather for the sake of the errors which these persons openly profess and which they do all in their power to propagate.

15. There is yet another element in this part of their teaching which is absolutely contrary to Catholic truth. For what is laid down as to experience is also applied with destructive effect to tradition, which has always been maintained by the Catholic Church. Tradition, as understood by the Modernists, is a communication with others of an original experience, through preaching by means of the intellectual formula. To this formula, in addition to its representative value they attribute a species of suggestive efficacy which acts firstly in the believer by stimulating the religious sense, should it happen to have grown sluggish, and by renewing the experience once acquired, and secondly, in those who do not yet believe by awakening in them for the first time the religious sense and producing the experience. In this way is religious experience spread abroad among the nations; and not merely among contemporaries by preaching, but among future generations both by books and by oral transmission from one to another. Sometimes this communication of religious experience takes root and thrives, at other times it withers at once and dies. For the Modernists, to live is a proof of truth, since for them life and truth are one and the same thing. Thus we are once more led to infer that all existing religions are equally true, for otherwise they would not survive.

16. We have proceeded sufficiently far, Venerable Brethren, to have before us enough, and more than enough, to enable us to see what are the relations which Modernists establish between faith and science — including, as they are wont to do under that name, history. And in the first place it is to be held that the object-matter of the one is quite extraneous to and separate from the object-matter of the other. For faith occupies itself solely with something which science declares to be for it unknowable. Hence each has a separate scope assigned to it: science is entirely concerned with phenomena, into which faith does not at all enter; faith, on the contrary, concerns itself with the divine, which is entirely unknown to science. Thus it is contended that there can never be any dissension between faith and science, for if each keeps on its own ground they can never meet and therefore never can be in contradiction. And if it be objected that in the visible world there are some things which appertain to faith, such as the human life of Christ, the Modernists reply by denying this. For though such things come within the category of phenomena, still in as far as they are lived by faith and in the way already described have been by faith transfigured and disfigured, they have been removed from the world of sense and transferred into material for the divine. Hence should it be further asked whether Christ has wrought real miracles, and made real prophecies, whether He rose truly from the dead and ascended into Heaven, the answer of agnostic science will be in the negative and the answer of faith in the affirmative yet there will not be, on that account, any conflict between them. For it will be denied by the philosopher as a philosopher speaking to philosophers and considering Christ only in historical reality; and it will be affirmed by the believer as a believer speaking to believers and considering the life of Christ as lived again by the faith and in the faith.

17. It would be a great mistake, nevertheless, to suppose that, according to these theories, one is allowed to believe that faith and science are entirely independent of each other. On the side of science that is indeed quite true and correct, but it is quite otherwise with regard to faith, which is subject to science, not on one but on three grounds. For in the first place

it must be observed that in every religious fact, when one takes away the divine reality and the experience of it which the believer possesses, everything else, and especially the religious formulas, belongs to the sphere of phenomena and therefore falls under the control of science. Let the believer go out of the world if he will, but so long as he remains in it, whether he like it or not, he cannot escape from the laws, the observation, the judgments of science and of history. Further, although it is contended that God is the object of faith alone, the statement refers only to the divine reality, not to the idea of God. The latter also is subject to science which, while it philosophizes in what is called the logical order, soars also to the absolute and the ideal. It is therefore the right of philosophy and of science to form its knowledge concerning the idea of God, to direct it in its evolution and to purify it of any extraneous elements which may have entered into it. Hence we have the Modernist axiom that the religious evolution ought to be brought into accord with the moral and intellectual, or as one whom they regard as their leader has expressed it, ought to be subject to it. Finally, man does not suffer a dualism to exist in himself, and the believer therefore feels within him an impelling need so to harmonize faith with science that it may never oppose the general conception which science sets forth concerning the universe.

Thus it is evident that science is to be entirely independent of faith, while on the other hand, and notwithstanding that they are supposed to be strangers to each other, faith is made subject to science. All this, Venerable Brethren, is in formal opposition to the teachings of Our predecessor, Pius IX, where he lays it down that: "In matters of religion it is the duty of philosophy not to command but to serve, not to prescribe what is to be believed, but to embrace what is to be believed with reasonable obedience, not to scrutinize the depths of the mysteries of God, but to venerate them devoutly and humbly."[8]

The Modernists completely invert the parts, and of them may be applied the words which another of Our predecessors Gregory IX, addressed to some theologians of his time:

---

[8] Brief to the Bishop of Breslau, June 15, 1857.

"Some among you, puffed up like bladders with the spirit of vanity strive by profane novelties to cross the boundaries fixed by the Fathers, twisting the meaning of the sacred text...to the philosophical teaching of the rationalists, not for the profit of their hearer but to make a show of science...these men, led away by various and strange doctrines, turn the head into the tail and force the queen to serve the handmaid."[9]

18. This will appear more clearly to anybody who studies the conduct of Modernists, which is in perfect harmony with their teachings. In their writings and addresses they seem not unfrequently to advocate doctrines which are contrary one to the other, so that one would be disposed to regard their attitude as double and doubtful. But this is done deliberately and advisedly, and the reason of it is to be found in their opinion as to the mutual separation of science and faith. Thus in their books one finds some things which might well be approved by a Catholic, but on turning over the page one is confronted by other things which might well have been dictated by a rationalist. When they write history they make no mention of the divinity of Christ, but when they are in the pulpit they profess it clearly; again, when they are dealing with history they take no account of the Fathers and the Councils, but when they catechize the people, they cite them respectfully. In the same way they draw their distinctions between exegesis which is theological and pastoral and exegesis which is scientific and historical. So, too, when they treat of philosophy, history, and criticism, acting on the principle that science in no way depends upon faith, they feel no especial horror in treading in the footsteps of Luther[10] and

---

[9] Gregory IX Epist. ad Magistros theol. paris. July 7, 1223.

[10] Proposition 29, condemned by Leo X in the bull of May 16, 1520, *Exsurge Domine*: *Via nobis facta est enervandi auctoritatem Conciliorum et libere contradicendi eorum gestis et iudicandi eorum decreta, at confidenter confitendi quidquid verum videtur, sive probatum fuerit, sive reprobatum a quocumque Concilio.* (The way has been made for us to weaken the authority of councils and to freely contradict their actions and to judge their decrees, but confidently to declare whatever seems true, whether it has been approved or disapproved by any council.)

are wont to display a manifold contempt for Catholic doctrines, for the Holy Fathers, for the Ecumenical Councils, for the ecclesiastical magisterium; and should they be taken to task for this, they complain that they are being deprived of their liberty. Lastly, maintaining the theory that faith must be subject to science, they continuously and openly rebuke the Church on the ground that she resolutely refuses to submit and accommodate her dogmas to the opinions of philosophy; while they, on their side, having for this purpose blotted out the old theology, endeavor to introduce a new theology which shall support the aberrations of philosophers.

19. At this point, Venerable Brethren, the way is opened for us to consider the Modernists in the theological arena — a difficult task, yet one that may be disposed of briefly. It is a question of effecting the conciliation of faith with science, but always by making the one subject to the other. In this matter the Modernist theologian takes exactly the same principles which we have seen employed by the Modernist philosopher — the principles of immanence and symbolism — and applies them to the believer. The process is an extremely simple one. The philosopher has declared: The principle of faith is immanent; the believer has added: This principle is God; and the theologian draws the conclusion: God is immanent in man. Thus we have theological immanence. So, too, the philosopher regards it as certain that the representations of the object of faith are merely symbolical; the believer has likewise affirmed that the object of faith is God in himself; and the theologian proceeds to affirm that: The representations of the divine reality are symbolical. And thus we have theological symbolism. These errors are truly of the gravest kind and the pernicious character of both will be seen clearly from an examination of their consequences. For, to begin with symbolism, since symbols are but symbols in regard to their objects and only instruments in regard to the believer, it is necessary first of all, according to the teachings of the Modernists, that the believer does not lay too much stress on the formula, as formula, but avail himself of it only for the purpose of uniting himself to the absolute truth which the formula at once reveals and conceals, that is to say, endeavors to express but

without ever succeeding in doing so. They would also have the believer make use of the formulas only in as far as they are helpful to him, for they are given to be a help and not a hindrance; with proper regard, however, for the social respect due to formulas which the public magisterium has deemed suitable for expressing the common consciousness until such time as the same magisterium shall provide otherwise. Concerning immanence it is not easy to determine what Modernists precisely mean by it, for their own opinions on the subject vary. Some understand it in the sense that God working in man is more intimately present in him than man is even in himself; and this conception, if properly understood, is irreproachable. Others hold that the divine action is one with the action of nature, as the action of the first cause is one with the action of the secondary cause; and this would destroy the supernatural order. Others, finally, explain it in a way which savors of pantheism, and this, in truth, is the sense which best fits in with the rest of their doctrines.

20. With this principle of immanence is connected another which may be called the principle of divine permanence. It differs from the first in much the same way as the private experience differs from the experience transmitted by tradition. An example illustrating what is meant will be found in the Church and the sacraments. The Church and the sacraments according to the Modernists, are not to be regarded as having been instituted by Christ Himself. This is barred by agnosticism, which recognizes in Christ nothing more than a man whose religious consciousness has been, like that of all men, formed by degrees; it is also barred by the law of immanence, which rejects what they call external application; it is further barred by the law of evolution, which requires, for the development of the germs, time and a certain series of circumstances; it is finally, barred by history, which shows that such in fact has been the course of things. Still it is to he held that both Church and sacraments have been founded mediately by Christ. But how? In this way: All Christian consciences were, they affirm, in a manner virtually included in the conscience of Christ as the plant is included in the seed. But as the branches live the life of the seed, so,

too, all Christians are to be said to live the life of Christ. But the life of Christ, according to faith, is divine, and so, too, is the life of Christians. And if this life produced, in the course of ages, both the Church and the sacraments, it is quite right to say that their origin is from Christ and is divine. In the same way they make out that the Holy Scriptures and the dogmas are divine. And in this, the Modernist theology may be said to reach its completion. A slender provision, in truth, but more than enough for the theologian who professes that the conclusions of science, whatever they may be, must always be accepted! No one will have any difficulty in making the application of these theories to the other points with which We propose to deal.

21. Thus far We have touched upon the origin and nature of faith. But as faith has many branches, and chief among them the Church, dogma, worship, devotions, the Books which we call "sacred," it concerns us to know what the Modernists teach concerning them. To begin with dogma, We have already indicated its origin and nature. Dogma is born of a sort of impulse or necessity by virtue of which the believer elaborates his thought so as to render it clearer to his own conscience and that of others. This elaboration consists entirely in the process of investigating and refining the primitive mental formula, not indeed in itself and according to any logical explanation, but according to circumstances, or vitally as the Modernists somewhat less intelligibly describe it. Hence it happens that around this primitive formula secondary formulas, as We have already indicated, gradually continue to be formed, and these subsequently grouped into one body, or one doctrinal construction and further sanctioned by the public magisterium as responding to the common consciousness, are called dogma. Dogma is to be carefully distinguished from the speculations of theologians which, although not alive with the life of dogma, are not without their utility as serving both to harmonize religion with science and to remove opposition between them, and to illumine and defend religion from without, and it may be even to prepare the matter for future dogma. Concerning worship there would not be much to be said, were it not that under this head are comprised the sacraments, concerning

which the Modernist errors are of the most serious character. For them the sacraments are the resultant of a double impulse or need — for, as we have seen, everything in ttheir system is explained by inner impulses or necessities. The first need is that of giving some sensible manifestation to religion; the second is that of expressing it, which could not be done without some sensible form and consecrating acts, and these are called sacraments. But for the Modernists, sacraments are bare symbols or signs, though not devoid of a certain efficacy — an efficacy, they tell us, like that of certain phrases vulgarly described as having caught the popular ear, inasmuch as they have the power of putting certain leading ideas into circulation, and of making a marked impression upon the mind. What the phrases are to the ideas, that the sacraments are to the religious sense, that and nothing more. The Modernists would express their mind more clearly were they to affirm that the sacraments are instituted solely to foster the faith but this is condemned by the Council of Trent: If anyone says that these sacraments are instituted solely to foster the faith, let him be anathema.[11]

22. We have already touched upon the nature and origin of the Sacred Books. According to the principles of the Modernists they may be rightly described as a summary of experiences, not indeed of the kind that may now and again come to anybody, but those extraordinary and striking experiences which are the possession of every religion. And this is precisely what they teach about our books of the Old and New Testament. But to suit their own theories they note with remarkable ingenuity that, although experience is something belonging to the present, still it may draw its material in like manner from the past and the future inasmuch as the believer by memory lives the past over again after the manner of the present, and lives the future already by anticipation. This explains how it is that the historical and apocalyptic books are included among the Sacred Writings. God does indeed speak in these books through the medium of the believer, but according to Modernist theology, only by immanence and vital permanence. We may ask, what then

---

[11] Sess. Vll, De Sacramentis in genere, can. 5.

becomes of inspiration? Inspiration, they reply, is in nowise distinguished from that impulse which stimulates the believer to reveal the faith that is in him by words of writing, except perhaps by its vehemence. It is something like that which happens in poetical inspiration, of which it has been said: There is a God in us, and when he stirreth he sets us afire. It is in this sense that God is said to be the origin of the inspiration of the Sacred Books. The Modernists moreover affirm concerning this inspiration, that there is nothing in the Sacred Books which is devoid of it. In this respect some might be disposed to consider them as more orthodox than certain writers in recent times who somewhat restrict inspiration, as, for instance, in what have been put forward as so-called tacit citations. But in all this we have mere verbal conjuring. For if we take the Bible, according to the standards of agnosticism, namely, as a human work, made by men for men, albeit the theologian is allowed to proclaim that it is divine by immanence, what room is there left in it for inspiration? The Modernists assert a general inspiration of the Sacred Books, but they admit no inspiration in the Catholic sense.

23. A wider field for comment is opened when we come to what the Modernist school has imagined to be the nature of the Church. They begin with the supposition that the Church has its birth in a double need; first, the need of the individual believer to communicate his faith to others, especially if he has had some original and special experience, and secondly, when the faith has become common to many, the need of the collectivity to form itself into a society and to guard, promote, and propagate the common good. What, then, is the Church? It is the product of the collective conscience, that is to say, of the association of individual consciences which, by virtue of the principle of vital permanence, depend all on one first believer, who for Catholics is Christ. Now every society needs a directing authority to guide its members towards the common end, to foster prudently the elements of cohesion, which in a religious society are doctrine and worship. Hence the triple authority in the Catholic Church, disciplinary, dogmatic, liturgical. The nature of this authority is to be gathered from

its origin, and its rights and duties from its nature. In past times it was a common error that authority came to the Church from without, that is to say directly from God; and it was then rightly held to be autocratic. But this conception has now grown obsolete. For in the same way as the Church is a vital emanation of the collectivity of consciences, so too authority emanates vitally from the Church itself. Authority, therefore, like the Church, has its origin in the religious conscience, and, that being so, is subject to it. Should it disown this dependence it becomes a tyranny. For we are living in an age when the sense of liberty has reached its highest development. In the civil order the public conscience has introduced popular government. Now there is in man only one conscience, just as there is only one life. It is for the ecclesiastical authority, therefore, to adopt a democratic form, unless it wishes to provoke and foment an intestine conflict in the consciences of mankind. The penalty of refusal is disaster. For it is madness to think that the sentiment of liberty, as it now obtains, can recede. Were it forcibly pent up and held in bonds, the more terrible would be its outburst, sweeping away at once both Church and religion. Such is the situation in the minds of the Modernists, and their one great anxiety is, in consequence, to find a way of conciliation between the authority of the Church and the liberty of the believers.

24. But it is not only within her own household that the Church must come to terms. Besides her relations with those within, she has others with those who are outside. The Church does not occupy the world all by herself; there are other societies in the world., with which she must necessarily have dealings and contact. The rights and duties of the Church towards civil societies must, therefore, be determined, and determined, of course, by her own nature, that, to wit, which the Modernists have already described to us. The rules to be applied in this matter are clearly those which have been laid down for science and faith, though in the latter case the question turned upon the object, while in the present case we have one of ends. In the same way, then, as faith and science are alien to each other by reason of the diversity of their objects, Church and State are strangers by reason of the

diversity of their ends, that of the Church being spiritual while that of the State is temporal. Formerly it was possible to subordinate the temporal to the spiritual and to speak of some questions as mixed, conceding to the Church the position of queen and mistress in all such, because the Church was then regarded as having been instituted immediately by God as the author of the supernatural order. But this doctrine is today repudiated alike by philosophers and historians. The state must, therefore, be separated from the Church, and the Catholic from the citizen. Every Catholic, from the fact that he is also a citizen, has the right and the duty to work for the common good in the way he thinks best, without troubling himself about the authority of the Church, without paying any heed to its wishes, its counsels, its orders — nay, even in spite of its rebukes. For the Church to trace out and prescribe for the citizen any line of action, on any pretext whatsoever, is to be guilty of an abuse of authority, against which one is bound to protest with all one's might. Venerable Brethren, the principles from which these doctrines spring have been solemnly condemned by Our predecessor, Pius VI, in his Apostolic Constitution Auctorem fidei.[12]

25. But it is not enough for the Modernist school that the State should be separated from the Church. For as faith is to be subordinated to science as far as phenomenal elements are concerned, so too in temporal matters the Church must be subject to the State. This, indeed, Modernists may not yet say openly, but they are forced by the logic of their position to admit it. For granted the principle that in temporal matters the State possesses the sole power, it will follow that when the believer, not satisfied with merely internal acts of religion,

---

[12] Proposition 2: "Propositio, quae statuit, potestatem a Deo Datam Ecclesiae ut communicaretur Pastoribus, qui sunt eius ministri pro salute animarum; sic intellecta, ut a communitate fidelium in Pastores derivetur ecclesiastici ministerii ac regiminis potestas: haeretica." Proposition 3: "Insuper, quae statuit Romanun Pontificem esse caput ministeriale; sic explicata ut Romanus Pontifex non a Christo in persona beati Petri, sed ab Ecclesia potestatem ministerii accipiat, qua velut Petri successor, verus Christi vicarius ac totius Ecclesiae caput pollet in universa Ecclesia: haerectica."

proceeds to external acts — such for instance as the reception or administration of the sacraments — these will fall under the control of the State. What will then become of ecclesiastical authority, which can only be exercised by external acts? Obviously it will be completely under the dominion of the State. It is this inevitable consequence which urges many among liberal Protestants to reject all external worship — nay, all external religious fellowship, and leads them to advocate what they call individual religion. If the Modernists have not yet openly proceeded so far, they ask the Church in the meanwhile to follow of her own accord in the direction in which they urge her and to adapt herself to the forms of the State. Such are their ideas about disciplinary authority. But much more evil and pernicious are their opinions on doctrinal and dogmatic authority. The following is their conception of the magisterium of the Church: No religious society, they say, can be a real unit unless the religious conscience of its members be one, and also the formula which they adopt. But this double unity requires a kind of common mind whose office is to find and determine the formula that corresponds best with the common conscience; and it must have, moreover, an authority sufficient to enable it to impose on the community the formula which has been decided upon. From the combination and, as it were, fusion of these two elements, the common mind which draws up the formula and the authority which imposes it, arises, according to the Modernists, the notion of the ecclesiastical magisterium. And, as this magisterium springs, in its last analysis, from the individual consciences and possesses its mandate of public utility for their benefit, it necessarily follows that the ecclesiastical magisterium must be dependent upon them, and should therefore be made to bow to the popular ideals. To prevent individual consciences from expressing freely and openly the impulses they feel, to hinder criticism from urging forward dogma in the path of its necessary evolution, is not a legitimate use but an abuse of a power given for the public weal. So too a due method and measure must be observed in the exercise of authority. To condemn and proscribe a work without the knowledge of the author, without hearing his explanations, without discussion, is something approaching to tyranny. And here again it is a question of finding a way of reconciling the full rights of authority on the one hand and those of liberty on the other. In the meantime the proper course for the Catholic will be to proclaim publicly his profound respect for authority, while never ceasing to follow his own judgment. Their general direction for the Church is as follows: that the ecclesiastical authority, since its end is entirely spiritual, should strip itself of that external pomp which adorns it in the eyes of the public. In this, they forget that while religion is for the soul, it is not exclusively for the soul, and that the honor paid to authority is reflected back on Christ who instituted it.

26. To conclude this whole question of faith and its various branches, we have still to consider, Venerable Brethren, what the Modernists have to say about the development of the one and the other. First of all they lay down the general principle that in a living religion everything is subject to change, and must in fact be changed. In this way they pass to what is practically their principal doctrine, namely, evolution. To the laws of evolution everything is subject under penalty of death — dogma, Church, worship, the Books we revere as sacred, even faith itself. The enunciation of this principle will not be a matter of surprise to anyone who bears in mind what the Modernists have had to say about each of these subjects. Having laid down this law of evolution, the Modernists themselves teach us how it operates. And first, with regard to faith. The primitive form of faith, they tell us, was rudimentary and common to all men alike, for it had its origin in human nature and human life. Vital evolution brought with it progress, not by the accretion of new and purely adventitious forms from without, but by an increasing perfusion of the religious sense into the conscience. The progress was of two kinds: negative, by the elimination of all extraneous elements, such, for example, as those derived from the family or nationality; and positive, by that intellectual and moral refining of man, by means of which the idea of the divine became fuller and clearer, while the religious sense became more acute. For the progress of faith the same causes are to be assigned as those which are adduced above to explain its origin. But to them must be

added those extraordinary men whom we call prophets — of whom Christ was the greatest — both because in their lives and their words there was something mysterious which faith attributed to the divinity, and because it fell to their lot to have new and original experiences fully in harmony with the religious needs of their time. The progress of dogma is due chiefly to the fact that obstacles to the faith have to be surmounted, enemies have to be vanquished, and objections have to be refuted. Add to this a perpetual striving to penetrate ever more profoundly into those things which are contained in the mysteries of faith. Thus, putting aside other examples, it is found to have happened in the case of Christ: in Him that divine something which faith recognized in Him was slowly and gradually expanded in such a way that He was at last held to be God. The chief stimulus of the evolution of worship consists in the need of accommodation to the manners and customs of peoples, as well as the need of availing itself of the value which certain acts have acquired by usage. Finally, evolution in the Church itself is fed by the need of adapting itself to historical conditions and of harmonizing itself with existing forms of society. Such is their view with regard to each. And here, before proceeding further, We wish to draw attention to this whole theory of necessities or needs, for beyond all that we have seen, it is, as it were, the base and foundation of that famous method which they describe as historical.

27. Although evolution is urged on by needs or necessities, yet, if controlled by these alone, it would easily overstep the boundaries of tradition, and thus, separated from its primitive vital principle, would make for ruin instead of progress. Hence, by those who study more closely the ideas of the Modernists, evolution is described as a resultant from the conflict of two forces, one of them tending towards progress, the other towards conservation. The conserving force exists in the Church and is found in tradition; tradition is represented by religious authority, and this both by right and in fact. By right, for it is in the very nature of authority to protect tradition: and in fact, since authority, raised as it is above the contingencies of life, feels hardly, or not at all, the spurs of progress. The progressive force, on the contrary,

which responds to the inner needs, lies in the individual consciences and works in them — especially in such of them as are in more close and intimate contact with life. Already we observe, Venerable Brethren, the introduction of that most pernicious doctrine which would make of the laity the factor of progress in the Church. Now it is by a species of covenant and compromise between these two forces of conservation and progress, that is to say between authority and individual consciences, that changes and advances take place. The individual consciences, or some of them, act on the collective conscience, which brings pressure to bear on the depositories of authority to make terms and to keep to them.

With all this in mind, one understands how it is that the Modernists express astonishment when they are reprimanded or punished. What is imputed to them as a fault they regard as a sacred duty. They understand the needs of consciences better than anyone else, since they come into closer touch with them than does the ecclesiastical authority. Nay, they embody them, so to speak, in themselves. Hence, for them to speak and to write publicly is a bounden duty. Let authority rebuke them if it pleases — they have their own conscience on their side and an intimate experience which tells them with certainty that what they deserve is not blame but praise. Then they reflect that, after all, there is no progress without a battle and no battle without its victims; and victims they are willing to be like the prophets and Christ Himself. They have no bitterness in their hearts against the authority which uses them roughly, for after all they readily admit that it is only doing its duty as authority. Their sole grief is that it remains deaf to their warnings, for in this way it impedes the progress of souls, but the hour will most surely come when further delay will be impossible, for if the laws of evolution may be checked for a while they cannot be finally evaded. And thus they go their way, reprimands and condemnations notwithstanding, masking an incredible audacity under a mock semblance of humility. While they make a pretense of bowing their heads, their minds and hands are more boldly intent than ever on carrying out their purposes. And this policy they follow willingly and wittingly, both because it is part of their system that authority is to be stimulated but not dethroned, and because it is necessary for them to remain within the ranks of the Church in order that they may gradually transform the collective conscience. And in saying this, they fail to perceive that they are avowing that the collective conscience is not with them, and that they have no right to claim to be its interpreters.

28. It is thus, Venerable Brethren, that for the Modernists, whether as authors or propagandists, there is to be nothing stable, nothing immutable in the Church. Nor, indeed, are they without forerunners in their doctrines, for it was of these that Our predecessor Pius IX wrote: "These enemies of divine revelation extol human progress to the skies, and with rash and sacrilegious daring would have it introduced into the Catholic religion as if this religion were not the work of God but of man, or some kind of philosophical discovery susceptible of perfection by human efforts."[13] On the subject of revelation and dogma in particular, the doctrine of the Modernists offers nothing new. We find it condemned in the Syllabus of Pius IX, where it is enunciated in these terms: "Divine revelation is imperfect, and therefore subject to continual and indefinite progress, corresponding with the progress of human reason";[14] and condemned still more solemnly in the Vatican Council: "The doctrine of the faith which God has revealed has not been proposed to human intelligences to be perfected by them as if it were a philosophical system, but as a divine deposit entrusted to the Spouse of Christ to be faithfully guarded and infallibly interpreted. Hence also that sense of the sacred dogmas is to be perpetually retained which our Holy Mother the Church has once declared, nor is this sense ever to be abandoned on plea or pretext of a more profound comprehension of the truth."[15] Nor is the development of our knowledge, even concerning the faith, barred by this pronouncement; on the contrary, it is supported and maintained. For the same Council continues: "Let intelligence and science and wisdom, therefore, increase and

---

[13] Pius IX, encyclical of November 9, 1846, Qui pluribus.

[14] Syllabus, Prop. 5.

[15] Constitution Dei Filius, cap. 4.

progress abundantly and vigorously in individuals, and in the mass, in the believer and in the whole Church, throughout the ages and the centuries — but only in its own kind, that is, according to the same dogma, the same sense, the same acceptation."[16]

29. We have studied the Modernist as philosopher, believer, and theologian. It now remains for us to consider him as historian, critic, apologist, and reformer.

30. Some Modernists, devoted to historical studies, seem to be deeply anxious not to be taken for philosophers. About philosophy they profess to know nothing whatever, and in this they display remarkable astuteness, for they are particularly desirous not to be suspected of any prepossession in favor of philosophical theories which would lay them open to the charge of not being, as they call it, objective. And yet the truth is that their history and their criticism are saturated with their philosophy, and that their historico-critical conclusions are the natural outcome of their philosophical principles. This will be patent to anyone who reflects. Their three first laws are contained in those three principles of their philosophy already dealt with: the principle of agnosticism, the theorem of the transfiguration of things by faith, and that other which may be called the principle of disfiguration. Let us see what consequences flow from each of these. Agnosticism tells us that history, like science, deals entirely with phenomena, and the consequence is that God, and every intervention of God in human affairs, is to be relegated to the domain of faith as belonging to it alone. Wherefore in things where there is combined a double element, the divine and the human, as, for example, in Christ, or the Church, or the sacraments, or the many other objects of the same kind, a division and separation must be made and the human element must he left to history while the divine will he assigned to faith. Hence we have that distinction, so current among the Modernists, between the Christ of history and the Christ of faith; the Church of history and the Church of faith; the sacraments of history and the sacraments of faith, and so in similar matters. Next we find that the human element itself,

---

[16] Loc. cit.

which the historian has to work on, as it appears in the documents, is to be considered as having been transfigured by faith, that is to say, raised above its historical conditions. It becomes necessary, therefore, to eliminate also the accretions which faith has added, to relegate them to faith itself and to the history of faith. Thus, when treating of Christ, the historian must set aside all that surpasses man in his natural condition, according to what psychology tells us of him, or according to what we gather from the place and period of his existence. Finally, they require, by virtue of the third principle, that even those things which are not outside the sphere of history should pass through the sieve, excluding all and relegating to faith everything which, in their judgment, is not in harmony with what they call the logic of facts or not in character with the persons of whom they are predicated. Thus, they will not allow that Christ ever uttered those things which do not seem to be within the capacity of the multitudes that listened to Him. Hence they delete from His real history and transfer to faith all the allegories found in His discourses. We may peradventure inquire on what principle they make these divisions? Their reply is that they argue from the character of the man, from his condition of life, from his education, from the complexus of the circumstances under which the facts took place; in short, if We understand them aright, on a principle which in the last analysis is merely subjective. Their method is to put themselves into the position and person of Christ, and then to attribute to Him what they would have done under like circumstances. In this way, absolutely a priori and acting on philosophical principles which they hold but which they profess to ignore, they proclaim that Christ, according to what they call His real history, was not God and never did anything divine, and that as man He did and said only what they, judging from the time in which He lived, consider that He ought to have said or done.

31. As history takes its conclusions from philosophy, so too criticism takes its conclusions from history. The critic on the data furnished him by the historian, makes two parts of all his documents. Those that remain after the triple elimination above described go to form the real history; the

rest is attributed to the history of the faith or, as it is styled, to internal history. For the Modernists distinguish very carefully between these two kinds of history, and it is to be noted that they oppose the history of the faith to real history precisely as real. Thus, as we have already said, we have a twofold Christ: a real Christ, and a Christ, the one of faith, who never really existed; a Christ who has lived at a given time and in a given place, and a Christ who never lived outside the pious meditations of the believer — the Christ, for instance, whom we find in the Gospel of St. John, which, according to them, is mere meditation from beginning to end.

32. But the dominion of philosophy over history does not end here. Given that division, of which We have spoken, of the documents into two parts, the philosopher steps in again with his dogma of vital immanence, and shows how everything in the history of the Church is to be explained by vital emanation. And since the cause or condition of every vital emanation whatsoever is to be found in some need or want, it follows that no fact can be regarded as antecedent to the need which produced it — historically the fact must be posterior to the need. What, then, does the historian do in view of this principle? He goes over his documents again, whether they be contained in the Sacred Books or elsewhere, draws up from them his list of the particular needs of the Church, whether relating to dogma, or liturgy, or other matters which are found in the Church thus related, and then he hands his list over to the critic. The critic takes in hand the documents dealing with the history of faith and distributes them, period by period, so that they correspond exactly with the list of needs, always guided by the principle that the narration must follow the facts, as the facts follow the needs. It may at times happen that some parts of the Sacred Scriptures, such as the Epistles, themselves constitute the fact created by the need. Even so, the rule holds that the age of any document can only be determined by the age in which each need has manifested itself in the Church. Further, a distinction must be made between the beginning of a fact and its development, for what is born in one day requires time for growth. Hence the critic must once more go over his documents, ranged as they are through the different ages, and

divide them again into two parts, separating those that regard the origin of the facts from those that deal with their development, and these he must again arrange according to their periods.

33. Then the philosopher must come in again to enjoin upon the historian the obligation of following in all his studies the precepts and laws of evolution. It is next for the historian to scrutinize his documents once more, to examine carefully the circumstances and conditions affecting the Church during the different periods, the conserving force she has put forth, the needs both internal and external that have stimulated her to progress, the obstacles she has had to encounter, in a word, everything that helps to determine the manner in which the laws of evolution have been fulfilled in her. This done, he finishes his work by drawing up a history of the development in its broad lines. The critic follows and fits in the rest of the documents. He sets himself to write. The history is finished. Now We ask here: Who is the author of this history? The historian? The critic? Assuredly neither of these but the philosopher. From beginning to end everything in it is a priori, and an apriorism that reeks of heresy. These men are certainly to be pitied, of whom the Apostle might well say: "They became vain in their thoughts...professing themselves to be wise, they became fools."[17] At the same time, they excite resentment when they accuse the Church of arranging and confusing the texts after her own fashion, and for the needs of her cause. In this they are accusing the Church of something for which their own conscience plainly reproaches them.

34. The result of this dismembering of the records, and this partition of them throughout the centuries is naturally that the Scriptures can no longer be attributed to the authors whose names they bear. The Modernists have no hesitation in affirming generally that these books, and especially the Pentateuch and the first three Gospels, have been gradually formed from a primitive brief narration, by additions, by interpolations of theological or allegorical interpretations, or parts introduced only for the purpose of joining different

---

[17] Rom. 1:21-22.

passages together. This means, to put it briefly and clearly, that in the Sacred Books we must admit a vital evolution, springing from and corresponding with the evolution of faith. The traces of this evolution, they tell us, are so visible in the books that one might almost write a history of it. Indeed, this history they actually do write, and with such an easy assurance that one might believe them to have seen with their own eyes the writers at work through the ages amplifying the Sacred Books. To aid them in this they call to their assistance that branch of criticism which they call textual, and labor to show that such a fact or such a phrase is not in its right place, adducing other arguments of the same kind. They seem, in fact, to have constructed for themselves certain types of narration and discourses, upon which they base their assured verdict as to whether a thing is or is not out of place. Let him who can judge how far they are qualified in this way to make such distinctions. To hear them descant of their works on the Sacred Books, in which they have been able to discover so much that is defective, one would imagine that before them nobody ever even turned over the pages of Scripture. The truth is that a whole multitude of Doctors, far superior to them in genius, in erudition, in sanctity, have sifted the Sacred Books in every way, and so far from finding in them anything blameworthy have thanked God more and more heartily the more deeply they have gone into them, for His divine bounty in having vouchsafed to speak thus to men. Unfortunately. these great Doctors did not enjoy the same aids to study that are possessed by the Modernists for they did not have for their rule and guide a philosophy borrowed from the negation of God, and a criterion which consists of themselves.

We believe, then, that We have set forth with sufficient clearness the historical method of the Modernists. The philosopher leads the way, the historian follows, and then in due order come the internal and textual critics. And since it is characteristic of the primary cause to communicate its virtue to causes which are secondary, it is quite clear that the criticism with which We are concerned is not any kind of criticism, but that which is rightly called agnostic, immanentist, and evolutionist criticism. Hence anyone who adopts it and employs it makes profession thereby of the errors contained in it, and places himself in opposition to Catholic teaching. This being so, it is much a matter for surprise that it should have found acceptance to such an extent among certain Catholics. Two causes may be assigned for this: first, the close alliance which the historians and critics of this school have formed among themselves independent of all differences of nationality or religion; second, their boundless effrontery by which, if one then makes any utterance, the others applaud him in chorus, proclaiming that science has made another step forward, while if an outsider should desire to inspect the new discovery for himself, they form a coalition against him. He who denies it is decried as one who is ignorant, while he who embraces and defends it has all their praise. In this way they entrap not a few, who, did they but realize what they are doing, would shrink back with horror. The domineering overbearance of those who teach the errors, and the thoughtless compliance of the more shallow minds who assent to them, create a corrupted atmosphere which penetrates everywhere, and carries infection with it. But let Us pass to the apologist.

35. The Modernist apologist depends in two ways on the philosopher. First, indirectly, inasmuch as his subject-matter is history — history dictated, as we have seen, by the philosopher; and, secondly, directly, inasmuch as he takes both his doctrines and his conclusions from the philosopher. Hence that common axiom of the Modernist school that in the new apologetics controversies in religion must be determined by psychological and historical research. The Modernist apologists, then, enter the arena, proclaiming to the rationalists that, though they are defending religion, they have no intention of employing the data of the sacred books or the histories in current use in the Church, and written upon the old lines, but real history composed on modern principles and according to the modern method. In all this they assert that they are not using an argumentum ad hominem, because they are really of the opinion that the truth is to be found only in this kind of history. They feel that it is not necessary for them to make profession of their own sincerity in their writings. They are already known to and praised by the

rationalists as fighting under the same banner, and they not only plume themselves on these encomiums, which would only provoke disgust in a real Catholic, but use them as a counter-compensation to the reprimands of the Church. Let us see how the Modernist conducts his apologetics. The aim he sets before himself is to make one who is still without faith attain that experience of the Catholic religion which, according to the system, is the sole basis of faith. There are two ways open to him, the objective and the subjective. The first of them starts from agnosticism. It tends to show that religion, and especially the Catholic religion, is endowed with such vitality as to compel every psychologist and historian of good faith to recognize that its history hides some element of the unknown. To this end it is necessary to prove that the Catholic religion, as it exists today, is that which was founded by Jesus Christ; that is to say, that it is nothing else than the progressive development of the germ which He brought into the world. Hence it is imperative first of all to establish what this germ was, and this the Modernist claims to he able to do by the following formula: Christ announced the coming of the kingdom of God, which was to be realized within a brief lapse of time and of which He was to become the Messias, the divinely-given founder and ruler. Then it must be shown how this germ, always immanent and permanent in the Catholic religion, has gone on slowly developing in the course of history, adapting itself successively to the different circumstances through which it has passed, borrowing from them by vital assimilation all the doctrinal, cultural, ecclesiastical forms that served its purpose; whilst, on the other hand, it surmounted all obstacles, vanquished all enemies, and survived all assaults and all combats. Anyone who well and duly considers this mass of obstacles, adversaries, attacks, combats, and the vitality and fecundity which the Church has shown throughout them all, must admit that if the laws of evolution are visible in her life they fail to explain the whole of her history — the unknown rises forth from it and presents itself before Us. Thus do they argue, not perceiving that their determination of the primitive germ is only an a priori assumption of agnostic and evolutionist philosophy, and that the germ itself has been gratuitously defined so that it may fit in with their contention.

36. But while they endeavor by this line of reasoning to prove and plead for the Catholic religion, these new apologists are more than willing to grant and to recognize that there are in it many things which are repulsive. Nay, they admit openly, and with ill-concealed satisfaction, that they have found that even its dogma is not exempt from errors and contradictions. They add also that this is not only excusable but — curiously enough — that it is even right and proper. In the Sacred Books there are many passages referring to science or history where, according to them, manifest errors are to he found. But, they say, the subject of these books is not science or history, but only religion and morals. In them history and science serve only as a species of covering to enable the religious and moral experiences wrapped Up in them to penetrate more readily among the masses. The masses understood science and history as they are expressed in these books, and it is clear that the expression of science and history in a more perfect form would have proved not so much a help as a hindrance. Moreover, they add, the Sacred Books, being essentially religious, are necessarily quick with life. Now life has its own truths and its own logic — quite different from rational truth aand rational logic, belonging as they do to a different order, viz., truth of adaptation and of proportion both with what they call the medium in which it lives and with the end for which it lives. Finally, the Modernists, losing all sense of control, go so far as to proclaim as true and legitimate whatever is explained by life.

We, Venerable Brethren, for whom there is but one and only one truth, and who hold that the Sacred Books, "written under the inspiration of the Holy Ghost, have God for their author"[18] declare that this is equivalent to attributing to God Himself the lie of utility or officious lie, and We say with St. Augustine: "In an authority so high, admit but one officious lie, and there will not remain a single passage of those apparently difficult to practice or to believe, which on the same most pernicious rule may not be explained as a lie

---

[18] Vatican Council, De Revelatione con. 2.

uttered by the author willfully and to serve a purpose."[19] And thus it will come about, the holy Doctor continues, that "everybody will believe and refuse to believe what he likes or dislikes in them," namely, the Scriptures. But the Modernists pursue their way eagerly. They grant also that certain arguments adduced in the Sacred Books in proof of a given doctrine, like those, for example, which are based on the prophecies, have no rational foundation to rest on. But they defend even these as artifices of preaching, which are justified by life. More than that. They are ready to admit, nay, to proclaim that Christ Himself manifestly erred in determining the time when the coming of the Kingdom of God was to take place; and they tell us that we must not be surprised at this since even He Himself was subject to the laws of life! After this what is to become of the dogmas of the Church? The dogmas bristle with flagrant contradictions, but what does it matter since, apart from the fact that vital logic accepts them, they are not repugnant to symbolical truth. Are we not dealing with the infinite, and has not the infinite an infinite variety of aspects? In short, to maintain and defend these theories they do not hesitate to declare that the noblest homage that can be paid to the Infinite is to make it the object of contradictory statements! But when they justify even contradictions, what is it that they will refuse to justify?

37. But it is not solely by objective arguments that the non-believer may be disposed to faith. There are also those that are subjective, and for this purpose the modernist apologists return to the doctrine of immanence. They endeavor, in fact, to persuade their non-believer that down in the very depths of his nature and his life lie hidden the need and the desire for some religion, and this not a religion of any kind, but the specific religion known as Catholicism, which, they say, is absolutely postulated by the perfect development of life. And here again We have grave reason to complain that there are Catholics who, while rejecting immanence as a doctrine, employ it as a method of apologetics, and who do this so imprudently that they seem to admit, not merely a

---

[19] Epist. 28.

capacity and a suitability for the supernatural, such as has at all times been emphasized, within due limits, by Catholic apologists, but that there is in human nature a true and rigorous need for the supernatural order. Truth to tell, it is only the moderate Modernists who make this appeal to an exigency for the Catholic religion. As for the others, who might he called integralists, they would show to the non-believer, as hidden in his being, the very germ which Christ Himself had in His consciousness, and which He transmitted to mankind. Such, Venerable Brethren, is a summary description of the apologetic method of the Modernists, in perfect harmony with their doctrines — methods and doctrines replete with errors, made not for edification but for destruction, not for the making of Catholics but for the seduction of those who are Catholics into heresy; and tending to the utter subversion of all religion.

38. It remains for Us now to say a few words about the Modernist as reformer. From all that has preceded, it is abundantly clear how great and how eager is the passion of such men for innovation. In all Catholicism there is absolutely nothing on which it does not fasten. They wish philosophy to be reformed, especially in the ecclesiastical seminaries. They wish the scholastic philosophy to be relegated to the history of philosophy and to be classed among absolute systems, and the young men to be taught modern philosophy which alone is true and suited to the times in which we live. They desire the reform of theology: rational theology is to have modern philosophy for its foundation, and positive theology is to be founded on the history of dogma. As for history, it must be written and taught only according to their methods and modern principles. Dogmas and their evolution, they affirm, are to be harmonized with science and history. In the Catechism no dogmas are to be inserted except those that have been reformed and are within the capacity of the people. Regarding worship, they say, the number of external devotions is to he reduced, and steps must be taken to prevent their further increase, though, indeed, some of the admirers of symbolism are disposed to be more indulgent on this head. They cry out that ecclesiastical government requires to be reformed in all its branches, but especially in

its disciplinary and dogmatic departments They insist that both outwardly and inwardly it must be brought into harmony with the modern conscience which now wholly tends towards democracy; a share in ecclesiastical government should therefore be given to the lower ranks of the clergy and even to the laity and authority which is too much concentrated should be decentralized The Roman Congregations and especially the index and the Holy Office, must be likewise modified The ecclesiastical authority must alter its line of conduct in the social and political world; while keeping outside political organizations it must adapt itself to them in order to penetrate them with its spirit. With regard to morals, they adopt the principle of the Americanists, that the active virtues are more important than the passive, and are to be more encouraged in practice. They ask that the clergy should return to their primitive humility and poverty, and that in their ideas and action they should admit the principles of Modernism; and there are some who, gladly listening to the teaching of their Protestant masters, would desire the suppression of the celibacy of the clergy. What is there left in the Church which is not to be reformed by them and according to their principles?

39. It may, perhaps, seem to some, Venerable Brethren, that We have dealt at too great length on this exposition of the doctrines of the Modernists. But it was necessary that We should do so, both in order to meet their customary charge that We do not understand their ideas, and to show that their system does not consist in scattered and unconnected theories, but, as it were, in a closely connected whole, so that it is not possible to admit one without admitting all. For this reason, too, We have had to give to this exposition a somewhat didactic form, and not to shrink from employing certain unwonted terms which the Modernists have brought into use. And now with Our eyes fixed upon the whole system, no one will be surprised that We should define it to be the synthesis of all heresies. Undoubtedly, were anyone to attempt the task of collecting together all the errors that have been broached against the faith and to concentrate into one the sap and substance of them all, he could not succeed in doing so better than the Modernists have done. Nay, they

have gone farther than this, for, as We have already intimated, their system means the destruction not of the Catholic religion alone, but of all religion. Hence the rationalists are not wanting in their applause, and the most frank and sincere among them congratulate themselves on having found in the Modernists the most valuable of all allies.

Let us turn for a moment, Venerable Brethren, to that most disastrous doctrine of agnosticism. By it every avenue to God on the side of the intellect is barred to man, while a better way is supposed to be opened from the side of a certain sense of the soul and action. But who does not see how mistaken is such a contention? For the sense of the soul is the response to the action of the thing which the intellect or the outward senses set before it. Take away the intelligence, and man, already inclined to follow the senses, becomes their slave. Doubly mistaken, from another point of view, for all these fantasies of the religious sense will never be able to destroy common sense, and common sense tells us that emotion and everything that leads the heart captive proves a hindrance instead of a help to the discovery of truth. We speak of truth in itself — for that other purely subjective truth, the fruit of the internal sense and action, if it serves its purpose for the play of words, is of no benefit to the man who wants above all things to know whether outside himself there is a God into whose hands he is one day to fall. True, the Modernists call in experience to eke out their system, but what does this experience add to that sense of the soul? Absolutely nothing beyond a certain intensity and a proportionate deepening of the conviction of the reality of the object. But these two will never make the sense of the soul into anything but sense, nor will they alter its nature, which is liable to deception when the intelligence is not there to guide it; on the contrary, they but confirm and strengthen this nature, for the more intense the sense is the more it is really sense. And as we are here dealing with religious sense and the experience involved in it, it is known to you, Venerable Brethren, how necessary in such a matter is prudence, and the learning by which prudence is guided. You know it from your own dealings with souls, and especially with souls in whom sentiment predominates; you know it also from your reading of works of ascetical theology — works for which the Modernists have but little esteem, but which testify to a science and a solidity far greater than theirs, and to a refinement and subtlety of observation far beyond any which the Modernists take credit to themselves for possessing. It seems to Us nothing short of madness, or at the least consummate temerity to accept for true, and without investigation, these incomplete experiences which are the vaunt of the Modernist. Let Us for a moment put the question: If experiences have so much force and value in their estimation, why do they not attach equal weight to the experience that so many thousands of Catholics have that the Modernists are on the wrong path? Is it that the Catholic experiences are the only ones which are false and deceptive? The vast majority of mankind holds and always will hold firmly that sense and experience alone, when not enlightened and guided by reason, cannot reach to the knowledge of God. What, then, remains but atheism and the absence of all religion? Certainly it is not the doctrine of symbolism that will save us from this. For if all the intellectual elements, as they call them, of religion are nothing more than mere symbols of God, will not the very name of God or of divine personality be also a symbol, and if this be admitted, the personality of God will become a matter of doubt and the gate will be opened to pantheism? And to pantheism pure and simple that other doctrine of the divine immanence leads directly. For this is the question which We ask: Does or does not this immanence leave God distinct from man? If it does, in what does it differ from the Catholic doctrine, and why does it reject the doctrine of external revelation? If it does not, it is pantheism. Now the doctrine of immanence in the Modernist acceptation holds and professes that every phenomenon of conscience proceeds from man as man. The rigorous conclusion from this is the identity of man with God, which means pantheism. The distinction which Modernists make between science and faith leads to the same conclusion. The object of science, they say, is the reality of the knowable; the object of faith, on the contrary, is the reality of the unknowable. Now, what makes the unknowable unknowable is the fact that there is no proportion between its object and the intellect — a defect of proportion which nothing whatever, even in the doctrine of the Modernist, can suppress. Hence the unknowable remains and will eternally remain unknowable to the believer as well as to the philosopher. Therefore if any religion at all is possible, it can only be the religion of an unknowable reality. And why this might not be that soul of the universe, of which certain rationalists speak, is something which certainly does not seem to Us apparent. These reasons suffice to show superabundantly by how many roads Modernism leads to atheism and to the annihilation of all religion. The error of Protestantism made the first step on this path; that of Modernism makes the second; atheism makes the next.

40. To penetrate still deeper into the meaning of Modernism and to find a suitable remedy for so deep a sore, it behooves Us, Venerable Brethren, to investigate the causes which have engendered it and which foster its growth. That the proximate and immediate cause consists in an error of the mind cannot be open to doubt. We recognize that the remote causes may be reduced to two: curiosity and pride. Curiosity by itself, if not prudently regulated, suffices to account for all errors. Such is the opinion of Our predecessor, Gregory XVI, who wrote: "A lamentable spectacle is that presented by the aberrations of human reason when it yields to the spirit of novelty, when against the warning of the Apostle it seeks to know beyond what it is meant to know, and when relying too much on itself it thinks it can find the truth outside the Catholic Church wherein truth is found without the slightest shadow of error."[20]

But it is pride which exercises an incomparably greater sway over the soul to blind it and lead it into error, and pride sits in Modernism as in its own house, finding sustenance everywhere in its doctrines and lurking in its every aspect. It is pride which fills Modernists with that self-assurance by which they consider themselves and pose as the rule for all. It is pride which puffs them up with that vainglory which allows them to regard themselves as the sole possessors of knowledge, and makes them say, elated and inflated with

---

[20] Gregory XVI, encyclical of June 25, 1834, Singulari Nos.

presumption, "We are not as the rest of men," and which, lest they should seem as other men, leads them to embrace and to devise novelties even of the most absurd kind. It is pride which rouses in them the spirit of disobedience and causes them to demand a compromise between authority and liberty. It is owing to their pride that they seek to be the reformers of others while they forget to reform themselves, and that they are found to be utterly wanting in respect for authority, even for the supreme authority. Truly there is no road which leads so directly and so quickly to Modernism as pride. When a Catholic layman or a priest forgets the precept of the Christian life which obliges us to renounce ourselves if we would follow Christ and neglects to tear pride from his heart, then it is he who most of all is a fully ripe subject for the errors of Modernism. For this reason, Venerable Brethren, it will be your first duty to resist such victims of pride, to employ them only in the lowest and obscurest offices. The higher they try to rise, the lower let them be placed, so that the lowliness of their position may limit their power of causing damage. Examine most carefully your young clerics by yourselves and by the directors of your seminaries, and when you find the spirit of pride among them reject them without compunction from the priesthood. Would to God that this had always been done with the vigilance and constancy which were required!

41. If we pass on from the moral to the intellectual causes of Modernism, the first and the chief which presents itself is ignorance. Yes, these very Modernists who seek to be esteemed as Doctors of the Church, who speak so loftily of modern philosophy and show such contempt for scholasticism, have embraced the one with all its false glamour, precisely because their ignorance of the other has left them without the means of being able to recognize confusion of thought and to refute sophistry. Their whole system, containing as it does errors so many and so great, has been born of the union between faith and false philosophy.

42. Would that they had but displayed less zeal and energy in propagating it! But such is their activity and such their unwearying labor on behalf of their cause, that one cannot but be pained to see them waste such energy in

endeavoring to ruin the Church when they might have been of such service to her had their efforts been better directed. Their artifices to delude men's minds are of two kinds, the first to remove obstacles from their path, the second to devise and apply actively and patiently every resource that can serve their purpose. They recognize that the three chief difficulties which stand in their way are the scholastic method of philosophy, the authority and tradition of the Fathers, and the magisterium of the Church, and on these they wage unrelenting war. Against scholastic philosophy and theology they use the weapons of ridicule and contempt. Whether it is ignorance or fear, or both, that inspires this conduct in them, certain it is that the passion for novelty is always united in them with hatred of scholasticism, and there is no surer sign that a man is tending to Modernism than when he begins to show his dislike for the scholastic method. Let the Modernists and their admirers remember the proposition condemned by Pius IX: "The method and principles which have served the ancient doctors of scholasticism when treating of theology no longer correspond with the exigencies of our time or the progress of science."[21] They exercise all their ingenuity in an effort to weaken the force and falsify the character of tradition, so as to rob it of all its weight and authority. But for Catholics nothing will remove the authority of the second Council of Nicea, where it condemns those "who dare, after the impious fashion of heretics, to deride the ecclesiastical traditions, to invent novelties of some kind…or endeavor by malice or craft to overthrow any one of the legitimate traditions of the Catholic Church"; nor that of the declaration of the fourth Council of Constantinople: "We therefore profess to preserve and guard the rules bequeathed to the Holy Catholic and Apostolic Church, by the Holy and most illustrious Apostles, by the orthodox Councils, both general and local, and by everyone of those divine interpreters, the Fathers and Doctors of the Church." Wherefore the Roman Pontiffs, Pius IV and Pius IX, ordered the insertion in the profession of faith of the following declaration: "I most firmly admit and embrace the apostolic

---

[21] Syllabus, Prop. 13.

and ecclesiastical traditions and other observances and constitutions of the Church."

The Modernists pass judgment on the holy Fathers of the Church even as they do upon tradition. With consummate temerity they assure the public that the Fathers, while personally most worthy of all veneration, were entirely ignorant of history and criticism, for which they are only excusable on account of the time in which they lived. Finally, the Modernists try in every way to diminish and weaken the authority of the ecclesiastical magisterium itself by sacrilegiously falsifying its origin, character, and rights, and by freely repeating the calumnies of its adversaries. To the entire band of Modernists may be applied those words which Our predecessor sorrowfully wrote: "To bring contempt and odium on the mystic Spouse of Christ, who is the true light, the children of darkness have been wont to cast in her face before the world a stupid calumny, and perverting the meaning and force of things and words, to depict her as the friend of darkness and ignorance, and the enemy of light, science, and progress."[22] This being so, Venerable Brethren, there is little reason to wonder that the Modernists vent all their bitterness and hatred on Catholics who zealously fight the battles of the Church. There is no species of insult which they do not heap upon them, but their usual course is to charge them with ignorance or obstinacy. When an adversary rises up against them with an erudition and force that renders them redoubtable, they seek to make a conspiracy of silence around him to nullify the effects of his attack. This policy towards Catholics is the more invidious in that they belaud with admiration which knows no bounds the writers who range themselves on their side, hailing their works, exuding novelty in every page, with a chorus of applause. For them the scholarship of a writer is in direct proportion to the recklessness of his attacks on antiquity, and of his efforts to undermine tradition and the ecclesiastical magisterium. When one of their number falls under the condemnations of the Church the rest of them, to the disgust of good Catholics, gather round him, loudly and publicly applaud him, and hold

---

[22] Motu Proprio of March 14, 1891, Ut mysticam.

him up in veneration as almost a martyr for truth. The young, excited and confused by all this clamor of praise and abuse, some of them afraid of being branded as ignorant, others ambitious to rank among the learned, and both classes goaded internally by curiosity and pride, not infrequently surrender and give themselves up to Modernism.

43. And here we have already some of the artifices employed by Modernists to exploit their wares. What efforts do they not make to win new recruits! They seize upon professorships in the seminaries and universities, and gradually make of them chairs of pestilence. In sermons from the pulpit they disseminate their doctrines, although possibly in utterances which are veiled. In congresses they express their teachings more openly. In their social gatherings they introduce them and commend them to others. Under their own names and under pseudonyms they publish numbers of books, newspapers, reviews, and sometimes one and the same writer adopts a variety of pseudonyms to trap the incautious reader into believing in a multitude of Modernist writers. In short, with feverish activity they leave nothing untried in act, speech, and writing. And with what result? We have to deplore the spectacle of many young men, once full of promise and capable of rendering great services to the Church, now gone astray. It is also a subject of grief to Us that many others who, while they certainly do not go so far as the former, have yet been so infected by breathing a poisoned atmosphere, as to think, speak, and write with a degree of laxity which ill becomes a Catholic. They are to be found among the laity, and in the ranks of the clergy, and they are not wanting even in the last place where one might expect to meet them, in religious communities If they treat of biblical questions, it is upon Modernist principles; if they write history, they carefully, and with ill-concealed satisfaction, drag into the light, on the plea of telling the whole truth, everything that appears to cast a stain upon the Church. Under the sway of certain a priori conceptions they destroy as far as they can the pious traditions of the people, and bring into disrespect certain relics highly venerable from their antiquity. They are possessed by the empty desire of having their names upon the lips of the public, and they know

they would never succeed in this were they to say only what has always been said by all men. Meanwhile it may be that they have persuaded themselves that in all this they are really serving God and the Church. In reality they only offend both, less perhaps by their works in themselves than by the spirit in which they write, and by the encouragement they thus give to the aims of the Modernists.

44. Against this host of grave errors, and its secret and open advance, Our predecessor Leo Xlll, of happy memory, worked strenuously, both in his words and his acts, especially as regards the study of the Bible. But, as we have seen, the Modernists are not easily deterred by such weapons. With an affectation of great submission and respect, they proceeded to twist the words of the Pontiff to their own sense, while they described his action as directed against others than themselves. Thus the evil has gone on increasing from day to day. We, therefore, Venerable Brethren, have decided to suffer no longer delay, and to adopt measures which are more efficacious. We exhort and conjure you to see to it that in this most grave matter no one shall be in a position to say that you have been in the slightest degree wanting in vigilance, zeal, or firmness. And what We ask of you and expect of you, We ask and expect also of all other pastors of souls, of all educators and professors of clerics, and in a very special way of the superiors of religious communities.

45. In the first place, with regard to studies, We will and strictly ordain that scholastic philosophy be made the basis of the sacred sciences. It goes without saying that "if anything is met with among the scholastic doctors which may be regarded as something investigated with an excess of subtlety, or taught without sufficient consideration; anything which is not in keeping with the certain results of later times; anything, in short, which is altogether destitute of probability, We have no desire whatever to propose it for the imitation of present generations."[23] And let it be clearly understood above all things that when We prescribe scholastic philosophy We understand chiefly that which the Angelic Doctor has bequeathed to us, and We, therefore, declare that all the

---

[23] Leo Xlll, encyclical of August 4, 1879, Aeterni Patris.

ordinances of Our predecessor on this subject continue fully in force, and, as far as may be necessary, We do decree anew, and confirm, and order that they shall be strictly observed by all. In seminaries where they have been neglected it will be for the Bishops to exact and require their observance in the future; and let this apply also to the superiors of religious orders. Further, We admonish professors to bear well in mind that they cannot set aside St. Thomas, especially in metaphysical questions, without grave disadvantage.

46. On this philosophical foundation the theological edifice is to be carefully raised. Promote the study of theology, Venerable Brethren, by all means in your power, so that your clerics on leaving the seminaries may carry with them a deep admiration and love of it, and always find in it a source of delight. For "in the vast and varied abundance of studies opening before the mind desirous of truth, it is known to everyone that theology occupies such a commanding place, that according to an ancient adage of the wise it is the duty of the other arts and sciences to serve it, and to wait upon it after the manner of handmaidens."[24] We will add that We deem worthy of praise those who with full respect for tradition, the Fathers, and the ecclesiastical magisterium, endeavor, with well-balanced judgment, and guided by Catholic principles (which is not always the case), to illustrate positive theology by throwing upon it the light of true history. It is certainly necessary that positive theology should be held in greater appreciation than it has been in the past, but this must be done without detriment to scholastic theology; and those are to be disapproved as Modernists who exalt positive theology in such a way as to seem to despise the scholastic.

47. With regard to secular studies, let it suffice to recall here what our predecessor has admirably said: "Apply yourselves energetically to the study of natural sciences: in which department the things that have been so brilliantly discovered, and so usefully applied, to the admiration of the present age, will be the object of praise and commendation to

---

[24] Leo XIII, Apostolic letter of December 10, 1889, In magna.

those who come after us."[25] But this is to be done without interfering with sacred studies, as Our same predecessor prescribed in these most weighty words: "If you carefully search for the cause of those errors you will find that it lies in the fact that in these days when the natural sciences absorb so much study, the more severe and lofty studies have been proportionately neglected — some of them have almost passed into oblivion, some of them are pursued in a half-hearted or superficial way, and, sad to say, now that the splendor of the former estate is dimmed, they have been disfigured by perverse doctrines and monstrous errors."[26] We ordain, therefore, that the study of natural sciences in the seminaries be carried out according to this law.

48. All these prescriptions, both Our own and those of Our predecessor, are to be kept in view whenever there is question of choosing directors and professors for seminaries and Catholic Universities. Anyone who in any way is found to be tainted with Modernism is to be excluded without compunction from these offices, whether of government or of teaching, and those who already occupy them are to be removed. The same policy is to be adopted towards those who openly or secretly lend countenance to Modernism either by extolling the Modernists and excusing their culpable conduct, or by carping at scholasticism, and the Fathers, and the magisterium of the Church, or by refusing obedience to ecclesiastical authority in any of its depositories; and towards those who show a love of novelty in history, archaeology, biblical exegesis; and finally towards those who neglect the sacred sciences or appear to prefer to them the secular. In all this question of studies, Venerable Brethren, you cannot be too watchful or too constant, but most of all in the choice of professors, for as a rule the students are modeled after the pattern of their masters. Strong in the consciousness of your duty, act always in this matter with prudence and with vigor.

49. Equal diligence and severity are to be used in examining and selecting candidates for Holy Orders. Far, far

---

[25] Leo XIII, allocution of March 7, 1880.
[26] Loc. cit.

from the clergy be the love of novelty! God hateth the proud and the obstinate mind. For the future the doctorate of theology and canon law must never be conferred on anyone who has not first of all made the regular course of scholastic philosophy; if conferred, it shall be held as null and void. The rules laid down in 1896 by the Sacred Congregation of Bishops and Regulars for the clerics, both secular and regular, of Italy, concerning the frequenting of the Universities, We now decree to be extended to all nation.[27] Clerics and priests inscribed in a Catholic Institute or University must not in the future follow in civil Universities those courses for which there are chairs in the Catholic Institutes to which they belong. If this has been permitted anywhere in the past, We ordain that it be not allowed for the future. Let the Bishops who form the Governing Board of such Catholic Institutes or Universities watch with all care that these Our commands be constantly observed.

50. It is also the duty of the Bishops to prevent writings of Modernists, or whatever savors of Modernism or promotes it, from being read when they have been published, and to hinder their publication when they have not. No books or papers or periodicals whatever of this kind are to be permitted to seminarists or university students. The injury to them would be not less than that which is caused by immoral reading — nay, it would be greater, for such writings poison Christian life at its very fount. The same decision is to be taken concerning the writings of some Catholics, who, though not evilly disposed themselves, are ill-instructed in theological studies and imbued with modern philosophy, and strive to make this harmonize with the faith, and, as they say, to turn it to the profit of the faith. The name and reputation of these authors cause them to read without suspicion, and they are, therefore, all the more dangerous in gradually preparing the way for Modernism.

51. To add some more general directions, Venerable Brethren, in a matter of such moment, We order that you do everything in your power to drive out of your dioceses, even by solemn interdict, any pernicious books that may be in

---

[27] Cf. ASS, 29:359ff.

circulation there. The Holy See neglects no means to remove writings of this kind, but their number has now grown to such an extent that it is hardly possible to subject them all to censure. Hence it happens sometimes that the remedy arrives too late, for the disease has taken root during the delay. We will, therefore, that the Bishops putting aside all fear and the prudence of the flesh, despising the clamor of evil men, shall, gently, by all means, but firmly, do each his own part in this work, remembering the injunctions of Leo XIII in the Apostolic Constitution Officiorum: "Let the Ordinaries, acting in this also as Delegates of the Apostolic See, exert themselves to proscribe and to put out of reach of the faithful injurious books or other writings printed or circulated in their dioceses."[28] In this passage the Bishops, it is true, receive an authorization, but they have also a charge laid upon them. Let no Bishop think that he fulfills his duty by denouncing to Us one or two books, while a great many others of the same kind are being published and circulated. Nor are you to be deterred by the fact that a book has obtained elsewhere the permission which is commonly called the Imprimatur, both because this may be merely simulated, and because it may have been granted through carelessness or too much indulgence or excessive trust placed in the author, which last has perhaps sometimes happened in the religious orders. Besides, just as the same food does not agree with everyone, it may happen that a book, harmless in one place, may, on account of the different circumstances, be hurtful in another. Should a Bishop, therefore, after having taken the advice of prudent persons, deem it right to condemn any of such books in his diocese, We give him ample faculty for the purpose and We lay upon him the obligation of doing so. Let all this be done in a fitting manner, and in certain cases it will suffice to restrict the prohibition to the clergy; but in all cases it will be obligatory on Catholic booksellers not to put on sale books condemned by the Bishop. And while We are treating of this subject, We wish the Bishops to see to it that booksellers do not, through desire for gain, engage in evil trade. It is certain that in the catalogs of some of them the books of the

---

[28] Cf. ASS, 30:39ff.

Pascendi Dominici Gregis

Modernists are not infrequently announced with no small praise. If they refuse obedience, let the Bishops, after due admonition, have no hesitation in depriving them of the title of Catholic booksellers. This applies, and with still more reason, to those who have the title of Episcopal booksellers. If they have that of Pontifical booksellers, let them be denounced to the Apostolic See. Finally, We remind all of Article XXVI of the above-mentioned Constitution Officiorum: "All those who have obtained an apostolic faculty to read and keep forbidden books, are not thereby authorized to read and keep books and periodicals forbidden by the local Ordinaries unless the apostolic faculty expressly concedes permission to read and keep books condemned by anyone whomsoever."

52. It is not enough to hinder the reading and the sale of bad books — it is also necessary to prevent them from being published. Hence, let the Bishops use the utmost strictness in granting permission to print. Under the rules of the Constitution Officiorum, many publications require the authorization of the Ordinary, and in certain dioceses (since the Bishop cannot personally make himself acquainted with them all) it has been the custom to have a suitable number of official censors for the examination of writings. We have the highest esteem for this institution of censors, and We not only exhort, but We order that it be extended to all dioceses. In all episcopal Curias, therefore, let censors be appointed for the revision of works intended for publication, and let the censors be chosen from both ranks of the clergy — secular and regular — men whose age, knowledge, and prudence will enable them to follow the safe and golden means in their judgments. It shall be their office to examine everything which requires permission for publication according to Articles XLI and XLII of the above-mentioned Constitution. The censor shall give his verdict in writing. If it be favorable, the Bishop will give the permission for publication by the word Imprimatur, which must be preceded by the *Nihil obstat* and the name of the censor. In the Roman Curia official censors shall be appointed in the same way as elsewhere, and the duty of nominating them shall appertain to the Master of the Sacred Palace, after they have been proposed to the

Cardinal Vicar and have been approved and accepted by the Sovereign Pontiff. It will also be the office of the Master of the Sacred Palace to select the censor for each writing. Permission for publication will be granted by him as well as by the Cardinal Vicar or his Vicegerent, and this permission, as above prescribed, must he preceded by the Nihil obstat and the name of the censor. Only on a very rare and exceptional occasion, and on the prudent decision of the Bishop, shall it be possible to omit mention of the censor. The name of the censor shall never be made known to the authors until he shall have given a favorable decision, so that he may not have to suffer inconvenience either while he is engaged in the examination of a writing or in case he should withhold his approval. Censors shall never be chosen from the religious orders until the opinion of the Provincial, or in Rome, of the General, has been privately obtained, and the Provincial or the General must give a conscientious account of the character, knowledge, and orthodoxy of the candidate. We admonish religious superiors of their most solemn duty never to allow anything to be published by any of their subjects without permission from themselves and from the Ordinary. Finally, We affirm and declare that the title of censor with which a person may be honored has no value whatever, and can never be adduced to give credit to the private opinions of him who holds it.

53. Having said this much in general, We now ordain in particular a more careful observance of Article XLII of the above-mentioned Constitution Officiorum, according to which "it is forbidden to secular priests, without the previous consent of the Ordinary, to undertake the editorship of papers or periodicals." This permission shall be withdrawn from any priest who makes a wrong use of it after having received an admonition thereupon. With regard to priests who are correspondents or collaborators of periodicals, as it happens not infrequently that they contribute matter infected with Modernism to their papers or periodicals, let the Bishops see to it that they do not offend in this manner; and if they do, let them warn the offenders and prevent them from writing. We solemnly charge in like manner the superiors of religious orders that they fulfill the same duty, and should they fail in

it, let the Bishops make due provision with authority from the Supreme Pontiff. Let there be, as far as this is possible, a special censor for newspapers and periodicals written by Catholics. It shall be his office to read in due time each number after it has been published, and if he find anything dangerous in it let him order that it be corrected as soon as possible. The Bishop shall have the same right even when the censor has seen nothing objectionable in a publication.

54. We have already mentioned congresses and public gatherings as among the means used by the Modernists to propagate and defend their opinions. In the future, Bishops shall not permit congresses of priests except on very rare occasions. When they do permit them it shall only be on condition that matters appertaining to the Bishops or the Apostolic See be not treated in them, and that no resolutions or petitions be allowed that would imply a usurpation of sacred authority, and that absolutely nothing be said in them which savors of Modernism, presbyterianism, or laicism. At congresses of this kind, which can only be held after permission in writing has been obtained in due time and for each case it shall not be lawful for priests of other dioceses to be present without the written permission of their Ordinary. Further, no priest must lose sight of the solemn recommendation of Leo XIII: "Let priests hold as sacred the authority of their pastors, let them take it for certain that the sacerdotal ministry, if not exercised under the guidance of the Bishops, can never be either holy, or very fruitful, or worthy of respect."[29]

55. But of what avail, Venerable Brethren, will be all Our commands and prescriptions if they be not dutifully and firmly carried out? In order that this may be done it has seemed expedient to us to extend to all dioceses the regulations which the Bishops of Umbria, with great wisdom, laid down for theirs many years ago. "In order," they say, "to extirpate the errors already propagated and to prevent their further diffusion, and to remove those teachers of impiety through whom the pernicious effects of such diffusion are being perpetuated, this sacred Assembly, following the

---

[29] Leo XIII, encyclical of February 10, 1884, Nobilissima Gallorum.

example of St. Charles Borromeo, has decided to establish in each of the dioceses a Council consisting of approved members of both branches of the clergy, which shall be charged with the task of noting the existence of errors and the devices by which new ones are introduced and propagated, and to inform the Bishop of the whole, so that he may take counsel with them as to the best means for suppressing the evil at the outset and preventing it spreading for the ruin of souls or, worse still, gaining strength and growth."[30] We decree, therefore, that in every diocese a council of this kind, which We are pleased to name the "Council of Vigilance," be instituted without delay. The priests called to form part in it shall be chosen somewhat after the manner above prescribed for the censors, and they shall meet every two months on an appointed day in the presence of the Bishop. They shall be bound to secrecy as to their deliberations and decisions, and in their functions shall be included the following: they shall watch most carefully for every trace and sign of Modernism both in publications and in teaching, and to preserve the clergy and the young from it they shall take all prudent, prompt, and efficacious measures. Let them combat novelties of words, remembering the admonitions of Leo XIII: "It is impossible to approve in Catholic publications a style inspired by unsound novelty which seems to deride the piety of the faithful and dwells on the introduction of a new order of Christian life, on new directions of the Church, on new aspirations of the modern soul, on a new social vocation of the clergy, on a new Christian civilization, and many other things of the same kind."[31] Language of the kind here indicated is not to be tolerated either in books or in lectures. The Councils must not neglect the books treating of the pious traditions of different places or of sacred relics. Let them not permit such questions to be discussed in journals or periodicals destined to foster piety, either with expressions savoring of mockery or contempt, or by dogmatic

---

[30] Acts of the Congress of the Bishops of Umbria, November, 1849, tit. 2, art. 6
[31] Instruction of the Sacred Congregation of Extraordinary Ecclesiastical Affairs, January 27, 1902.

pronouncements, especially when, as is often the case, what is stated as a certainty either does not pass the limits of probability or is based on prejudiced opinion. Concerning sacred relics, let this be the rule: if Bishops, who alone are judges in such matters, know for certain that a relic is not genuine, let them remove it at once from the veneration of the faithful; if the authentications of a relic happen to have been lost through civil disturbances, or in any other way, let it not be exposed for public veneration until the Bishop has verified it. The argument of prescription or well-founded presumption is to have weight only when devotion to a relic is commendable by reason of its antiquity, according to the sense of the Decree issued in 1896 by the Congregation of Indulgences and Sacred Relics: "Ancient relics are to retain the veneration they have always enjoyed except when in individual instances there are clear arguments that they are false or superstitious." In passing judgment on pious traditions let it always be borne in mind that in this matter the Church uses the greatest prudence, and that she does not allow traditions of this kind to be narrated in books except with the utmost caution and with the insertion of the declaration imposed by Urban VIII; and even then she does not guarantee the truth of the fact narrated; she simply does not forbid belief in things for which human evidence is not wanting. On this matter the Sacred Congregation of Rites, thirty years ago, decreed as follows: "These apparitions or revelations have neither been approved nor condemned by the Holy See, which has simply allowed them to be believed on purely human faith, on the tradition which they relate, corroborated by testimony and documents worthy of credence."[32] Anyone who follows this rule has no cause to fear. For the devotion based on any apparition, in so far as it regards the fact itself, that is to say, in so far as the devotion is relative, always implies the condition of the fact being true; while in so far as it is absolute, it is always based on the truth, seeing that its object is the persons of the saints who are honored. The same is true of relics. Finally, We entrust to the Councils of Vigilance the duty of overlooking assiduously

---

[32] Decree of May 2, 1877.

and diligently social institutions as well as writings on social questions so that they may harbor no trace of Modernism, but obey the prescriptions of the Roman Pontiffs.

56. Lest what We have laid down thus far should pass into oblivion, We will and ordain that the Bishops of all dioceses, a year after the publication of these letters and every three years thenceforward, furnish the Holy See with a diligent and sworn report on the things which have been decreed in this Our Letter, and on the doctrines that find currency among the clergy, and especially in the seminaries and other Catholic institutions, those not excepted which are not subject to the Ordinary, and We impose the like obligation on the Generals of religious orders with regard to those who are under them.

57. This, Venerable Brethren, is what We have thought it Our duty to write to you for the salvation of all who believe. The adversaries of the Church will doubtless abuse what We have said to refurbish the old calumny by which We are traduced as the enemy of science and of the progress of humanity. As a fresh answer to such accusations, which the history of the Christian religion refutes by never-failing evidence, it is Our intention to establish by every means in our power a special Institute in which, through the co-operation of those Catholics who are most eminent for their learning, the advance of science and every other department of knowledge may be promoted under the guidance and teaching of Catholic truth. God grant that We may happily realize Our design with the assistance of all those who bear a sincere love for the Church of Christ. But of this We propose to speak on another occasion.

Meanwhile, Venerable Brethren, fully confident in your zeal and energy, We beseech for you with Our whole heart the abundance of heavenly light, so that in the midst of this great danger to souls from the insidious invasions of error upon every hand, you may see clearly what ought to be done, and labor to do it with all your strength and courage. May Jesus Christ, the author and finisher of our faith, be with you in His power; and may the Immaculate Virgin, the destroyer of all heresies, be with you by her prayers and aid. And We, as a pledge of Our affection and of the Divine solace in adversity, most lovingly grant to you, your clergy and people, the Apostolic Benediction.

Given at St. Peter's, Rome, September 8, 1907, in the fifth year of Our Pontificate.

✠

Other Papal Pronouncments
related to Freemasonry

The following list includes other papal statements that warn against the errors of Masonic teachings and/or the adverse effects of their realization, though Freemasonry is not specifically mentioned. Sample quotes from each are included here, and copies of the full documents can be found online.

1. *Quibus quantisque malis*, papal allocution of Bl. Pope Pius IX on April 20, 1849

    To all, then, it is evident that these darkest and most destructive societies and sects have been founded at various times by fabricators of falsehood, followers of perverse doctrines, to instill in spirits their deliriums, systems and plots more deeply, to corrupt the hearts of the simple and to open a broad road to committing all sorts of wickedness with impunity. These abominable sects of perdition, most pernicious not only to the salvation of souls, but also to the good and the peace of society, which have always been detested by Us, and already condemned by Our Predecessors, We also condemned in the encyclical to the Bishops of the Catholic world given November 9, 1846, and now also, with supreme apostolic authority, We again condemn, forbid, and proscribe.

2. *Noscitis et nobiscum*, encyclical on the Church in the Pontifical States, by Bl. Pope Pius IX on December 8, 1849.

    As regards this teaching and these theories, it is now generally known that the special goal of their proponents is to introduce to the people the pernicious fictions of *Socialism* and *Communism* by misapplying the terms "liberty" and "equality." The final goal shared by these teachings, whether of *Communism* or

> *Socialism*, even if approached differently, is to excite by continuous disturbances workers and others, especially those of the lower class, whom they have deceived by their lies and deluded by the promise of a happier condition. They are preparing them for plundering, stealing, and usurping first the Church's and then everyone's property. After this they will profane all law, human and divine, to destroy divine worship and to subvert the entire ordering of civil societies.

3. *Singulari quadam*, allocution of Bl. Pope Pius IX on December 9, 1854.

    > We have still to lament the existence of an impious race of unbelievers who would exterminate all religious worship, if that were possible for them; and we must count amongst them, before all, the members of secret societies, who, bound together by a criminal compact, neglect no means of overthrowing and destroying the Church and the State by the violation of every law. It is against them, assuredly, that the words of the Divine Redeemer are directed:—" You are children of the Devil, and you do the works of your father."

4. *Quanto conficiamur moerore*, letter to the Church in Italy on promotion of false doctrines, by Bl. Pope Pius IX on August 10, 1863.

    > You are certainly aware, our beloved sons and venerable brothers, that every kind of impious and deceitful writing, lies, calumny, and blasphemy has been let loose from hell. No pain has been spared to transfer schools to non-Catholic teachers and to appropriate churches for non-Catholic worship. With a multiple of other, surely diabolical treacheries, arts, and undertakings, the enemies of God employ every effort to destroy completely-if that were possible — the Catholic Church, seduce and corruupt the people, especially guileless youth, and uproot our holy faith and religion from the souls of all.

✠

www.ingramcontent.com/pod-product-compliance
Lightning Source LLC
Chambersburg PA
CBHW020340010526
44119CB00048B/536